CONTENTS

VEGETABLE & VEGETARIAN RECIPES

Grilled Corn With Honey Butter

Servings: 6
Cooking Time: 10 Minutes
Ingredients:
- 6 pieces corn, husked
- 2 tablespoons olive oil
- Salt and pepper to taste
- ½ cup butter, room temperature
- ½ cup honey

Directions:
1. Fire the Grill to 350F. Use desired wood pellets when cooking. Close the lid and preheat for 15 minutes.
2. Brush the corn with oil and season with salt and pepper to taste.
3. Place the corn on the grill grate and cook for 10 minutes. Make sure to flip the corn halfway through the cooking time for even cooking.
4. Meanwhile, mix the butter and honey on a small bowl. Set aside.
5. Once the corn is cooked, remove from the grill and brush with the honey butter sauce.

Nutrition Info: Calories per serving: 387; Protein: 5g; Carbs: 51.2g; Fat: 21.6g Sugar: 28.2g

Smoked Mushrooms

Servings: 2
Cooking Time: 45 Minutes
Ingredients:
- 4 cups whole baby portobello, cleaned
- 1 tbsp canola oil
- 1 tbsp onion powder
- 1 tbsp garlic, granulated
- 1 tbsp salt
- 1 tbsp pepper

Directions:
1. Place all the ingredients in a bowl, mix, and combine.
2. Set your to 180F.
3. Place the mushrooms on the grill directly and smoke for about 30 minutes.
4. Increase heat to high and cook the mushroom for another 15 minutes.
5. Serve warm and enjoy!

Nutrition Info: Calories 118, Total fat 7.6g, Saturated fat 0.6g, Total carbs 10.8g, Net carbs 8.3g, Protein 5.4g, Sugars 3.7g, Fiber 2.5g, Sodium 3500mg, Potassium 536mg

Twice-smoked Potatoes

Servings: 16
Cooking Time: 1 Hour 35 Minutes
Ingredients:
- 8 Idaho, Russet, or Yukon Gold potatoes
- 1 (12-ounce) can evaporated milk, heated
- 1 cup (2 sticks) butter, melted
- ½ cup sour cream, at room temperature
- 1 cup grated Parmesan cheese
- ½ pound bacon, cooked and crumbled
- ¼ cup chopped scallions
- Salt
- Freshly ground black pepper
- 1 cup shredded Cheddar cheese

Directions:
1. Supply your smoker with wood pellets and follow the manufacturer's specific start-up procedure. Preheat, with the lid closed, to 400°F.
2. Poke the potatoes all over with a fork. Arrange them directly on the grill grate, close the lid, and smoke for 1 hour and 15 minutes, or until cooked through and they have some give when pinched.
3. Let the potatoes cool for 10 minutes, then cut in half lengthwise.
4. Into a medium bowl, scoop out the potato flesh, leaving ¼ inch in the shells; place the shells on a baking sheet.
5. Using an electric mixer on medium speed, beat the potatoes, milk, butter, and sour cream until smooth.
6. Stir in the Parmesan cheese, bacon, and scallions, and season with salt and pepper.
7. Generously stuff each shell with the potato mixture and top with Cheddar cheese.
8. Place the baking sheet on the grill grate, close the lid, and smoke for 20 minutes, or until the cheese is melted.

Roasted Parmesan Cheese Broccoli

Servings: 3 To 4
Cooking Time: 45 Minutes
Ingredients:
- 3cups broccoli, stems trimmed
- 1tbsp lemon juice
- 1tbsp olive oil
- 2garlic cloves, minced
- 1/2 tsp kosher salt
- 1/2 tsp ground black pepper
- 1tsp lemon zest
- 1/8 cup parmesan cheese, grated

Directions:
1. Preheat pellet grill to 375°F.

2. Place broccoli in a resealable bag. Add lemon juice, olive oil, garlic cloves, salt, and pepper. Seal the bag and toss to combine. Let the mixture marinate for 30 minutes.
3. Pour broccoli into a grill basket. Place basket on grill grates to roast. Grill broccoli for 14-18 minutes, flipping broccoli halfway through. Grill until tender yet a little crispy on the outside.
4. Remove broccoli from grill and place on a serving dish—zest with lemon and top with grated parmesan cheese. Serve immediately and enjoy!
Nutrition Info: Calories: 82.6 Fat: 4.6 g Cholesterol: 1.8 mg Carbohydrate: 8.1 g Fiber: 4.6 g Sugar: 0 Protein: 5.5

Wood Pellet Grilled Zucchini Squash Spears

Servings: 5
Cooking Time: 10 Minutes
Ingredients:
- 4 zucchini, cleaned and ends cut
- 2 tbsp olive oil
- 1 tbsp sherry vinegar
- 2 thyme, leaves pulled
- Salt and pepper to taste

Directions:
1. Cut the zucchini into halves then cut each half thirds.
2. Add the rest of the ingredients in a ziplock bag with the zucchini pieces. Toss to mix well.
3. Preheat the wood pellet temperature to 350°F with the lid closed for 15 minutes.
4. Remove the zucchini from the bag and place them on the grill grate with the cut side down.
5. Cook for 4 minutes per side or until the zucchini are tender.
6. Remove from grill and serve with thyme leaves. Enjoy.
Nutrition Info: Calories 74, Total fat 5.4g, Saturated fat 0.5g, Total Carbs 6.1g, Net Carbs 3.8g, Protein 2.6g, Sugar 3.9g, Fiber 2.3g, Sodium: 302mg, Potassium 599mg

Cajun Style Grilled Corn

Servings: 4
Cooking Time: 25 Minutes
Ingredients:
- 4 ears corn, with husks
- 1tsp dried oregano
- 1tsp paprika
- 1tsp garlic powder
- 1tsp onion powder

- 1/2 tsp kosher salt
- 1/2 tsp ground black pepper
- 1/4 tsp dried thyme
- 1/4 tsp cayenne pepper
- 2tsp butter, melted

Directions:
1. Preheat pellet grill to 375°F.
2. Peel husks back but do not remove. Scrub and remove silks.
3. Mix oregano, paprika, garlic powder, onion powder, salt, pepper, thyme, and cayenne in a small bowl.
4. Brush melted butter over corn.
5. Rub seasoning mixture over each ear of corn. Pull husks up and place corn on grill grates. Grill for about 12-15 minutes, turning occasionally.
6. Remove from grill and allow to cool for about 5 minutes. Remove husks, then serve and enjoy!
Nutrition Info: Calories: 278 Fat: 17.4 g Cholesterol: 40.7 mg Carbohydrate: 30.6 g Fiber: 4.5 g Sugar: 4.6 g Protein: 5.4 g

Smoked Brussels Sprouts

Servings: 6
Cooking Time: 45 Minutes
Ingredients:
- 1-1/2 pounds Brussels sprouts
- 2 cloves of garlic minced
- 2 tbsp extra virgin olive oil
- Sea salt and cracked black pepper

Directions:
1. Rinse sprouts
2. Remove the outer leaves and brown bottoms off the sprouts.
3. Place sprouts in a large bowl then coat with olive oil.
4. Add a coat of garlic, salt, and pepper and transfer them to the pan.
5. Add to the top rack of the smoker with water and woodchips.
6. Smoke for 45 minutes or until reaches 250°F temperature.
7. Serve
Nutrition Info: Calories: 84 Cal Fat: 4.9 g Carbohydrates: 7.2 g Protein: 2.6 g Fiber: 2.9 g

Sweet Potato Chips

Servings: 3
Cooking Time: 35 To 45 Minutes
Ingredients:
- 2 sweet potatoes
- 1 quart warm water
- 1 tablespoon cornstarch, plus 2 teaspoons

- ¼ cup extra-virgin olive oil
- 1 tablespoon salt
- 1 tablespoon packed brown sugar
- 1 teaspoon ground cinnamon
- 1 teaspoon freshly ground black pepper
- ½ teaspoon cayenne pepper

Directions:
1. Using a mandolin, thinly slice the sweet potatoes.
2. Pour the warm water into a large bowl and add 1 tablespoon of cornstarch and the potato slices. Let soak for 15 to 20 minutes.
3. Supply your smoker with wood pellets and follow the manufacturer's specific start-up procedure. Preheat, with the lid closed, to 375°F.
4. Drain the potato slices, then arrange in a single layer on a perforated pizza pan or a baking sheet lined with aluminum foil. Brush the potato slices on both sides with the olive oil.
5. In a small bowl, whisk together the salt, brown sugar, cinnamon, black pepper, cayenne pepper, and the remaining 2 teaspoons of cornstarch. Sprinkle this seasoning blend on both sides of the potatoes.
6. Place the pan or baking sheet on the grill grate, close the lid, and smoke for 35 to 45 minutes, flipping after 20 minutes, until the chips curl up and become crispy.
7. Store in an airtight container.

Kale Chips

Servings: 6
Cooking Time: 20 Minutes
Ingredients:
- 2 bunches of kale, stems removed
- ½ teaspoon of sea salt
- 4 tablespoons olive oil

Directions:
1. Switch on the grill, fill the grill hopper with apple-flavored wood pellets, power the grill on by using the control panel, select 'smoke' on the temperature dial, or set the temperature to 250 degrees F and let it preheat for a minimum of 15 minutes.
2. Meanwhile, rinse the kale leaves, pat dry, spread the kale on a sheet tray, drizzle with oil, season with salt and toss until well coated.
3. When the grill has preheated, open the lid, place sheet tray on the grill grate, shut the grill and smoke for 20 minutes until crisp.
4. Serve straight away.
Nutrition Info: Calories: 110 Cal ;Fat: 5 g ;Carbs: 15.8 g ;Protein: 5.3 g ;Fiber: 5.6 g

Wood Pellet Grilled Vegetables

Servings: 8
Cooking Time: 15 Minutes
Ingredients:
- 1 veggie tray
- 1/4 cup vegetable oil
- 2 tbsp veggie seasoning

Directions:
1. Preheat the wood pellet grill to 375°F
2. Toss the vegetables in oil then place on a sheet pan.
3. Sprinkle with veggie seasoning then place on the hot grill.
4. Grill for 15 minutes or until the veggies are cooked.
5. Let rest then serve. Enjoy.
Nutrition Info: Calories 44, Total fat 5g, Saturated fat 0g, Total Carbs 1g, Net Carbs 1g, Protein 0g, Sugar 0g, Fiber 0g, Sodium: 36mg, Potassium 10mg

Smoked Pickles

Servings: 6
Cooking Time: 15 Minutes
Ingredients:
- 1-quart water
- ¼ cup sugar
- ½ quart white vinegar
- ½ cup salt
- ½ teaspoon peppercorns
- 1 ½ teaspoons celery seeds
- 1 ½ teaspoons coriander seeds
- 1 teaspoon mustard seeds
- 8 cloves of garlic, minced
- 1 bunch dill weed
- 12 small cucumbers

Directions:
1. Place the water, sugar, vinegar, salt, and peppercorns in a saucepan. Bring to a boil over medium flame.
2. Transfer to a bowl and allow to cool. Add in the rest of the ingredients.
3. Allow the cucumber to soak in the brine for at least 3 days.
4. When ready to cook, fire the Grill to 500F. Use desired wood pellets when cooking. Close the lid and preheat for 15 minutes.
5. Pat dry the cucumber with paper towel and place on the grill grate. Smoke for 15 minutes.
Nutrition Info: Calories per serving: 67; Protein: 2.4g; Carbs: 12.9g; Fat: 1.1g Sugar:8.5 g

Wood Pellet Smoked Vegetables

Servings: 6
Cooking Time: 15 Minutes
Ingredients:
- 1 ear corn, fresh, husks and silk strands removed
- 1yellow squash, sliced
- 1 red onion, cut into wedges
- 1 green pepper, cut into strips
- 1 red pepper, cut into strips
- 1 yellow pepper, cut into strips
- 1 cup mushrooms, halved
- 2 tbsp oil
- 2 tbsp chicken seasoning

Directions:
1. Soak the pecan wood pellets in water for an hour. Remove the pellets from water and fill the smoker box with the wet pellets.
2. Place the smoker box under the grill and close the lid. Heat the grill on high heat for 10 minutes or until smoke starts coming out from the wood chips.
3. Meanwhile, toss the veggies in oil and seasonings then transfer them into a grill basket.
4. Grill for 10 minutes while turning occasionally. Serve and enjoy.

Nutrition Info: Calories 97, Total fat 5g, Saturated fat 2g, Total Carbs 11g, Net Carbs 8g, Protein 2g, Sugar 1g, Fiber 3g, Sodium: 251mg, Potassium 171mg

Garlic And Rosemary Potato Wedges

Servings: 4
Cooking Time: 1 Hour 30 Minutes
Ingredients:
- 4-6 large russet potatoes, cut into wedges
- ¼ cup olive oil
- 2garlic cloves, minced
- 2tablespoons rosemary leaves, chopped
- 2teaspoon salt
- 1teaspoon fresh ground black pepper
- 1teaspoon sugar
- 1teaspoon onion powder

Directions:
1. Preheat your smoker to 250 degrees Fahrenheit using maple wood
2. Take a large bowl and add potatoes and olive oil
3. Toss well
4. Take another small bowl and stir garlic, salt, rosemary, pepper, sugar, onion powder
5. Sprinkle the mix on all sides of the potato wedge
6. Transfer the seasoned wedge to your smoker rack and smoke for 1 and a ½ hours
7. Serve and enjoy!

Nutrition Info: Calories: 291 Fats: 10g Carbs: 46g Fiber: 2g

Wood Pellet Grilled Stuffed Zucchini

Servings: 8
Cooking Time: 11 Minutes
Ingredients:
- 4 zucchini
- 5 tbsp olive oil
- 2 tbsp red onion, chopped
- 1/4 tbsp garlic, minced
- 1/2 cup bread crumbs
- 1/2 cup mozzarella cheese, shredded
- 1 tbsp fresh mint
- 1/2 tbsp salt
- 3 tbsp parmesan cheese

Directions:
1. Cut the zucchini lengthwise and scoop out the pulp then brush the shells with oil.
2. In a non-stick skillet sauté pulp, onion, and remaining oil. Add garlic and cook for a minute.
3. Add bread crumbs and cook until golden brown. Remove from heat and stir in mozzarella cheese, fresh mint, and salt.
4. Spoon the mixture into the shells and sprinkle parmesan cheese.
5. Place in a grill and grill for 10 minutes or until the zucchini are tender.

Nutrition Info: Calories 186, Total fat 10g, Saturated fat 5g, Total Carbs 17g, Net Carbs 14g, Protein 9g, Sugar 4g, Fiber 3g, Sodium: 553mg

Smoked Watermelon

Servings: 5
Cooking Time: 45-90 Minutes
Ingredients:
- 1 small seedless watermelon
- Balsamic vinegar
- Wooden skewers

Directions:
1. Slice ends of small seedless watermelons
2. Slice the watermelon in 1-inch cubes. Put the cubes in a container and drizzle vinegar on the cubes of watermelon.
3. Preheat the smoker to 225°F. Add wood chips and water to the smoker before starting preheating.
4. Place the cubes on the skewers.
5. Place the skewers on the smoker rack for 50 minutes.
6. Cook
7. Remove the skewers.
8. Serve!

Nutrition Info: Calories: 20 Cal Fat: 0 g Carbohydrates: 4 g Protein: 1 g Fiber: 0.2 g

Nutrition Info: Calories: 231 Fats: 10g Carbs: 26g Fiber: 1g

Roasted Hasselback Potatoes

Servings: 6
Cooking Time: 30 Minutes
Ingredients:
- 6 large russet potatoes
- 1-pound bacon
- ½ cup butter
- Salt to taste
- 1 cup cheddar cheese
- 3 whole scallions, chopped

Directions:
1. Fire the Grill to 350F. Use desired wood pellets when cooking. Close the lid and preheat for 15 minutes.
2. Place two wooden spoons on either side of the potato and slice the potato into thin strips without completely cutting through the potato.
3. Chop the bacon into small pieces and place in between the cracks or slices of the potatoes.
4. Place potatoes in a cast iron skillet. Top the potatoes with butter, salt, and cheddar cheese.
5. Place the skillet on the grill grate and cook for 30 minutes. Make sure to baste the potatoes with melted cheese 10 minutes before the cooking time ends.

Nutrition Info: Calories per serving: 662; Protein: 16.1g; Carbs: 71.5g; Fat: 38g Sugar: 2.3g

Smoked Healthy Cabbage

Servings: 5
Cooking Time: 2 Hours
Ingredients:
- 1head cabbage, cored
- 4tablespoons butter
- 2tablespoons rendered bacon fat
- 1chicken bouillon cube
- 1teaspoon fresh ground black pepper
- 1garlic clove, minced

Directions:
1. Preheat your smoker to 240 degrees Fahrenheit using your preferred wood
2. Fill the hole of your cored cabbage with butter, bouillon cube, bacon fat, pepper and garlic
3. Wrap the cabbage in foil about two-thirds of the way up
4. Make sure to leave the top open
5. Transfer to your smoker rack and smoke for 2 hours
6. Unwrap and enjoy!

Roasted Spicy Tomatoes

Servings: 4
Cooking Time: 1 Hour And 30 Minutes
Ingredients:
- 2 lb. large tomatoes, sliced in half
- Olive oil
- 2 tablespoons garlic, chopped
- 3 tablespoons parsley, chopped
- Salt and pepper to taste
- Hot pepper sauce

Directions:
1. Set the temperature to 400 degrees F.
2. Preheat it for 15 minutes while the lid is closed.
3. Add tomatoes to a baking pan.
4. Drizzle with oil and sprinkle with garlic, parsley, salt and pepper.
5. Roast for 1 hour and 30 minutes.
6. Drizzle with hot pepper sauce and serve.
7. Tips: You can also puree the roasted tomatoes and use as sauce for pasta or as dip for chips.

Roasted Sheet Pan Vegetables

Servings: 6
Cooking Time: 20 Minutes
Ingredients:
- 1 small purple cauliflower, cut into florets
- 1 small yellow cauliflower, cut into florets
- 4 cups butternut squash
- 2 cups mushroom, fresh
- 3 tablespoons extra virgin olive oil
- 2 teaspoons salt
- 2 teaspoons black pepper

Directions:
1. Fire the Grill to 350F. Use desired wood pellets when cooking. Close the lid and preheat for 15 minutes.
2. Place the vegetables in a baking tray and season with olive oil, salt, and pepper. Toss to coat all vegetables.
3. Place in the grill and cook for 20 minutes. Make sure to shake the tray halfway through the cooking time for even cooking.

Nutrition Info: Calories per serving: 101; Protein: 3.8g; Carbs: 16.9g; Fat: 3.5g Sugar: 4.4g

Roasted Peach Salsa

Servings: 6
Cooking Time: 10 Minutes

Ingredients:

- 6 whole peaches, pitted and halved
- 3 tomatoes, chopped
- 2 whole onions, chopped
- ½ cup cilantro, chopped
- 2 cloves garlic, minced
- 5 teaspoons apple cider vinegar
- ½ teaspoon salt
- ¼ teaspoon black pepper
- 2 tablespoons olive oil

Directions:

1. Fire the Grill to 300F. Use desired wood pellets when cooking. Close the lid and preheat for 15 minutes.
2. Place the peaches on the grill grate and cook for 5 minutes on each side. Remove from the grill and allow to rest for 5 minutes.
3. Place the peaches, tomatoes, onion, and cilantro in a salad bowl. On a smaller bowl, stir in the garlic, apple cider vinegar, salt, pepper, and olive oil. Stir until well-combined. Pour into the salad and toss to coat.

Nutrition Info: Calories per serving: 155 ; Protein: 3.1g; Carbs: 27.6 g; Fat: 5.1g Sugar: 20g

Smoked Pumpkin Soup

Servings: 6
Cooking Time: 1 Hour And 33 Minutes
Ingredients:

- 5 pounds pumpkin, seeded and sliced
- 3 tablespoons butter
- 1 onion, diced
- 2 cloves garlic, minced
- 1 tablespoon brown sugar
- 1 teaspoon paprika
- ¼ teaspoon ground cinnamon
- ¼ teaspoon ground nutmeg
- ½ cup apple cider
- 5 cups broth
- ½ cup cream

Directions:

1. Fire the Grill to 180F. Use desired wood pellets when cooking. Close the lid and preheat for 15 minutes.
2. Place the pumpkin on the grill grate and smoke for an hour or until tender. Allow to cool.
3. Melt the butter in a large saucepan over medium heat and sauté the onion and garlic for 3 minutes. Stir in the rest of the ingredients including the smoked pumpkin. Cook for another 30 minutes.
4. Transfer to a blender and pulse until smooth.

Nutrition Info: Calories per serving: 246; Protein: 8.8g; Carbs: 32.2g; Fat: 11.4g Sugar: 15.5g

Smoked Mashed Red Potatoes

Servings: 8
Cooking Time: 30 Minutes
Ingredients:

- 8 large potatoes
- Salt and pepper to taste
- ½ cup heavy cream
- ¼ cup butter

Directions:

1. Fire the Grill to 180F. Use desired wood pellets when cooking. Close the lid and preheat for 15 minutes.
2. Slice the potatoes into half and season with salt and pepper to taste. Place on a baking tray.
3. Place the tray with the potatoes on the grill grate and cook for 30 minutes. Be sure to flip the potatoes halfway through the cooking time.
4. Once cooked, remove from the grill and place on a bowl. Add the rest of the ingredients and mash until well-combined.

Nutrition Info: Calories per serving: 363 ; Protein: 7.8g; Carbs: 65.2g; Fat: 8.9g Sugar: 3.4g

Smokey Roasted Cauliflower

Servings: 4 To 6
Cooking Time: 1 Hour 20 Minutes
Ingredients:

- 1head cauliflower
- cup parmesan cheese
- Spice Ingredients:
- 1tbsp olive oil
- 2cloves garlic, chopped
- 1tsp kosher salt
- 1tsp smoked paprika

Directions:

1. Preheat pellet grill to 180°F. If applicable, set smoke setting to high.
2. Cut cauliflower into bite-size flowerets and place in a grill basket. Place basket on the grill grate and smoke for an hour.
3. Mix spice Ingredients In a small bowl while the cauliflower is smoking. Remove cauliflower from the grill after an hour and let cool.
4. Change grill temperature to 425°F. After the cauliflower has cooled, put cauliflower in a resealable bag, and pour marinade in the bag. Toss to combine in the bag.
5. Place cauliflower back in a grill basket and return to grill. Roast in the grill basket for 10-12 minutes or until the outsides begin to get crispy and golden brown.
6. Remove from grill and transfer to a serving dish. Sprinkle parmesan cheese over the cauliflower and

rest for a few minutes so the cheese can melt. Serve and enjoy!
Nutrition Info: Calories: 70 Fat: 35 g Cholesterol: 0 Carbohydrate: 7 g Fiber: 3 g Sugar: 3 g Protein: 3 g

Grilled Cherry Tomato Skewers

Servings: 4
Cooking Time: 50 Minutes
Ingredients:
- 24 cherry tomatoes
- 1/4 cup olive oil
- 3tbsp balsamic vinegar
- 4garlic cloves, minced
- 1tbsp fresh thyme, finely chopped
- 1tsp kosher salt
- 1tsp ground black pepper
- 2tbsp chives, finely chopped

Directions:
1. Preheat pellet grill to 425°F.
2. In a medium-sized bowl, mix olive oil, balsamic vinegar, garlic, and thyme. Add tomatoes and toss to coat.
3. Let tomatoes sit in the marinade at room temperature for about 30 minutes.
4. Remove tomatoes from marinade and thread 4 tomatoes per skewer.
5. Season both sides of each skewer with kosher salt and ground pepper.
6. Place on grill grate and grill for about 3 minutes on each side, or until each side is slightly charred.
7. Remove from grill and allow to rest for about 5 minutes. Garnish with chives, then serve and enjoy!
Nutrition Info: Calories: 228 Fat: 10 g Cholesterol: 70 mg Carbohydrate: 7 g Fiber: 2 g Sugar: 3 g Protein: 27 g

Wood Pellet Smoked Mushrooms

Servings: 5
Cooking Time: 45 Minutes
Ingredients:
- 4 cup portobello, whole and cleaned
- 1 tbsp canola oil
- 1 tbsp onion powder
- 1 tbsp granulated garlic
- 1tbsp salt
- 1 tbsp pepper

Directions:
1. In a mixing bowl, add all the ingredients and mix well.
2. Set the wood pellet temperature to 180°F then place the mushrooms directly on the grill.
3. Smoke the mushrooms for 30 minutes.

4. Increase the temperature to high and cook the mushrooms for a further 15 minutes.
5. Serve and enjoy.
Nutrition Info: Calories 1680, Total fat 30g, Saturated fat 2g, Total Carbs 10g, Net Carbs 10g, Protein 4g, Sugar 0g, Fiber 0g, Sodium: 514mg, Potassium 0mg

Whole Roasted Cauliflower With Garlic Parmesan Butter

Servings: 5
Cooking Time: 45 Minutes
Ingredients:
- 1/4 cup olive oil
- Salt and pepper to taste
- 1 cauliflower, fresh
- 1/2 cup butter, melted
- 1/4 cup parmesan cheese, grated
- 2 garlic cloves, minced
- 1/2 tbsp parsley, chopped

Directions:
1. Preheat the wood pellet grill with the lid closed for 15 minutes.
2. Meanwhile, brush the cauliflower with oil then season with salt and pepper.
3. Place the cauliflower in a cast iron and place it on a grill grate.
4. Cook for 45 minutes or until the cauliflower is golden brown and tender.
5. Meanwhile, mix butter, cheese, garlic, and parsley in a mixing bowl.
6. In the last 20 minutes of cooking, add the butter mixture.
7. Remove the cauliflower from the grill and top with more cheese and parsley if you desire. Enjoy.
Nutrition Info: Calories 156, Total fat 11.1g, Saturated fat 3.4g, Total Carbs 8.8g, Net Carbs 5.1g, Protein 8.2g, Sugar 0g, Fiber 3.7g, Sodium: 316mg, Potassium 468.2mg

Zucchini With Red Potatoes

Servings: 4
Cooking Time: 4 Hours
Ingredients:
- 2 zucchinis, sliced in 3/4-inch-thick disks
- 1 red pepper, cut into strips
- 2 yellow squash, sliced in 3/4-inch-thick disks
- 1 medium red onion, cut into wedges
- 6 small red potatoes, cut into chunks
- Balsamic Vinaigrette:
- 1/3 cup extra virgin olive oil
- 1/4 teaspoon salt

- 1/4 cup balsamic vinegar
- 2 tsp Dijon mustard
- 1/8 teaspoon pepper

Directions:

1. For Vinaigrette: Take a medium-sized bowl and blend together olive oil, Dijon mustard, salt, pepper, and balsamic vinegar.
2. Place all the veggies into a large bowl and pour the vinaigrette mixture over it and evenly toss.
3. Put the vegetable in a pan and then smoke for 4 hours at a temperature of 225°F.
4. Serve and enjoy the food.

Nutrition Info: Calories: 381 Cal Fat: 17.6 g Carbohydrates: 49 g Protein: 6.7 g Fiber: 6.5 g

Minestrone Soup

Servings: 4
Cooking Time: 35 Minutes
Ingredients:

- 1/4 tsp. Black Pepper
- 2tbsp. Olive Oil
- 15 oz. Cannellini Beans
- 1Onion quartered
- 1/2 tsp. Salt
- 2Garlic cloves, minced
- 1/3 cup Parmesan Cheese, grated
- 2Rosemary sprigs, minced
- 1cup Kale leaves, chopped
- 4cups Vegetable Stock
- Juice and Zest of 1 Lemon

Directions:

1. Begin by keeping oil, onion, and garlic in the pitcher of the blender.
2. Next, select the 'saute' button.
3. Once sautéed, stir in celery, rosemary, vegetable stock, lemon zest, lemon juice, kale, parmesan, salt, and pepper.
4. Then, press the 'hearty soup' button.
5. When it takes only 5 to 6 minutes to finish, add the beans and continue cooking.

Nutrition Info: Calories: 34 Fat: 1 g Total Carbs: 4.7 g Fiber: 0.4 g Sugar: 0 g Protein: 1.8 g Cholesterol: 1 mg

Baked Parmesan Mushrooms

Servings: 8
Cooking Time: 15 Minutes
Ingredients:

- 8 mushroom caps
- 1/2 cup Parmesan cheese, grated
- 1/2 teaspoon garlic salt
- 1/4 cup mayonnaise

- Pinch paprika
- Hot sauce

Directions:

1. Place mushroom caps in a baking pan.
2. Mix the remaining ingredients in a bowl.
3. Scoop the mixture onto the mushroom.
4. Place the baking pan on the grill.
5. Cook in the wood pellet grill at 350 degrees F for 15 minutes while the lid is closed.
6. Tips: You can also add chopped sausage to the mixture.

Grilled Asparagus With Wild Mushrooms

Servings: 4
Cooking Time: 10 Minutes
Ingredients:

- 2 bunches fresh asparagus, trimmed
- 4 cups wild mushrooms, sliced
- 1 large shallots, sliced into rings
- Extra virgin oil as needed
- 2 tablespoons butter, melted

Directions:

1. Fire the Grill to 500F. Use desired wood pellets when cooking. Close the lid and preheat for 15 minutes.
2. Place the asparagus, mushrooms, and shallots on a baking tray. Drizzle with oil and butter and season with salt and pepper to taste.
3. Place on a baking tray and cook for 10 minutes. Make sure to give the asparagus a good stir halfway through the cooking time for even browning.

Nutrition Info: Calories per serving: 218; Protein: 15.2g; Carbs: 26.6 g; Fat: 10g Sugar: 12.9g

Smoked And Smashed New Potatoes

Servings: 4
Cooking Time: 8 Hours
Ingredients:

- 1-1/2 pounds small new red potatoes or fingerlings
- Extra virgin olive oil
- Sea salt and black pepper
- 2 tbsp softened butter

Directions:

1. Let the potatoes dry. Once dried, put in a pan and coat with salt, pepper, and extra virgin olive oil.
2. Place the potatoes on the topmost rack of the smoker.
3. Smoke for 60 minutes.
4. Once done, take them out and smash each one
5. Mix with butter and season

Nutrition Info: Calories: 258 Cal Fat: 2.0 g Carbohydrates: 15.5 g Protein: 4.1 g Fiber: 1.5 g

Grilled Baby Carrots And Fennel

Servings: 8
Cooking Time: 30 Minutes
Ingredients:
- 1-pound slender rainbow carrots, washed and peeled
- 2 whole fennel bulbs, chopped
- 2 tablespoons extra virgin olive oil
- 1 teaspoon salt
- Salt to taste

Directions:
1. Fire the Grill to 500F. Use desired wood pellets when cooking. Close the lid and preheat for 15 minutes.
2. Place all ingredients in a sheet tray and toss to coat with oil and seasoning.
3. Place on the grill grate and cook for 30 minutes.

Nutrition Info: Calories per serving:52 ; Protein: 1.2g; Carbs: 8.9g; Fat: 1.7g Sugar: 4.3g

Smoked Hummus

Servings: 6
Cooking Time: 20 Minutes
Ingredients:
- 1 ½ cups chickpeas, rinsed and drained
- ¼ cup tahini
- 1 tablespoon garlic, minced
- 2 tablespoons extra virgin olive oil
- 1 teaspoon salt
- 4 tablespoons lemon juice

Directions:
1. Fire the Grill to 350F. Use desired wood pellets when cooking. Close the lid and preheat for 15 minutes.
2. Spread the chickpeas on a sheet tray and place on the grill grate. Smoke for 20 minutes.
3. Let the chickpeas cool at room temperature.
4. Place smoked chickpeas in a blender or food processor. Add in the rest of the ingredients. Pulse until smooth.
5. Serve with roasted vegetables if desired.

Nutrition Info: Calories per serving: 271; Protein: 12.1g; Carbs: 34.8g; Fat: 10.4g Sugar: 5.7g

Wood Pellet Bacon Wrapped Jalapeno Poppers

Servings: 6
Cooking Time: 20 Minutes
Ingredients:
- 6 jalapenos, fresh
- 4 oz cream cheese
- 1/2 cup cheddar cheese, shredded
- 1 tbsp vegetable rub
- 12 slices cut bacon

Directions:
1. Preheat the wood pellet smoker and grill to375°F.
2. Slice the jalapenos lengthwise and scrape the seed and membrane. Rinse them with water and set aside.
3. In a mixing bowl, mix cream cheese, cheddar cheese, vegetable rub until well mixed.
4. Fill the jalapeno halves with the mixture then wrap with the bacon pieces.
5. Smoke for 20 minutes or until the bacon crispy.
6. Serve and enjoy.

Nutrition Info: Calories 1830, Total fat 11g, Saturated fat 6g, Total Carbs 5g, Net Carbs 4g, Protein 6g, Sugar 4g, Fiber 1g

Grilled Scallions

Servings: 6
Cooking Time: 20 Minutes
Ingredients:
- 10 whole scallions, chopped
- ¼ cup olive oil
- Salt and pepper to taste
- 2 tablespoons rice vinegar
- 1 whole jalapeno, sliced into rings

Directions:
1. Fire the Grill to 500F. Use desired wood pellets when cooking. Close the lid and preheat for 15 minutes.
2. Place on a bowl all ingredients and toss to coat. Transfer to a parchment-lined baking tray.
3. Place on the grill grate and cook for 20 minutes or until the scallions char.

Nutrition Info: Calories per serving: 135; Protein: 2.2 g; Carbs: 9.7 g; Fat: 10.1g Sugar: 4.6g

Feisty Roasted Cauliflower

Servings: 4
Cooking Time: 10 Minutes
Ingredients:
- 1cauliflower head, cut into florets
- 1tablespoon oil
- 1cup parmesan, grated
- 2garlic cloves, crushed
- ½ teaspoon pepper
- ½ teaspoon salt
- ¼ teaspoon paprika

Directions:

1. Preheat your Smoker to 180 degrees F
2. Transfer florets to smoker and smoke for 1 hour
3. Take a bowl and add all ingredients except cheese
4. Once smoking is done, remove florets
5. Increase temperature to 450 degrees F, brush florets with the brush and transfer to grill
6. Smoke for 10 minutes more
7. Sprinkle cheese on top and let them sit (Lid closed) until cheese melts
8. Serve and enjoy!

Nutrition Info: Calories: 45 Fats: 2g Carbs: 7g Fiber: 1g

Grilled Carrots And Asparagus

Servings: 6
Cooking Time: 30 Minutes
Ingredients:
- 1 pound whole carrots, with tops
- 1 bunch of asparagus, ends trimmed
- Sea salt as needed
- 1 teaspoon lemon zest
- 2 tablespoons honey
- 2 tablespoons olive oil

Directions:
1. Switch on the grill, fill the grill hopper with flavored wood pellets, power the grill on by using the control panel, select 'smoke' on the temperature dial, or set the temperature to 450 degrees F and let it preheat for a minimum of 15 minutes.
2. Meanwhile, take a medium dish, place asparagus in it, season with sea salt, drizzle with oil and toss until mixed.
3. Take a medium bowl, place carrots in it, drizzle with honey, sprinkle with sea salt and toss until combined.
4. When the grill has preheated, open the lid, place asparagus and carrots on the grill grate, shut the grill and smoke for 30 minutes.
5. When done, transfer vegetables to a dish, sprinkle with lemon zest, and then serve.

Nutrition Info: Calories: 79.8 Cal ;Fat: 4.8 g ;Carbs: 8.6 g ;Protein: 2.6 g ;Fiber: 3.5 g

Bacon-wrapped Jalapeno Poppers

Servings: 6
Cooking Time: 20 Minutes
Ingredients:
- 6 jalapenos, Fresh
- 1/2 cup shredded cheddar cheese
- 4 oz soft cream cheese
- 1-1/2 tbsp veggie rub
- 12 bacon slices, thin cut

Directions:
1. Preheat your grill to 375F.
2. Halve the jalapenos lengthwise then scrape membrane and seeds using a spoon. rinse them and set aside.
3. Meanwhile, combine cheddar cheese, cream cheese, and veggie rub in a bowl, medium stirring until incorporated fully.
4. Fill the jalapenos with your cheese mixture then wrap each half with a bacon slice.
5. Place on your grill and grill for about 15-20 minutes until bacon becomes crispy and peppers are soft.
6. Serve and enjoy.

Nutrition Info: Calories 329, Total fat 25.7g, Saturated fat 11.4g, Total carbs 5g, Net carbs 4.6g, Protein 18.1g, Sugars 0.6g, Fiber 0.4g, Sodium 1667mg, Potassium 277mg

Blt Pasta Salad

Servings: 6
Cooking Time: 35 To 45 Minutes
Ingredients:
- 1 pound thick-cut bacon
- 16 ounces bowtie pasta, cooked according to package directions and drained
- 2 tomatoes, chopped
- ½ cup chopped scallions
- ½ cup Italian dressing
- ½ cup ranch dressing
- 1 tablespoon chopped fresh basil
- 1 teaspoon salt
- 1 teaspoon freshly ground black pepper
- 1 teaspoon garlic powder
- 1 head lettuce, cored and torn

Directions:
1. Supply your smoker with wood pellets and follow the manufacturer's specific start-up procedure. Preheat, with the lid closed, to 225°F.
2. Arrange the bacon slices on the grill grate, close the lid, and cook for 30 to 45 minutes, flipping after 20 minutes, until crisp.
3. Remove the bacon from the grill and chop.
4. In a large bowl, combine the chopped bacon with the cooked pasta, tomatoes, scallions, Italian dressing, ranch dressing, basil, salt, pepper, and garlic powder. Refrigerate until ready to serve.
5. Toss in the lettuce just before serving to keep it from wilting.

Garlic And Herb Smoke Potato

Servings: 6
Cooking Time: 2 Hours

Ingredients:

- 1.5 pounds bag of Gemstone Potatoes
- 1/4 cup Parmesan, fresh grated
- For the Marinade
- 2 tbsp olive oil
- 6 garlic cloves, freshly chopped
- 1/2 tsp dried oregano
- 1/2 tsp dried basil
- 1/2 tsp dried dill
- 1/2 tsp salt
- 1/2 tsp dried Italian seasoning
- 1/4 tsp ground pepper

Directions:

1. Preheat the smoker to 225°F.
2. Wash the potatoes thoroughly and add them to a sealable plastic bag.
3. Add garlic cloves, basil, salt, Italian seasoning, dill, oregano, and olive oil to the zip lock bag. Shake.
4. Place in the fridge for 2 hours to marinate.
5. Next, take an Aluminum foil and put 2 tbsp of water along with the coated potatoes. Fold the foil so that the potatoes are sealed in
6. Place in the preheated smoker.
7. Smoke for 2 hours
8. Remove the foil and pour the potatoes into a bowl.
9. Serve with grated Parmesan cheese.

Nutrition Info: Calories: 146 Cal Fat: 6 g Carbohydrates: 19 g Protein: 4 g Fiber: 2.1 g

Caldereta Stew

Servings: 12
Cooking Time: 4 Hours

Ingredients:

- 2lb. chuck roast, sliced into cubes
- 2tablespoons olive oil
- 1carrot, sliced into cubes
- 2potatoes, sliced into cubes
- 4garlic cloves, chopped
- 2tablespoons tomato paste
- 2cups tomato sauce
- 2red bell peppers, sliced into strips
- 2green bell peppers, sliced into strips
- 2cups of water
- 1/2 cup cheddar cheese, grated
- 1/4 cup liver spread
- Salt to taste

Directions:

1. Put the beef in a cast iron pan.
2. Place this in the smoking cabinet.
3. Open the side dampers and sear slide.
4. Set the temperature to 375 degrees F.
5. Smoke the beef for 1 hour and 30 minutes.

6. Flip the beef and smoke for another 1 hour and 30 minutes.
7. Add a Dutch oven on top of the grill.
8. Pour in the olive oil.
9. Add the carrots and potatoes.
10. Cook for 5 minutes.
11. Stir in the garlic and cook for 1 minute.
12. Transfer the beef to the Dutch oven.
13. Stir in the tomato paste, tomato sauce, bell peppers, and water.
14. Bring to a boil.
15. Reduce temperature to 275 degrees F.
16. Simmer for 1 hour.
17. Add the cheese and liver.
18. Season with the salt.

Nutrition Info: Calories: 191.1 Fat: 9.3 g Cholesterol: 34 mg Carbohydrates: 15.4 g Fiber: 1.8 g Sugars: 1.3 g Protein: 11.3 g

Bacon-wrapped Jalapeño Poppers

Servings: 8 To 12
Cooking Time: 40 Minutes

Ingredients:

- 12 large jalapeño peppers
- 8 oz cream cheese, softened
- 1cup pepper jack cheese, shredded
- Juice of 1 lemon1/2 tsp garlic powder
- 1/4 tsp kosher salt
- 1/4 tsp ground black pepper
- 12 bacon slices, cut in half

Directions:

1. Preheat pellet grill to 400°F.
2. Slice jalapeños in half lengthwise. Remove seeds and scrape sides with a spoon to remove the membrane.
3. In a medium bowl, mix cream cheese, pepper jack cheese, garlic powder, salt, and pepper until thoroughly combined.
4. Use a spoon or knife to place the cream cheese mixture into each jalapeño half. Make sure not to fill over the sides of the jalapeño half.
5. Wrap each cheese-filled pepper with a half slice of bacon. If you can't get a secure wrap, then hold bacon and pepper together with a toothpick.
6. Place assembled poppers on the grill and cook for 15-20 minutes or until bacon is crispy.
7. Remove from grill, allow to cool, then serve and enjoy!

Nutrition Info: Calories: 78.8 Fat: 7.2 g Cholesterol: 19.2 mg Carbohydrate: 1 g Fiber: 0.2 g Sugar: 0.7 g Protein: 2.5 g

Easy Smoked Vegetables

Servings: 6
Cooking Time: 1 ½ Hour
Ingredients:
- 1 cup of pecan wood chips
- 1 ear fresh corn, silk strands removed, and husks, cut corn into 1-inch pieces
- 1 medium yellow squash, 1/2-inch slices
- 1 small red onion, thin wedges
- 1 small green bell pepper, 1-inch strips
- 1 small red bell pepper, 1-inch strips
- 1 small yellow bell pepper, 1-inch strips
- 1 cup mushrooms, halved
- 2 tbsp vegetable oil
- Vegetable seasonings

Directions:
1. Take a large bowl and toss all the vegetables together in it. Sprinkle it with seasoning and coat all the vegetables well with it.
2. Place the wood chips and a bowl of water in the smoker.
3. Preheat the smoker at 100°F or ten minutes.
4. Put the vegetables in a pan and add to the middle rack of the electric smoker.
5. Smoke for thirty minutes until the vegetable becomes tender.
6. When done, serve, and enjoy.

Nutrition Info: Calories: 97 Cal Fat: 5 g
Carbohydrates: 11 g Protein: 2 g Fiber: 3 g

Smoked Baked Beans

Servings: 12
Cooking Time: 3 Hours
Ingredients:
- 1 medium yellow onion diced
- 3 jalapenos
- 56 oz pork and beans
- 3/4 cup barbeque sauce
- 1/2 cup dark brown sugar
- 1/4 cup apple cider vinegar
- 2 tbsp Dijon mustard
- 2 tbsp molasses

Directions:
1. Preheat the smoker to 250°F. Pour the beans along with all the liquid in a pan. Add brown sugar, barbeque sauce, Dijon mustard, apple cider vinegar, and molasses. Stir. Place the pan on one of the racks. Smoke for 3 hours until thickened. Remove after 3 hours. Serve

Nutrition Info: Calories: 214 Cal Fat: 2 g
Carbohydrates: 42 g Protein: 7 g Fiber: 7 g

Cauliflower With Parmesan And Butter

Servings: 4
Cooking Time: 45 Minutes
Ingredients:
- 1 medium head of cauliflower
- 1 teaspoon minced garlic
- 1 teaspoon salt
- ½ teaspoon ground black pepper
- 1/4 cup olive oil
- 1/2 cup melted butter, unsalted
- 1/2 tablespoon chopped parsley
- 1/4 cup shredded parmesan cheese

Directions:
1. Switch on the grill, fill the grill hopper with flavored wood pellets, power the grill on by using the control panel, select 'smoke' on the temperature dial, or set the temperature to 450 degrees F and let it preheat for a minimum of 15 minutes.
2. Meanwhile, brush the cauliflower head with oil, season with salt and black pepper and then place in a skillet pan.
3. When the grill has preheated, open the lid, place prepared skillet pan on the grill grate, shut the grill and smoke for 45 minutes until golden brown and the center has turned tender.
4. Meanwhile, take a small bowl, place melted butter in it, and then stir in garlic, parsley, and cheese until combined.
5. Baste cheese mixture frequently in the last 20 minutes of cooking and, when done, remove the pan from heat and garnish cauliflower with parsley.
6. Cut it into slices and then serve.

Nutrition Info: Calories: 128 Cal ;Fat: 7.6 g ;Carbs: 10.8 g ;Protein: 7.4 g ;Fiber: 5 g

Split Pea Soup With Mushrooms

Servings: 4
Cooking Time: 35 Minutes
Ingredients:
- 2tbsp. Olive Oil
- 3Garlic cloves, minced
- 3tbsp. Parsley, fresh and chopped
- 2Carrots chopped
- 1.2/3 cup Green Peas
- 9cups Water
- 2tsp. Salt
- 1/4 tsp. Black Pepper
- 1lb. Portobello Mushrooms
- 1Bay Leaf
- 2Celery Ribs, chopped
- 1Onion quartered
- 1/2 tsp. Thyme, dried
- 6tbsp. Parmesan Cheese, grated

Directions:

1. First, keep oil, onion, and garlic in the blender pitcher.
2. Next, select the 'saute' button.
3. Once sautéed, stir in the rest of the ingredients, excluding parsley and cheese.
4. Then, press the 'hearty soup' button.
5. Finally, transfer the soup among the serving bowls and garnish it with parsley and cheese.

Nutrition Info: Calories: 61 Fat: 1.1 g Total Carbs: 10 g Fiber: 1.9 g Sugar: 3.2 g Protein: 3.2 g Cholesterol: 0

Roasted Veggies & Hummus

Servings: 4
Cooking Time: 20 Minutes
Ingredients:
- 1 white onion, sliced into wedges
- 2 cups butternut squash
- 2 cups cauliflower, sliced into florets
- 1 cup mushroom buttons
- Olive oil
- Salt and pepper to taste
- Hummus

Directions:
1. Set the wood pellet grill to high.
2. Preheat it for 10 minutes while the lid is closed.
3. Add the veggies to a baking pan.
4. Roast for 20 minutes.
5. Serve roasted veggies with hummus.
6. Tips: You can also spread a little hummus on the vegetables before roasting.

Grilled Zucchini Squash Spears

Servings: 4
Cooking Time: 10 Minutes
Ingredients:
- 4 zucchini, medium
- 2 tbsp olive oil
- 1 tbsp sherry vinegar
- 2 thyme, leaves pulled
- Salt to taste
- Pepper to taste

Directions:
1. Clean zucchini, cut ends off, half each lengthwise, and cut each half into thirds.
2. Combine all the other ingredients in a zip lock bag, medium, then add spears.
3. Toss well and mix to coat the zucchini.
4. Preheat to 350F with the lid closed for about 15 minutes.
5. Remove spears from the zip lock bag and place them directly on your grill grate with the cut side down.

6. Cook for about 3-4 minutes until zucchini is tender and grill marks show.
7. Remove them from the grill and enjoy.

Nutrition Info: Calories 93, Total fat 7.4g, Saturated fat 1.1g, Total carbs 7.1g, Net carbs 4.9g, Protein 2.4g, Sugars 3.4g, Fiber 2.2g, Sodium 59mg, Potassium 515mg

Baked Sweet And Savory Yams

Servings: 6
Cooking Time: 55 Minutes
Ingredients:
- 3 pounds yams, scrubbed
- 3 tablespoons extra virgin olive oil
- Honey to taste
- Goat cheese as needed
- ½ cup brown sugar
- ½ cup pecans, chopped

Directions:
1. Fire the Grill to 350F. Use desired wood pellets when cooking. Close the lid and preheat for 15 minutes.
2. Poke holes on the yams using a fork. Wrap yams in foil and place on the grill grate. Cook for 45 minutes until tender.
3. Remove the yams from the grill and allow to cool. Once cooled, peel the yam and slice to ¼" rounds.
4. Place on a parchment-lined baking tray and brush with olive oil. Drizzle with honey, cheese, brown sugar, and pecans.
5. Place in the grill and cook for another 10 minutes.

Nutrition Info: Calories per serving: 421; Protein: 4.3g; Carbs: 82.4g; Fat: 9.3g Sugar:19.3 g

Roasted Butternut Squash

Servings: 4
Cooking Time: 30 Minutes
Ingredients:
- 2-pound butternut squash
- 3 tablespoon extra-virgin olive oil
- Veggie Rub, as needed

Directions:
1. Fire the Grill to 350F. Use desired wood pellets when cooking. Close the lid and preheat for 15 minutes.
2. Slice the butternut squash into ½ inch thick and remove the seeds. Season with oil and veggie rub.
3. Place the seasoned squash in a baking tray.
4. Grill for 30 minutes.

Nutrition Info: Calories per serving: 131; Protein: 1.9g; Carbs: 23.6g; Fat: 4.7g Sugar: 0g

Carolina Baked Beans

Servings: 12 To 15 Minutes
Cooking Time: 2 To 3 Hours
Ingredients:
- 3 (28-ounce) cans baked beans (I like Bush's brand)
- 1 large onion, finely chopped
- 1 cup The Ultimate BBQ Sauce
- ½ cup light brown sugar
- ¼ cup Worcestershire sauce
- 3 tablespoons yellow mustard
- Nonstick cooking spray or butter, for greasing
- 1 large bell pepper, cut into thin rings
- ½ pound thick-cut bacon, partially cooked and cut into quarters

Directions:
1. Supply your smoker with wood pellets and follow the manufacturer's specific start-up procedure. Preheat, with the lid closed, to 300°F.
2. In a large mixing bowl, stir together the beans, onion, barbecue sauce, brown sugar, Worcestershire sauce, and mustard until well combined
3. Coat a 9-by-13-inch aluminum pan with cooking spray or butter.
4. Pour the beans into the pan and top with the bell pepper rings and bacon pieces, pressing them down slightly into the sauce.
5. Place a layer of heavy-duty foil on the grill grate to catch drips, and place the pan on top of the foil. Close the lid and cook for 2 hours 30 minutes to 3 hours, or until the beans are hot, thick, and bubbly.
6. Let the beans rest for 5 minutes before serving.

Potato Fries With Chipotle Peppers

Servings: 4
Cooking Time: 30 Minutes
Ingredients:
- 4 potatoes, sliced into strips
- 3 tablespoons olive oil
- Salt and pepper to taste
- 1 cup mayonnaise
- 2 chipotle peppers in adobo sauce
- 2 tablespoons lime juice

Directions:
1. Set the wood pellet grill to high.
2. Preheat it for 15 minutes while the lid is closed.
3. Coat the potato strips with oil.
4. Sprinkle with salt and pepper.
5. Put a baking pan on the grate.
6. Transfer potato strips to the pan.
7. Cook potatoes until crispy.

8. Mix the remaining ingredients.
9. Pulse in a food processor until pureed.
10. Serve potato fries with chipotle dip.
11. Tips: You can also use sweet potatoes instead of potatoes.

Chicken Tortilla Soup

Servings: 4
Cooking Time: 35 Minutes
Ingredients:
- 1/2 cup Black Beans, canned
- 1Jalapeno Pepper, halved and seeds removed
- 1-1/2 cup Chicken Stock
- 2Carrots, sliced into ¼-inch pieces
- 1/2 of 1 Onion, peeled and halved
- 1/2 cup Corn
- 3 Garlic cloves
- 14-1/2 oz. Fire Roasted Tomatoes
- 1/4 cup Cilantro Leaves
- 10 oz. Chicken Breast, diced into ½ inch
- For the seasoning mix:
- 1/4 tsp. Chipotle
- 1tsp. Cuminutes
- 1/2 tsp. Sea Salt
- 1/2 tsp. Smoked Paprika

Directions:
1. Place pepper, carrots, onion, garlic cloves, and cilantro in the blender pitcher.
2. Pulse the mixture for 3 minutes and then pour the chicken stock to it.
3. Pulse again for another 3 minutes.
4. Next, stir in the remaining ingredients and press the 'hearty soup' button.
5. Finally, transfer to the serving bowl.

Nutrition Info: Calories: 260 Fat: 4 g Total Carbs: 40 g Fiber: 5.9 g Sugar: 8 g Protein: 14 g Cholesterol: 20 mg

Smoked Tofu

Servings: 4
Cooking Time: 41 Hour And 30 Minutes
Ingredients:
- 400g plain tofu
- Sesame oil

Directions:
1. Preheat the smoker to 225°F while adding wood chips and water to it.
2. Till that time, take the tofu out of the packet and let it rest
3. Slice the tofu in one-inch thick pieces and apply sesame oil

4. Place the tofu inside the smoker for 45 minutes while adding water and wood chips after one hour.
5. Once cooked, take them out and serve!
Nutrition Info: Calories: 201 Cal Fat: 13 g Carbohydrates: 1 g Protein: 20 g Fiber: 0 g

Grilled Sugar Snap Peas

Servings: 4
Cooking Time: 10 Minutes
Ingredients:
* 2-pound sugar snap peas, ends trimmed
* ½ teaspoon garlic powder
* 1 teaspoon salt
* 2/3 teaspoon ground black pepper
* 2 tablespoons olive oil

Directions:
1. Switch on the grill, fill the grill hopper with apple-flavored wood pellets, power the grill on by using the control panel, select 'smoke' on the temperature dial, or set the temperature to 450 degrees F and let it preheat for a minimum of 15 minutes.
2. Meanwhile, take a medium bowl, place peas in it, add garlic powder and oil, season with salt and black pepper, toss until mixed and then spread on the sheet pan.
3. When the grill has preheated, open the lid, place the prepared sheet pan on the grill grate, shut the grill and smoke for 10 minutes until slightly charred.
4. Serve straight away.
Nutrition Info: Calories: 91 Cal ;Fat: 5 g ;Carbs: 9 g ;Protein: 4 g ;Fiber: 3 g

Grilled Broccoli

Servings: 1-2
Cooking Time: 3 Minutes
Ingredients:
* 2cups of broccoli, fresh
* 1tablespoon of canola oil
* 1teaspoon of lemon pepper

Directions:
1. Place the grill; grate inside the unit and close the hood.
2. Preheat the grill by turning at high for 10 minutes.
3. Meanwhile, mix broccoli with lemon pepper and canola oil.
4. Toss well to coat the Ingredients: thoroughly.
5. Place it on a grill grade once add food appears.
6. Lock the unit and cook for 3 minutes at medium.
7. Take out and serve.
Nutrition Info: Calories: 96 Total Fat: 7.3g Saturated Fat: 0.5g Cholesterol: 0mg Sodium: 30mg Total

Carbohydrate: 6.7g Dietary Fiber 2.7g Total Sugars: 1.6g Protein: 2.7g

Roasted Root Vegetables

Servings: 6
Cooking Time: 45 Minutes
Ingredients:
* 1 large red onion, peeled
* 1 bunch of red beets, trimmed, peeled
* 1 large yam, peeled
* 1 bunch of golden beets, trimmed, peeled
* 1 large parsnips, peeled
* 1 butternut squash, peeled
* 1 large carrot, peeled
* 6 garlic cloves, peeled
* 3 tablespoons thyme leaves
* Salt as needed
* 1 cinnamon stick
* Ground black pepper as needed
* 3 tablespoons olive oil
* 2 tablespoons honey

Directions:
1. Switch on the grill, fill the grill hopper with hickory flavored wood pellets, power the grill on by using the control panel, select 'smoke' on the temperature dial, or set the temperature to 450 degrees F and let it preheat for a minimum of 15 minutes.
2. Meanwhile, cut all the vegetables into ½-inch pieces, place them in a large bowl, add garlic, thyme, and cinnamon, drizzle with oil and toss until mixed.
3. Take a large cookie sheet, line it with foil, spread with vegetables, and then season with salt and black pepper.
4. When the grill has preheated, open the lid, place prepared cookie sheet on the grill grate, shut the grill and smoke for 45 minutes until tender.
5. When done, transfer vegetables to a dish, drizzle with honey, and then serve.
Nutrition Info: Calories: 164 Cal ;Fat: 4 g ;Carbs: 31.7 g ;Protein: 2.7 g ;Fiber: 6.4 g

Smoked Balsamic Potatoes And Carrots

Servings: 6
Cooking Time: 10 Minutes
Ingredients:
* 2 large carrots, peeled and chopped roughly
* 2 large Yukon Gold potatoes, peeled and wedged
* 5 tablespoons olive oil
* 5 tablespoons balsamic vinegar
* Salt and pepper to taste

Directions:

1. Fire the Grill to 400F. Use desired wood pellets when cooking. Close the lid and preheat for 15 minutes.
2. Place all ingredients in a bowl and toss to coat the vegetables with the seasoning.
3. Place on a baking tray lined with foil.
4. Place on the grill grate and close the lid. Cook for 30 minutes.
Nutrition Info: Calories per serving: 219; Protein: 2.9g; Carbs: 27g; Fat: 11.4g Sugar:4.5 g

Smoked Deviled Eggs

Servings: 4 To 6
Cooking Time: 50 Minutes
Ingredients:
- 6 large eggs
- 1slice bacon
- 1/4 cup mayonnaise
- 1tsp Dijon mustard
- 1tsp apple cider vinegar
- 1/4 tsp paprika
- Pinch of kosher salt
- 1tbsp chives, chopped

Directions:
1. Preheat pellet grill to 180°F and turn smoke setting on, if applicable.
2. Bring a pot of water to a boil. Add eggs and hard boil eggs for about 12 minutes.
3. Remove eggs from pot and place them into an ice-water bath. Once eggs have cooled completely, peel them and slice in half lengthwise.
4. Place sliced eggs on grill, yolk side up. Smoke for 30 to 45 minutes, depending on how much smoky flavor you want.
5. While eggs smoke, cook bacon until it's crispy.
6. Remove eggs from the grill and allow to cool on a plate.
7. Remove the yolks and place all of them in a small bowl. Place the egg whites on a plate.
8. Mash yolks with a fork and add mayonnaise, mustard, apple cider vinegar, paprika, and salt. Stir until combined.
9. Spoon a scoop of yolk mixture back into each egg white.
10. Sprinkle paprika, chives, and crispy bacon bits to garnish. Serve and enjoy!
Nutrition Info: Calories: 140 Fat: 12 g Cholesterol: 190 mg Carbohydrate: 1 g Fiber: 0 Sugar: 0 Protein: 6 g

Mexican Street Corn With Chipotle Butter 2

Servings: 6

Cooking Time: 45 Minutes
Ingredients:
- 16 to 20 long toothpicks
- 1 pound Brussels sprouts, trimmed and wilted, leaves removed
- ½ pound bacon, cut in half
- 1 tablespoon packed brown sugar
- 1 tablespoon Cajun seasoning
- ¼ cup balsamic vinegar
- ¼ cup extra-virgin olive oil
- ¼ cup chopped fresh cilantro
- 2 teaspoons minced garlic

Directions:
1. Soak the toothpicks in water for 15 minutes.
2. Supply your smoker with wood pellets and follow the manufacturer's specific start-up procedure. Preheat, with the lid closed, to 300°F.
3. Wrap each Brussels sprout in a half slice of bacon and secure with a toothpick.
4. In a small bowl, combine the brown sugar and Cajun seasoning. Dip each wrapped Brussels sprout in this sweet rub and roll around to coat.
5. Place the sprouts on a Frogmat or parchment paper–lined baking sheet on the grill grate, close the lid, and smoke for 45 minutes to 1 hour, turning as needed, until cooked evenly and the bacon is crisp.
6. In a small bowl, whisk together the balsamic vinegar, olive oil, cilantro, and garlic.
7. Remove the toothpicks from the Brussels sprouts, transfer to a plate and serve drizzled with the cilantro-balsamic sauce.

Smoked Potato Salad

Servings: 4
Cooking Time: 40 Minutes
Ingredients:
- 2 lb. potatoes
- 2 tablespoons olive oil
- 2 cups mayonnaise
- 1 tablespoon white wine vinegar
- 1 tablespoon dry mustard
- 1/2 onion, chopped
- 2 celery stalks, chopped
- Salt and pepper to taste

Directions:
1. Coat the potatoes with oil.
2. Smoke the potatoes in the wood pellet grill at 180 degrees F for 20 minutes.
3. Increase temperature to 450 degrees F and cook for 20 more minutes.
4. Transfer to a bowl and let cool.
5. Peel potatoes.
6. Slice into cubes.
7. Refrigerate for 30 minutes.

8. Stir in the rest of the ingredients.
9. Tips: You can also add chopped hard-boiled eggs to the mixture.

Grilled Corn With Honey & Butter

Servings: 4
Cooking Time: 10 Minutes
Ingredients:
- 6 pieces corn
- 2 tablespoons olive oil
- 1/2 cup butter
- 1/2 cup honey
- 1 tablespoon smoked salt
- Pepper to taste

Directions:
1. Preheat the wood pellet grill to high for 15 minutes while the lid is closed.
2. Brush the corn with oil and butter.
3. Grill the corn for 10 minutes, turning from time to time.
4. Mix honey and butter.
5. Brush corn with this mixture and sprinkle with smoked salt and pepper.
6. Tips: Slice off the kernels and serve as side dish to a main course.

Grilled Asparagus & Honey-glazed Carrots

Servings: 4
Cooking Time: 35 Minutes
Ingredients:
- 1 bunch asparagus, woody ends removed
- 2 tbsp olive oil
- 1 lb peeled carrots
- 2 tbsp honey
- Sea salt to taste
- Lemon zest to taste

Directions:
1. Rinse the vegetables under cold water.
2. Splash the asparagus with oil and generously with a splash of salt.
3. Drizzle carrots generously with honey and splash lightly with salt.
4. Preheat your to 350F with the lid closed for about 15 minutes.
5. Place the carrots first on the grill and cook for about 10-15 minutes.
6. Now place asparagus on the grill and cook both for about 15-20 minutes or until done to your liking.
7. Top with lemon zest and enjoy.
Nutrition Info: Calories 184, Total fat 7.3g, Saturated fat 1.1g, Total carbs 28.6g, Net carbs 21g, Protein 6g, Sugars 18.5g, Fiber 7.6g, Sodium 142mg, Potassium 826mg

Smoked Acorn Squash

Servings: 6
Cooking Time: 2 Hours
Ingredients:
- 3 acorn squash, seeded and halved
- 3 tbsp olive oil
- 1/4 cup butter, unsalted
- 1 tbsp cinnamon, ground
- 1 tbsp chili powder
- 1 tbsp nutmeg, ground
- 1/4 cup brown sugar

Directions:
1. Brush the cut sides of your squash with olive oil then cover with foil poking holes for smoke and steam to get through.
2. Preheat your to 225F.
3. Place the squash halves on the grill with the cut side down and smoke for about 1½- 2 hours. Remove from the Traeger.
4. Let it sit while you prepare spiced butter. Melt butter in a saucepan then add spices and sugar stirring to combine.
5. Remove the foil form the squash halves.
6. Place 1 tbsp of the butter mixture onto each half.
7. Serve and enjoy!
Nutrition Info: Calories 149, Total 10g, Saturated fat 5g, Total carbs 14g, Net carbs 12g, Protein 2g, Sugars 2g, Fiber 2g, Sodium 19mg, Potassium 101m

Vegetable Skewers

Servings: 4
Cooking Time: 20 Minutes
Ingredients:
- 2 cups whole white mushrooms
- 2 large yellow squash, peeled, chopped
- 1 cup chopped pineapple
- 1 cup chopped red pepper
- 1 cup halved strawberries
- 2 large zucchini, chopped
- For the Dressing:
- 2 lemons, juiced
- ½ teaspoon ground black pepper
- 1/2 teaspoon sea salt
- 1 teaspoon red chili powder
- 1 tablespoon maple syrup
- 1 tablespoon orange zest
- 2 tablespoons apple cider vinegar
- 1/4 cup olive oil

Directions:
1. Switch on the grill, fill the grill hopper with flavored wood pellets, power the grill on by using the

control panel, select 'smoke' on the temperature dial, or set the temperature to 450 degrees F and let it preheat for a minimum of 5 minutes.

2. Meanwhile, prepared thread vegetables and fruits on skewers alternately and then brush skewers with oil.

3. When the grill has preheated, open the lid, place vegetable skewers on the grill grate, shut the grill, and smoke for 20 minutes until tender and lightly charred.

4. Meanwhile, prepare the dressing and for this, take a small bowl, place all of its ingredients in it and then whisk until combined.

5. When done, transfer skewers to a dish, top with prepared dressing and then serve.

Nutrition Info: Calories: 130 Cal ;Fat: 2 g ;Carbs: 20 g ;Protein: 2 g ;Fiber: 0.3 g

Wood Pellet Grilled Mexican Street Corn

Servings: 6
Cooking Time: 25 Minutes
Ingredients:
- 6 ears of corn on the cob, shucked
- 1 tbsp olive oil
- Kosher salt and pepper to taste
- 1/4 cup mayo
- 1/4cup sour cream
- 1 tbsp garlic paste
- 1/2 tbsp chili powder
- Pinch of ground red pepper
- 1/2 cup cotija cheese, crumbled
- 1/4 cup cilantro, chopped
- 6 lime wedges

Directions:
1. Brush the corn with oil and sprinkle with salt.
2. Place the corn on a wood pellet grill set at 350°F. Cook for 25 minutes as you turn it occasionally.
3. Meanwhile mix mayo, cream, garlic, chili, and red pepper until well combined.
4. When the corn is cooked remove from the grill, let it rest for some minutes then brush with the mayo mixture.
5. Sprinkle cotija cheese, more chili powder, and cilantro. Serve with lime wedges. Enjoy.

Nutrition Info: Calories 144, Total fat 5g, Saturated fat 2g, Total Carbs 10g, Net Carbs 10g, Protein 0g, Sugar 0g, Fiber 0g, Sodium: 136mg, Potassium 173mg

Fries With Chipotle Ketchup

Servings: 6
Cooking Time: 10 Minutes
Ingredients:

- 6 Yukon Gold potatoes, scrubbed and cut into thick strips
- 1 tablespoon Beef Rub
- 1 tablespoon extra-virgin olive oil
- 1 teaspoon onion powder
- 1 teaspoon garlic powder
- ½ cup chipotle peppers, chopped
- 1 cup ketchup
- 1 tablespoon sugar
- 1 tablespoon cumin
- 1 tablespoon chili powder
- 1 whole lime
- 2 tablespoons butter

Directions:
1. Place the potatoes in a bowl and stir in the Beef Rub, olive oil, onion powder, and garlic powder. Toss to coat the potatoes with the spices.
2. Fire the Grill to 500F. Use desired wood pellets when cooking. Close the lid and preheat for 15 minutes.
3. Place the potatoes on a baking sheet lined with foil.
4. Place on the grill grate and cook for 10 minutes.
5. Meanwhile, place the rest of the ingredients in a small bowl and mix until well-combined.
6. Serve the fries with the chipotle ketchup sauce.

Nutrition Info: Calories per serving: 387 ; Protein: 8.6g; Carbs: 79.3g; Fat: 5.6g Sugar: 13.7g

Grilled Zucchini Squash

Servings: 6
Cooking Time: 10 Minutes
Ingredients:
- 3 medium zucchinis, sliced into ¼ inch thick lengthwise
- 2 tablespoons olive oil
- 1 tablespoon sherry vinegar
- 2 thyme leaves, pulled
- Salt and pepper to taste

Directions:
1. Fire the Grill to 350F. Use desired wood pellets when cooking. Close the lid and preheat for 15 minutes.
2. Place zucchini in a bowl and all ingredients. Gently massage the zucchini slices to coat with the seasoning.
3. Place the zucchini on the grill grate and cook for 5 minutes on each side.

Nutrition Info: Calories per serving: 44; Protein: 0.3 g; Carbs: 0.9 g; Fat: 4g Sugar: 0.1g

Corn Chowder

Servings: 3 To 4
Cooking Time: 35 Minutes
Ingredients:
- 1/4 tsp. Cajun Seasoning
- 2tbsp. Butter, unsalted
- 2tbsp. Parsley, fresh and minced
- 1Onion quartered
- 1/2 cup Celery Stalks, diced
- 1/4 tsp. Sea Salt
- 2Garlic cloves
- 1/4 cup Heavy Cream
- 1/2 cup Carrot, diced
- 3cups Corn Kernels, frozen
- 2-1/2 cups Vegetable Broth
- 1/4 tsp. Black Pepper, grounded
- 1Red Potato, chopped

Directions:
1. To start with, keep butter, onion, and garlic in the pitcher of the blender.
2. After that, press the 'saute' button.
3. Next, stir in all the remaining ingredients to the pitcher and select the 'hearty soup' button.
4. Once the program gets over, transfer the soup to serving bowls and serve immediately.
5. Garnish with parsley leaves.

Nutrition Info: Calories: 499 Fat: 40 g Total Carbs: 32 g Fiber: 2.5 g Sugar: 7.3 g Protein: 6.8 g Cholesterol: 120 mg

Vegan Smoked Carrot Dogs

Servings: 2
Cooking Time: 35 Minutes
Ingredients:
- 4 carrots, thick
- 2 tbsp avocado oil
- 1/2 tbsp garlic powder
- 1 tbsp liquid smoke
- Pepper to taste
- Kosher salt to taste

Directions:
1. Preheat your to 425F then line a parchment paper on a baking sheet.
2. Peel the carrots to resemble a hot dog. Round the edges when peeling.
3. Whisk together oil, garlic powder, liquid smoke, pepper and salt in a bowl, small.
4. Now place carrots on the baking sheet and pour the mixture over. Roll your carrots in the mixture to massage seasoning and oil into them. Use fingertips.
5. Roast the carrots in the until fork tender for about 35 minutes. Brush the carrots using the marinade mixture every 5 minutes.

6. Remove and place into hot dog buns then top with hot dog toppings of your choice.
7. Serve and enjoy!

Nutrition Info: Calories 76, Total fat 1.8g, Saturated 0.4g, Total 14.4g, Net carbs 10.6g, Protein 1.5g, Sugar 6.6g, Fiber 3.8g, Sodium 163mg, Potassium 458mg

Shiitake Smoked Mushrooms

Servings: 4-6
Cooking Time: 45 Minutes
Ingredients:
- 4 Cup Shiitake Mushrooms
- 1 tbsp canola oil
- 1 tsp onion powder
- 1 tsp granulated garlic
- 1 tsp salt
- 1 tsp pepper

Directions:
1. Combine all the ingredients together
2. Apply the mix over the mushrooms generously.
3. Preheat the smoker at 180°F. Add wood chips and half a bowl of water in the side tray.
4. Place it in the smoker and smoke for 45 minutes.
5. Serve warm and enjoy.

Nutrition Info: Calories: 301 Cal Fat: 9 g Carbohydrates: 47.8 g Protein: 7.1 g Fiber: 4.8 g

Southern Slaw

Servings: 10
Cooking Time: 1 Hour And 10 Minutes
Ingredients:
- 1 head cabbage, shredded
- ¼ cup white vinegar
- ¼ cup sugar
- 1 teaspoon paprika
- ½ teaspoon salt
- ½ teaspoon freshly ground black pepper
- 1 cup heavy (whipping) cream

Directions:
1. Place the shredded cabbage in a large bowl.
2. In a small bowl, combine the vinegar, sugar, paprika, salt, and pepper.
3. Pour the vinegar mixture over the cabbage and mix well.
4. Fold in the heavy cream and refrigerate for at least 1 hour before serving.

Grilled Baby Carrots And Fennel With Romesco

Servings: 8 To 12

Cooking Time: 45 Minutes
Ingredients:
- 1 Pound Slender Rainbow Carrots
- 2 Whole Fennel, bulb
- 2 Tablespoon extra-virgin olive oil
- 1 Teaspoon salt
- 2 Tablespoon extra-virgin olive oil
- To Taste salt
- 1 Tablespoon fresh thyme

Directions:
1. When ready to cook, set temperature to High and preheat, lid closed for 15 minutes. For optimal results, set to 500°F if available.
2. Trim the carrot tops to 1". Peel the carrots and halve any larger ones so they are all about 1/2" thick. Cut the fennel bulbs lengthwise into 1/2" thick slices.
3. Place the fennel and potato slices in a large mixing bowl. Drizzle with 2 Tbsp of the olive oil and a teaspoon of salt.
4. Toss to coat the vegetables evenly with the oil.
5. Place the carrots on a sheet pan. Drizzle with the additional 2 Tbsp of olive oil and a generous pinch of salt. Brush the olive oil over the carrots to distribute evenly.
6. Add the potatoes and fennel slices to the sheet pan. Nestle a few sprigs of herbs into the vegetables as well.
7. Place the pan directly on the grill grate and cook, stirring occasionally until the vegetables are browned and softened, about 35-45 minutes.
8. Allow to cool and serve with the Smoked Romesco Sauce. Enjoy!

Grilled Vegetables

Servings: 12
Cooking Time: 15 Minutes
Ingredients:
- 1 veggie tray
- 1/4 cup vegetable oil
- 1-2 tbsp veggie seasoning

Directions:
1. Preheat your to 375F.
2. Meanwhile, toss the veggies in oil placed on a sheet pan, large, then splash with the seasoning.
3. Place on the and grill for about 10-15 minutes.
4. Remove, serve, and enjoy.

Nutrition Info: Calories 44, Total fat 5g, Saturated fat 0g, Total carbs 1g, Net carbs 1g, Protein 0g, Sugars 0g, Fiber 0g, Sodium 36mg, Potassium 116mg

Bunny Dogs With Sweet And Spicy Jalapeño Relish

Servings: 8

Cooking Time: 35 To 40 Minutes
Ingredients:
- 8 hot dog-size carrots, peeled
- ¼ cup honey
- ¼ cup yellow mustard
- Nonstick cooking spray or butter, for greasing
- Salt
- Freshly ground black pepper
- 8 hot dog buns
- Sweet and Spicy Jalapeño Relish

Directions:
1. Prepare the carrots by removing the stems and slicing in half lengthwise.
2. In a small bowl, whisk together the honey and mustard.
3. Supply your smoker with wood pellets and follow the manufacturer's specific start-up procedure. Preheat, with the lid closed, to 375°F.
4. Line a baking sheet with aluminum foil and coat with cooking spray.
5. Brush the carrots on both sides with the honey mustard and season with salt and pepper; put on the baking sheet.
6. Place the baking sheet on the grill grate, close the lid, and smoke for 35 to 40 minutes, or until tender and starting to brown.
7. To serve, lightly toast the hot dog buns on the grill and top each with two slices of carrot and some relish.

Wood Pellet Smoked Asparagus

Servings: 4
Cooking Time: 1 Hour
Ingredients:
- 1 bunch fresh asparagus, ends cut
- 2 tbsp olive oil
- Salt and pepper to taste

Directions:
1. Fire up your wood pellet smoker to 230°F
2. Place the asparagus in a mixing bowl and drizzle with olive oil. Season with salt and pepper.
3. Place the asparagus in a tinfoil sheet and fold the sides such that you create a basket.
4. Smoke the asparagus for 1 hour or until soft turning after half an hour.
5. Remove from the grill and serve. Enjoy.

Nutrition Info: Calories 43, Total fat 2g, Saturated fat 0g, Total Carbs 4g, Net Carbs 2g, Protein 3g, Sugar 2g, Fiber 2g, Sodium: 148mg

Roasted Green Beans With Bacon

Servings: 6
Cooking Time: 20 Minutes

Ingredients:
- 1-pound green beans
- 4 strips bacon, cut into small pieces
- 4 tablespoons extra virgin olive oil
- 2 cloves garlic, minced
- 1 teaspoon salt

Directions:
1. Fire the Grill to 400F. Use desired wood pellets when cooking. Close the lid and preheat for 15 minutes.
2. Toss all ingredients on a sheet tray and spread out evenly.
3. Place the tray on the grill grate and roast for 20 minutes.

Nutrition Info: Calories per serving: 65 ; Protein: 1.3g; Carbs: 3.8g; Fat: 5.3g Sugar: 0.6g

Apple Veggie Burger

Servings: 6
Cooking Time: 35 Minutes
Ingredients:
- 3 tbsp ground flax or ground chia
- 1/3 cup of warm water
- 1/2 cups rolled oats
- 1 cup chickpeas, drained and rinsed
- 1 tsp cumin
- 1/2 cup onion
- 1 tsp dried basil
- 2 granny smith apples
- 1/3 cup parsley or cilantro, chopped
- 2 tbsp soy sauce
- 2 tsp liquid smoke
- 2 cloves garlic, minced
- 1 tsp chili powder
- 1/4 tsp black pepper

Directions:
1. Preheat the smoker to 225°F while adding wood chips and water to it.
2. In a separate bowl, add chickpeas and mash. Mix together the remaining ingredients along with the dipped flax seeds.
3. Form patties from this mixture.
4. Put the patties on the rack of the smoker and smoke them for 20 minutes on each side.
5. When brown, take them out, and serve.

Nutrition Info: Calories: 241 Cal Fat: 5 g Carbohydrates: 40 g Protein: 9 g Fiber: 10.3 g

Crispy Maple Bacon Brussels Sprouts

Servings: 6
Cooking Time: 1 Hour
Ingredients:

- 1lb brussels sprouts, trimmed and quartered
- 6 slices thick-cut bacon
- 3tbsp maple syrup
- 1tsp olive oil
- 1/2 tsp kosher salt
- 1/2 tsp ground black pepper

Directions:
1. Preheat pellet grill to 425°F.
2. Cut bacon into 1/2 inch thick slices.
3. Place brussels sprouts in a single layer in the cast iron skillet. Drizzle with olive oil and maple syrup, then toss to coat. Sprinkle bacon slices on top then season with kosher salt and black pepper.
4. Place skillet in the pellet grill and roast for about 40 to 45 minutes, or until the brussels sprouts are caramelized and brown.
5. Remove skillet from grill and allow brussels sprouts to cool for about 5 to 10 minutes. Serve and enjoy!

Nutrition Info: Calories: 175.3 Fat: 12.1 g Cholesterol: 6.6 mg Carbohydrate: 13.6 g Fiber: 2.9 g Sugar: 7.6 g Protein: 4.8 g

Grilled Romaine Caesar Salad

Servings: 6
Cooking Time: 5 Minutes
Ingredients:
- ¼ cup extra virgin olive oil
- 2 cloves garlic, minced
- 1 teaspoon Dijon mustard
- 1 cup mayonnaise
- Salt and pepper to taste
- 2 head Romaine lettuce
- ¼ cup parmesan cheese
- Croutons, optional

Directions:
1. In a small bowl, combine the olive oil, garlic, mustard, and mayonnaise. Season with salt and pepper to taste. Mix and set aside.
2. Cut the Romaine in half lengthwise leaving the ends intact so that it does not come apart.
3. Fire the Grill to 400F. Use desired wood pellets when cooking. Close the lid and preheat for 15 minutes.
4. Brush the Romaine lettuce with oil and place cut side down on the grill grate. Cook for 5 minutes.
5. Once cooked, chop the lettuce and place on a bowl. Toss with the salad dressing, parmesan cheese, and croutons.

Nutrition Info: Calories per serving: 235 ; Protein: 7.5g; Carbs: 19.4 g; Fat: 9.7g Sugar: 8.3g

Stuffed Grilled Zucchini

Servings: 4
Cooking Time: 10 Minutes
Ingredients:
- 4 zucchini, medium
- 5 tbsp olive oil, divided
- 2 tbsp red onion, finely chopped
- 1/4 tbsp garlic, minced
- 1/2 cup bread crumbs, dry
- 1/2 cup shredded mozzarella cheese, part-skim
- 1/2 tbsp salt
- 1 tbsp fresh mint, minced
- 3 tbsp parmesan cheese, grated

Directions:
1. Halve zucchini lengthwise and scoop pulp ou. Leave 1/4 -inch shell. Now brush using 2 tbsp oil, set aside, and chop the pulp.
2. Saute onion and pulp in a skillet, large, then add garlic and cook for about 1 minute.
3. Add bread crumbs and cook while stirring for about 2 minutes until golden brown.
4. Remove everything from heat then stir in mozzarella cheese, salt, and mint. Scoop into the zucchini shells and splash with parmesan cheese.
5. Preheat your to 375F.
6. Place stuffed zucchini on the grill and grill while covered for about 8-10 minutes until tender.
7. Serve warm and enjoy.

Nutrition Info: Calories 186, Total fat 10g, Saturated fat 3g, Total carbs 17g, Net carbs 14g, Protein 9g, Sugars 4g, Fiber 3g, Sodium 553mg, Potassium 237mg

Potluck Salad With Smoked Cornbread

Servings: 6
Cooking Time: 35 To 45 Minutes
Ingredients:
- 1 cup all-purpose flour
- 1 cup yellow cornmeal
- 1 tablespoon sugar
- 2 teaspoons baking powder
- 1 teaspoon salt
- 1 cup milk
- 1 egg, beaten, at room temperature
- 4 tablespoons (½ stick) unsalted butter, melted and cooled
- Nonstick cooking spray or butter, for greasing
- ½ cup milk
- ½ cup sour cream
- 2 tablespoons dry ranch dressing mix
- 1 pound bacon, cooked and crumbled
- 3 tomatoes, chopped
- 1 bell pepper, chopped
- 1 cucumber, seeded and chopped
- 2 stalks celery, chopped (about 1 cup)
- ½ cup chopped scallions

Directions:
1. For the cornbread:
2. In a medium bowl, combine the flour, cornmeal, sugar, baking powder, and salt.
3. In a small bowl, whisk together the milk and egg. Pour in the butter, then slowly fold this mixture into the dry ingredients.
4. Supply your smoker with wood pellets and follow the manufacturer's specific start-up procedure. Preheat, with the lid closed, to 375°F.
5. Coat a cast iron skillet with cooking spray or butter.
6. Pour the batter into the skillet, place on the grill grate, close the lid, and smoke for 35 to 45 minutes, or until the cornbread is browned and pulls away from the side of the skillet.
7. Remove the cornbread from the grill and let cool, then coarsely crumble.
8. For the salad:
9. In a small bowl, whisk together the milk, sour cream, and ranch dressing mix.
10. In a medium bowl, combine the crumbled bacon, tomatoes, bell pepper, cucumber, celery, and scallions.
11. In a large serving bowl, layer half of the crumbled cornbread, half of the bacon-veggie mixture, and half of the dressing. Toss lightly.
12. Repeat the layering with the remaining cornbread, bacon-veggie mixture, and dressing. Toss again.
13. Refrigerate the salad for at least 1 hour. Serve cold.

Spinach Soup

Servings: 4
Cooking Time: 35 Minutes
Ingredients:
- 2cups Chicken Stock
- 2tbsp. Vegetable Oil
- 1Onion quartered
- 2 ½ cup Spinach
- ½ lb. Red Potatoes, sliced thinly
- 2cups Milk, whole
- 1Leek, large and sliced thinly
- Black Pepper and Sea Salt, as needed
- 1Thyme Sprigs
- 1Bay Leaf

Directions:
1. For making this healthy soup, place the oil, onion, bay leaf, and thyme in the blender pitcher.
2. Now, press the 'saute' button.

3. Once sautéed, stir in the rest of the ingredients and press the 'smooth soup' button.
4. Finally, transfer the soup to the serving bowls and serve it hot.

Nutrition Info: Calories: 403 Fat: 24 g Total Carbs: 32 g Fiber: 3 g Sugar: 5.5 g Protein: 15 g Cholesterol: 66 mg

Georgia Sweet Onion Bake

Servings: 6
Cooking Time: 1 Hour
Ingredients:
- Nonstick cooking spray or butter, for greasing
- 4 large Vidalia or other sweet onions
- 8 tablespoons (1 stick) unsalted butter, melted
- 4 chicken bouillon cubes
- 1 cup grated Parmesan cheese

Directions:
1. Supply your smoker with wood pellets and follow the manufacturer's specific start-up procedure. Preheat, with the lid closed, to 350°F.
2. Coat a high-sided baking pan with cooking spray or butter.
3. Peel the onions and cut into quarters, separating into individual petals.
4. Spread the onions out in the prepared pan and pour the melted butter over them.
5. Crush the bouillon cubes and sprinkle over the buttery onion pieces, then top with the cheese.
6. Transfer the pan to the grill, close the lid, and smoke for 30 minutes.
7. Remove the pan from the grill, cover tightly with aluminum foil, and poke several holes all over to vent.
8. Place the pan back on the grill, close the lid, and smoke for an additional 30 to 45 minutes.
9. Uncover the onions, stir, and serve hot.

Scampi Spaghetti Squash

Servings: 4
Cooking Time: 40 Minutes
Ingredients:
- 1 spaghetti squash
- 2 tablespoons extra-virgin olive oil
- 1 teaspoon salt
- 1 teaspoon freshly ground black pepper
- 2 teaspoons garlic powder
- 4 tablespoons (½ stick) unsalted butter
- ½ cup white wine
- 1 tablespoon minced garlic
- 2 teaspoons chopped fresh parsley
- 1 teaspoon red pepper flakes
- ½ teaspoon salt

- ½ teaspoon freshly ground black pepper

Directions:
1. For the squash:
2. Supply your smoker with wood pellets and follow the manufacturer's specific start-up procedure. Preheat, with the lid closed, to 375°F.
3. Cut off both ends of the squash, then cut it in half lengthwise. Scoop out and discard the seeds.
4. Rub the squash flesh well with the olive oil and sprinkle on the salt, pepper, and garlic powder.
5. Place the squash cut-side up on the grill grate, close the lid, and smoke for 40 minutes, or until tender
6. For the sauce:
7. On the stove top, in a medium saucepan over medium heat, combine the butter, white wine, minced garlic, parsley, red pepper flakes, salt, and pepper, and cook for about 5 minutes, or until heated through. Reduce the heat to low and keep the sauce warm.
8. Remove the squash from the grill and let cool slightly before shredding the flesh with a fork; discard the skin.
9. Stir the shredded squash into the garlic-wine butter sauce and serve immediately.

Smoked 3-bean Salad

Servings: 6
Cooking Time: 20 Minutes
Ingredients:
- 1 can Great Northern Beans, rinsed and drained
- 1 can Red Kidney Beans, rinsed and drained
- 1pound fresh green beans, trimmed
- 2 tablespoons olive oil
- Salt and pepper to taste
- 1 shallot, sliced thinly
- 2 tablespoons red wine vinegar
- 1 teaspoon Dijon mustard

Directions:
1. Fire the Grill to 500F. Use desired wood pellets when cooking. Close the lid and preheat for 15 minutes.
2. Place the beans in a sheet tray and drizzle with olive oil. Season with salt and pepper to taste.
3. Place in the grill and cook for 20 minutes. Make sure to shake the tray for even cooking.
4. Once cooked, remove the beans and place in a bowl. Allow to cool first.
5. Add the shallots and the rest of the ingredients. Season with more salt and pepper if desired. Toss to coat the beans with the seasoning.

Nutrition Info: Calories per serving: 179; Protein: 8.2 g; Carbs: 23.5g; Fat: 6.5g Sugar: 2.2g

Smoked Stuffed Mushrooms

Servings: 12
Cooking Time: 1 Hour 15 Minutes
Ingredients:
- 12-16 white mushrooms, large, cleaned and stems removed
- 1/2 cup parmesan cheese
- 1/2 cup bread crumbs, Italian
- 2 minced garlic cloves
- 2 tbsp fresh parsley, chopped
- 1/4 -1/3 cup olive oil
- Salt and pepper to taste

Directions:
1. Preheat your 375F.
2. Remove mushroom very bottom stem then dice the rest into small pieces.
3. Combine mushroom stems, parmesan cheese, bread crumbs, garlic, parsley, 3 tbsp oil, pepper, and salt in a bowl, large. Combine until moist.
4. Layer mushrooms in a pan, disposable, then fill them with the mixture until heaping. Drizzle with more oil.
5. Place the pan on the grill.
6. Smoke for about 1 hour 20 minutes until filling browns and mushrooms become tender.
7. Remove from and serve.
8. Enjoy!

Nutrition Info: Calories 74, Total fat 6.1g, Saturated fat 1g, Total carbs 4.1g, Net carbs 3.7g, Protein 1.6g, Sugars 0.6g, Fiber 0.4g, Sodium 57mg, Potassium 72mg

Baked Cheesy Corn Pudding

Servings: 6
Cooking Time: 30 Minutes
Ingredients:
- 3 cloves of garlic, chopped
- 3 tablespoons butter
- 3 cups whole corn kernels
- 8 ounces cream cheese
- 1 cup cheddar cheese
- 1 cup parmesan cheese
- 1 tablespoon salt
- ½ tablespoon black pepper
- ½ cup dry breadcrumbs
- 1 cup mozzarella cheese, grated
- 1 tablespoon thyme, minced

Directions:
1. Fire the Grill to 350F. Use desired wood pellets when cooking. Close the lid and preheat for 15 minutes.
2. In a large saucepan, sauté the garlic and butter for 2 minutes until fragrant. Add the corn, cheddar cheese, parmesan cheese, salt, and pepper. Heat until the corn is melted then pour into a baking dish.
3. In a small bowl, combine the breadcrumbs, mozzarella cheese, and thyme.
4. Spread the cheese and bread crumb mixture on top of the corn mixture.
5. Place the baking dish on the grill grate and cook for 25 minutes.
6. Allow to rest before removing from the mold.

Nutrition Info: Calories per serving: 523; Protein: 29.4g; Carbs: 34g; Fat: 31.2g Sugar: 10.8g

Butter Braised Green Beans

Servings: 6
Cooking Time: 20 Minutes
Ingredients:
- 24 ounces Green Beans, trimmed
- 8 tablespoons butter, melted
- Salt and pepper to taste

Directions:
1. Fire the Grill to 500F. Use desired wood pellets when cooking. Close the lid and preheat for 15 minutes.
2. Place all ingredients in a bowl and toss to coat the beans with the seasoning.
3. Place the seasoned beans in a sheet tray.
4. Cook in the grill for 20 minutes.

Nutrition Info: Calories per serving: 164; Protein: 1.6g; Carbs: 5.6 g; Fat: 15.8g Sugar: 1.3g

Salt-crusted Baked Potatoes

Servings: 6
Cooking Time: 40 Minutes
Ingredients:
- 6 russet potatoes, scrubbed and dried
- 3 tablespoons oil
- 1 tablespoons salt
- Butter as needed
- Sour cream as needed

Directions:
1. Fire the Grill to 400F. Use desired wood pellets when cooking. Close the lid and preheat for 15 minutes.
2. In a large bowl, coat the potatoes with oil and salt. Place seasoned potatoes on a baking tray.
3. Place the tray with potatoes on the grill grate.
4. Close the lid and grill for 40 minutes.
5. Serve with butter and sour cream.

Nutrition Info: Calories per serving: 363; Protein: 8g; Carbs: 66.8g; Fat: 8.6g Sugar: 2.3g

Wood Pellet Grill Spicy Sweet Potatoes

Servings: 6
Cooking Time: 35 Minutes
Ingredients:
- 2 lb sweet potatoes, cut into chunks
- 1 red onion, chopped
- 2 tbsp oil
- 2 tbsp orange juice
- 1 tbsp roasted cinnamon
- 1 tbsp salt
- 1/4 tbsp Chiptole chili pepper

Directions:
1. Preheat the wood pellet grill to 425°F with the lid closed.
2. Toss the sweet potatoes with onion, oil, and juice.
3. In a mixing bowl, mix cinnamon, salt, and pepper then sprinkle the mixture over the sweet potatoes.
4. Spread the potatoes on a lined baking dish in a single layer.
5. Place the baking dish in the grill and grill for 30 minutes or until the sweet potatoes ate tender.
6. Serve and enjoy.

Nutrition Info: Calories 145, Total fat 5g, Saturated fat 0g, Total Carbs 23g, Net Carbs 19g, Protein 2g, Sugar 3g, Fiber 4g, Sodium: 428mg, Potassium 230mg

Smoked Eggs

Servings: 12
Cooking Time: 30 Minutes
Ingredients:
- 12 hardboiled eggs, peeled and rinsed

Directions:
1. Supply your smoker with wood pellets and follow the manufacturer's specific start-up procedure. Preheat the grill, with the lid closed, to 120°F.
2. Place the eggs directly on the grill grate and smoke for 30 minutes. They will begin to take on a slight brown sheen.
3. Remove the eggs and refrigerate for at least 30 minutes before serving. Refrigerate any leftovers in an airtight container for 1 or 2 weeks.

Smoked Mushrooms

Servings: 6
Cooking Time: 10 Minutes
Ingredients:
- 4 cups baby portobello, whole and cleaned
- 1 tablespoon canola oil
- 1 teaspoon onion powder
- 1 teaspoon garlic powder
- Salt and pepper to taste

Directions:
1. Place all ingredients in a bowl and toss to coat the mushrooms with the seasoning.
2. Fire the Grill to 350F. Use desired wood pellets when cooking. Close the lid and preheat for 15 minutes.
3. Place mushrooms on the grill grate and smoke for 10 minutes. Make sure to flip the mushrooms halfway through the cooking time.
4. Remove from the grill and serve.

Nutrition Info: Calories per serving: 62; Protein: 5.2g; Carbs: 6.6g; Fat: 2.9g Sugar: 0.3g

Sweet Potato Fries

Servings: 4
Cooking Time: 40 Minutes
Ingredients:
- 3 sweet potatoes, sliced into strips
- 4 tablespoons olive oil
- 2 tablespoons fresh rosemary, chopped
- Salt and pepper to taste

Directions:
1. Set the wood pellet grill to 450 degrees F.
2. Preheat it for 10 minutes.
3. Spread the sweet potato strips in the baking pan.
4. Toss in olive oil and sprinkle with rosemary, salt and pepper.
5. Cook for 15 minutes.
6. Flip and cook for another 15 minutes.
7. Flip and cook for 10 more minutes.
8. Tips: Soak sweet potatoes in water before cooking to prevent browning.

Wood Pellet Smoked Acorn Squash

Servings: 6
Cooking Time: 2 Hours
Ingredients:
- 3 tbsp olive oil
- 3 acorn squash, halved and seeded
- 1/4 cup unsalted butter
- 1/4 cup brown sugar
- 1 tbsp cinnamon, ground
- 1 tbsp chili powder
- 1 tbsp nutmeg, ground

Directions:
1. Brush olive oil on the acorn squash cut sides then cover the halves with foil. Poke holes on the foil to allow steam and smoke through.
2. Fire up the wood pellet to 225°F and smoke the squash for 1-1/2-2 hours.

3. Remove the squash from the smoker and allow it to sit.
4. Meanwhile, melt butter, sugar and spices in a saucepan. Stir well to combine.
5. Remove the foil from the squash and spoon the butter mixture in each squash half. Enjoy.
Nutrition Info: Calories 149, Total fat 10g, Saturated fat 5g, Total Carbs 14g, Net Carbs 12g, Protein 2g, Sugar 0g, Fiber 2g, Sodium: 19mg, Potassium 0mg

Roasted Vegetable Medley

Servings: 4 To 6
Cooking Time: 50 Minutes
Ingredients:
- 2medium potatoes, cut to 1 inch wedges
- 2red bell peppers, cut into 1 inch cubes
- 1small butternut squash, peeled and cubed to 1 inch cube
- 1red onion, cut to 1 inch cubes
- 1cup broccoli, trimmed
- 2tbsp olive oil
- 1tbsp balsamic vinegar
- 1tbsp fresh rosemary, minced
- 1tbsp fresh thyme, minced
- 1tsp kosher salt
- 1tsp ground black pepper

Directions:
1. Preheat pellet grill to 425°F.
2. In a large bowl, combine potatoes, peppers, squash, and onion.
3. In a small bowl, whisk together olive oil, balsamic vinegar, rosemary, thyme, salt, and pepper.
4. Pour marinade over vegetables and toss to coat. Allow resting for about 15 minutes.
5. Place marinated vegetables into a grill basket, and place a grill basket on the grill grate. Cook for about 30-40 minutes, occasionally tossing in the grill basket.
6. Remove veggies from grill and transfer to a serving dish. Allow to cool for 5 minutes, then serve and enjoy!
Nutrition Info: Calories: 158.6 Fat: 7.4 g Cholesterol: 0 Carbohydrate: 22 g Fiber: 7.2 g Sugar: 3.1 g Protein: 5.2 g

Wood Pellet Grilled Asparagus And Honey Glazed Carrots

Servings: 5
Cooking Time: 35 Minutes
Ingredients:
- 1 bunch asparagus, trimmed ends
- 1 lb carrots, peeled
- 2 tbsp olive oil
- Sea salt to taste
- 2 tbsp honey
- Lemon zest

Directions:
1. Sprinkle the asparagus with oil and sea salt. Drizzle the carrots with honey and salt.
2. Preheat the wood pellet to 165°F wit the lid closed for 15 minutes.
3. Place the carrots in the wood pellet and cook for 15 minutes. Add asparagus and cook for 20 more minutes or until cooked through.
4. Top the carrots and asparagus with lemon zest. Enjoy.
Nutrition Info: Calories 1680, Total fat 30g, Saturated fat 2g, Total Carbs 10g, Net Carbs 10g, Protein 4g, Sugar 0g, Fiber 0g, Sodium: 514mg, Potassium 0mg

Grilled Sweet Potato Planks

Servings: 8
Cooking Time: 30 Minutes
Ingredients:
- 5 sweet potatoes, sliced into planks
- 1 tablespoon olive oil
- 1 teaspoon onion powder
- Salt and pepper to taste

Directions:
1. Set the wood pellet grill to high.
2. Preheat it for 15 minutes while the lid is closed.
3. Coat the sweet potatoes with oil.
4. Sprinkle with onion powder, salt and pepper.
5. Grill the sweet potatoes for 15 minutes.
6. Tips: Grill for a few more minutes if you want your sweet potatoes crispier.

Vegetable Sandwich

Servings: 4
Cooking Time: 45 Minutes
Ingredients:
- For the Smoked Hummus:
- 1 1/2 cups cooked chickpeas
- 1 tablespoon minced garlic
- 1 teaspoon salt
- 4 tablespoons lemon juice
- 2 tablespoon olive oil
- 1/3 cup tahini
- For the Vegetables:
- 2 large portobello mushrooms
- 1 small eggplant, destemmed, sliced into strips
- 1 teaspoon salt
- 1 small zucchini, trimmed, sliced into strips

- ½ teaspoon ground black pepper
- 1 small yellow squash, peeled, sliced into strips
- ¼ cup olive oil
- For the Cheese:
- 1 lemon, juiced
- ½ teaspoon minced garlic
- ¼ teaspoon ground black pepper
- ¼ teaspoon salt
- 1/2 cup ricotta cheese
- To Assemble:
- 1 bunch basil, leaves chopped
- 2 heirloom tomatoes, sliced
- 4 ciabatta buns, halved

Directions:
1. Switch on the grill, fill the grill hopper with pecan flavored wood pellets, power the grill on by using the control panel, select 'smoke' on the temperature dial, or set the temperature to 180 degrees F and let it preheat for a minimum of 15 minutes.
2. Meanwhile, prepare the hummus, and for this, take a sheet tray and spread chickpeas on it.
3. When the grill has preheated, open the lid, place sheet tray on the grill grate, shut the grill and smoke for 20 minutes.
4. When done, transfer chickpeas to a food processor, add remaining ingredients for the hummus in it, and pulse for 2 minutes until smooth, set aside until required.
5. Change the smoking temperature to 500 degrees F, shut with lid, and let it preheat for 10 minutes.
6. Meanwhile, prepare vegetables and for this, take a large bowl, place all the vegetables in it, add salt and black pepper, drizzle with oil and lemon juice and toss until coated.
7. Place vegetables on the grill grate, shut with lid and then smoke for eggplant, zucchini, and squash for 15 minutes and mushrooms for 25 minutes.
8. Meanwhile, prepare the cheese and for this, take a small bowl, place all of its ingredients in it and stir until well combined.
9. Assemble the sandwich for this, cut buns in half lengthwise, spread prepared hummus on one side, spread cheese on the other side, then stuff with grilled vegetables and top with tomatoes and basil.
10. Serve straight away.

Nutrition Info: Calories: 560 Cal ;Fat: 40 g ;Carbs: 45 g ;Protein: 8.3 g ;Fiber: 6.8 g

Coconut Bacon

Servings: 2
Cooking Time: 30 Minutes
Ingredients:
- 3 1/2 cups flaked coconut

- 1 tbsp pure maple syrup
- 1 tbsp water
- 2 tbsp liquid smoke
- 1 tbsp soy sauce
- 1 tsp smoked paprika (optional)

Directions:
1. Preheat the smoker at 325°F.
2. Take a large mixing bowl and combine liquid smoke, maple syrup, soy sauce, and water.
3. Pour flaked coconut over the mixture. Add it to a cooking sheet.
4. Place in the middle rack of the smoker.
5. Smoke it for 30 minutes and every 7-8 minutes, keep flipping the sides.
6. Serve and enjoy.

Nutrition Info: Calories: 1244 Cal Fat: 100 g Carbohydrates: 70 g Protein: 16 g Fiber: 2 g

Grilled Zucchini

Servings: 6
Cooking Time: 10 Minutes
Ingredients:
- 4 medium zucchini
- 2 tablespoons olive oil
- 1 tablespoon sherry vinegar
- 2 sprigs of thyme, leaves chopped
- ½ teaspoon salt
- 1/3 teaspoon ground black pepper

Directions:
1. Switch on the grill, fill the grill hopper with oak flavored wood pellets, power the grill on by using the control panel, select 'smoke' on the temperature dial, or set the temperature to 350 degrees F and let it preheat for a minimum of 5 minutes.
2. Meanwhile, cut the ends of each zucchini, cut each in half and then into thirds and place in a plastic bag.
3. Add remaining ingredients, seal the bag, and shake well to coat zucchini pieces.
4. When the grill has preheated, open the lid, place zucchini on the grill grate, shut the grill and smoke for 4 minutes per side.
5. When done, transfer zucchini to a dish, garnish with more thyme and then serve.

Nutrition Info: Calories: 74 Cal ;Fat: 5.4 g ;Carbs: 6.1 g ;Protein: 2.6 g ;Fiber: 2.3 g

Broccoli-cauliflower Salad

Servings: 4
Cooking Time: 25 Minutes
Ingredients:
- 1½ cups mayonnaise
- ½ cup sour cream

- ¼ cup sugar
- 1 bunch broccoli, cut into small pieces
- 1 head cauliflower, cut into small pieces
- 1 small red onion, chopped
- 6 slices bacon, cooked and crumbled (precooked bacon works well)
- 1 cup shredded Cheddar cheese

Directions:
1. In a small bowl, whisk together the mayonnaise, sour cream, and sugar to make a dressing.
2. In a large bowl, combine the broccoli, cauliflower, onion, bacon, and Cheddar cheese.
3. Pour the dressing over the vegetable mixture and toss well to coat.
4. Serve the salad chilled.

Roasted Okra

Servings: 4
Cooking Time: 30 Minutes
Ingredients:
- Nonstick cooking spray or butter, for greasing
- 1 pound whole okra
- 2 tablespoons extra-virgin olive oil
- 2 teaspoons seasoned salt
- 2 teaspoons freshly ground black pepper

Directions:
1. Supply your smoker with wood pellets and follow the manufacturer's specific start-up procedure. Preheat, with the lid closed, to 400°F. Alternatively, preheat your oven to 400°F.
2. Line a shallow rimmed baking pan with aluminum foil and coat with cooking spray.
3. Arrange the okra on the pan in a single layer. Drizzle with the olive oil, turning to coat. Season on all sides with the salt and pepper.
4. Place the baking pan on the grill grate, close the lid, and smoke for 30 minutes, or until crisp and slightly charred. Alternatively, roast in the oven for 30 minutes.
5. Serve hot.

Green Beans With Bacon

Servings: 6
Cooking Time: 20 Minutes
Ingredients:

- 4 strips of bacon, chopped
- 1 1/2 pound green beans, ends trimmed
- 1 teaspoon minced garlic
- 1 teaspoon salt
- 4 tablespoons olive oil

Directions:
1. Switch on the grill, fill the grill hopper with flavored wood pellets, power the grill on by using the control panel, select 'smoke' on the temperature dial, or set the temperature to 450 degrees F and let it preheat for a minimum of 15 minutes.
2. Meanwhile, take a sheet tray, place all the ingredients in it and toss until mixed.
3. When the grill has preheated, open the lid, place prepared sheet tray on the grill grate, shut the grill and smoke for 20 minutes until lightly browned and cooked.
4. When done, transfer green beans to a dish and then serve.

Nutrition Info: Calories: 93 Cal ;Fat: 4.6 g ;Carbs: 8.2 g ;Protein: 5.9 g ;Fiber: 2.9 g

Grilled Ratatouille Salad

Servings: 6
Cooking Time: 25 Minutes
Ingredients:
- 1 Whole sweet potatoes
- 1 Whole red onion, diced
- 1 Whole zucchini
- 1 Whole Squash
- 1 Large Tomato, diced
- As Needed vegetable oil
- As Needed salt and pepper

Directions:
1. Preheat grill to high setting with the lid closed for 10-15 minutes.
2. Slice all vegetables to a ¼ inch thickness.
3. Lightly brush each vegetable with oil and season with Traeger's Veggie Shake or salt and pepper.
4. Place sweet potato, onion, zucchini, and squash on grill grate and grill for 20 minutes or until tender, turn halfway through.
5. Add tomato slices to the grill during the last 5 minutes of cooking time.
6. For presentation, alternate vegetables while layering them vertically. Enjoy!

POULTRY RECIPES

Hot And Sweet Spatchcocked Chicken

Servings: 8
Cooking Time: 55 Minutes
Ingredients:
- 1 whole chicken, spatchcocked
- ¼ cup Chicken Rub
- 2 tablespoons olive oil
- ½ cup Sweet and Heat BBQ Sauce

Directions:
1. Place the chicken breastbone-side down on a flat surface and press the breastbone to break it and flatten the chicken. Sprinkle the Chicken Rub all over the chicken and massage until the bird is seasoned well. Allow the chicken to rest in the fridge for at least 12 hours.
2. When ready to cook, fire the Grill to 350F. Use preferred wood pellets. Close the grill lid and preheat for 15 minutes.
3. Before cooking the chicken, baste with oil. Place on the grill grate and cook on both sides for 55 minutes.
4. 20 minutes before the cooking time, baste the chicken with Sweet and Heat BBQ Sauce.
5. Continue cooking until a meat thermometer inserted in the thickest part of the chicken reads at 165F.
6. Allow to rest before carving the chicken.
Nutrition Info: Calories per serving: 200; Protein: 30.6g; Carbs: 1.1g; Fat: 7.4g Sugar: 0.6g

Chicken Wings

Servings: 4
Cooking Time: 15 Minutes
Ingredients:
- Fresh chicken wings
- Salt to taste
- Pepper to taste
- Garlic powder
- Onion powder
- Cayenne
- Paprika
- Seasoning salt
- Barbeque sauce to taste

Directions:
1. Preheat the wood pellet grill to low. Mix seasoning and coat on chicken. Put the wings on the grill and cook. Place the wings on the grill and cook for 20 minutes or until the wings are fully cooked. Let rest to cool for 5 minutes then toss with barbeque sauce. Serve with orzo and salad. Enjoy.
Nutrition Info: Calories: 311 Cal Fat: 22 g
Carbohydrates: 22 g Protein: 22 g Fiber: 3 g

Smoked Chicken Drumsticks

Servings: 5
Cooking Time: 2 Hours 30 Minutes
Ingredients:
- 10 chicken drumsticks
- 2tsp garlic powder
- 1tsp salt
- 1tsp onion powder
- 1/2 tsp ground black pepper
- ½ tsp cayenne pepper
- 1tsp brown sugar
- 1/3 cup hot sauce
- 1tsp paprika
- ½ tsp thyme

Directions:
1. In a large mixing bowl, combine the garlic powder, sugar, hot sauce, paprika, thyme, cayenne, salt, and ground pepper. Add the drumsticks and toss to combine.
2. Cover the bowl and refrigerate for 1 hour.
3. Remove the drumsticks from the marinade and let them sit for about 1 hour until they are at room temperature.
4. Arrange the drumsticks into a rack.
5. Start your pellet grill on smoke, leaving the lid open for 5 minutes for the fire to start.
6. Close the lid and preheat grill to 250°F, using hickory or apple hardwood pellets.
7. Place the rack on the grill and smoke drumsticks for 2 hours, 30 minutes, or until the drumsticks' internal temperature reaches 180°F.
8. Remove drumsticks from heat and let them rest for a few minutes.
9. Serve.
Nutrition Info: Calories: 167 Total Fat: 5.4 g
Saturated Fat: 1.4 g Cholesterol: 81 mg Sodium: 946 mg Total Carbohydrate: 2.6 g Dietary Fiber: 0.5 g
Total Sugars: 1.3 g Protein: 25.7 g

Grilled Chicken

Servings: 6
Cooking Time: 1 Hour 10 Minutes;
Ingredients:
- 5 lb. whole chicken
- 1/2 cup oil
- chicken rub

Directions:
1. Preheat the on the smoke setting with the lid open for 5 minutes. Close the lid and let it heat for 15 minutes or until it reaches 450..

2. Use bakers twine to tie the chicken legs together then rub it with oil. Coat the chicken with the rub and place it on the grill.
3. Grill for 70 minutes with the lid closed or until it reaches an internal temperature of 165F.
4. Remove the chicken from the and let rest for 15 minutes. Cut and serve.
Nutrition Info: Calories 935, Total fat 53g, Saturated fat 15g, Total carbs 0g, Net carbs 0g Protein 107g, Sugars 0g, Fiber 0g, Sodium 320mg

Smoked Turkey Breast

Servings: 2 To 4
Cooking Time: 1 To 2 Hours
Ingredients:
- 1 (3-pound) turkey breast
- Salt
- Freshly ground black pepper
- 1 teaspoon garlic powder

Directions:
1. Supply your smoker with wood pellets and follow the manufacturer's specific start-up procedure. Preheat the grill, with the lid closed, to 180°F.
2. Season the turkey breast all over with salt, pepper, and garlic powder.
3. Place the breast directly on the grill grate and smoke for 1 hour.
4. Increase the grill's temperature to 350°F and continue to cook until the turkey's internal temperature reaches 170°F. Remove the breast from the grill and serve immediately.

Bourbon Bbq Smoked Chicken Wings

Servings: 8
Cooking Time: 24 Minutes
Ingredients:
- 4 pounds chicken wings, patted dry
- 2 tablespoons olive oil
- Salt and pepper to taste
- ½ medium yellow onions, minced
- 5 cloves garlic, mince
- ½ cup bourbon
- 2 cups ketchup
- 1/3 cup apple cider vinegar
- 2 tablespoons liquid smoke
- ½ teaspoon kosher salt
- ½ teaspoon black pepper
- A dash of hot sauce

Directions:
1. Place the chicken in a bowl and drizzle with olive oil. Season with salt and pepper to taste. In

another bowl, combine the rest of the ingredients and set aside.
2. Fire the Grill to 400F. Use hickory wood pellets. Close the lid and allow to preheat for 15 minutes.
3. Place the chicken on the grill grate and cook for 12 minutes on each side.
4. Using a brush, brush the chicken wings with bourbon sauce on all sides.
5. Flip the chicken and cook for another 12 minutes with the lid closed.
Nutrition Info: Calories per serving: 384 ; Protein: 50.7g; Carbs: 17.8 g; Fat: 11.5g Sugar: 13.1g

Sheet Pan Chicken Fajitas

Servings: 10
Cooking Time: 10 Minutes
Ingredients:
- 2 lb chicken breast
- 1 onion, sliced
- 1 red bell pepper, seeded and sliced
- 1 orange-red bell pepper, seeded and sliced
- 1 tbsp salt
- 1/2 tbsp onion powder
- 1/2 tbsp granulated garlic
- 2 tbsp Spiceologist Chile Margarita Seasoning
- 2 tbsp oil

Directions:
1. Preheat the to 450F and line a baking sheet with parchment paper.
2. In a mixing bowl, combine seasonings and oil then toss with the peppers and chicken.
3. Place the baking sheet in the and let heat for 10 minutes with the lid closed.
4. Open the lid and place the veggies and the chicken in a single layer. Close the lid and cook for 10 minutes or until the chicken is no longer pink.
5. Serve with warm tortillas and top with your favorite toppings.
Nutrition Info: Calories 211, Total fat 6g, Saturated fat 1g, Total carbs 5g, Net carbs 4g Protein 29g, Sugars 4g, Fiber 1g, Sodium 360mg

Mini Turducken Roulade

Servings: 6
Cooking Time: 2 Hours
Ingredients:
- 1 (16-ounce) boneless turkey breast
- 1 (8-to 10-ounce) boneless duck breast
- 1 (8-ounce) boneless, skinless chicken breast
- Salt
- Freshly ground black pepper
- 2 cups Italian dressing

- 2 tablespoons Cajun seasoning
- 1 cup prepared seasoned stuffing mix
- 8 slices bacon
- Butcher's string

Directions:
1. Butterfly the turkey, duck, and chicken breasts, cover with plastic wrap and, using a mallet, flatten each ½ inch thick.
2. Season all the meat on both sides with a little salt and pepper.
3. In a medium bowl, combine the Italian dressing and Cajun seasoning. Spread one-fourth of the mixture on top of the flattened turkey breast.
4. Place the duck breast on top of the turkey, spread it with one-fourth of the dressing mixture, and top with the stuffing mix.
5. Place the chicken breast on top of the duck and spread with one-fourth of the dressing mixture.
6. Supply your smoker with wood pellets and follow the manufacturer's specific start-up procedure. Preheat, with the lid closed, to 275°F.
7. Tightly roll up the stack, tie with butcher's string, and slather the whole thing with the remaining dressing mixture.
8. Wrap the bacon slices around the turducken and secure with toothpicks, or try making a bacon weave (see the technique for this in the Jalapeño-Bacon Pork Tenderloin recipe).
9. Place the turducken roulade in a roasting pan. Transfer to the grill, close the lid, and roast for 2 hours, or until a meat thermometer inserted in the turducken reads 165°F. Tent with aluminum foil in the last 30 minutes, if necessary, to keep from overbrowning.
10. Let the turducken rest for 15 to 20 minutes before carving. Serve warm.

Herb Roasted Turkey

Servings: 12
Cooking Time: 3 Hours And 30 Minutes
Ingredients:
- 14 pounds turkey, cleaned
- 2 tablespoons chopped mixed herbs
- Pork and poultry rub as needed
- 1/4 teaspoon ground black pepper
- 3 tablespoons butter, unsalted, melted
- 8 tablespoons butter, unsalted, softened
- 2 cups chicken broth

Directions:
1. Clean the turkey by removing the giblets, wash it inside out, pat dry with paper towels, then place it on a roasting pan and tuck the turkey wings by tiring with butcher's string.
2. Switch on the grill, fill the grill hopper with hickory flavored wood pellets, power the grill on by using the control panel, select 'smoke' on the temperature dial, or set the temperature to 325 degrees F and let it preheat for a minimum of 15 minutes.
3. Meanwhile, prepared herb butter and for this, take a small bowl, place the softened butter in it, add black pepper and mixed herbs and beat until fluffy.
4. Place some of the prepared herb butter underneath the skin of turkey by using a handle of a wooden spoon, and massage the skin to distribute butter evenly.
5. Then rub the exterior of the turkey with melted butter, season with pork and poultry rub, and pour the broth in the roasting pan.
6. When the grill has preheated, open the lid, place roasting pan containing turkey on the grill grate, shut the grill and smoke for 3 hours and 30 minutes until the internal temperature reaches 165 degrees F and the top has turned golden brown.
7. When done, transfer turkey to a cutting board, let it rest for 30 minutes, then carve it into slices and serve.

Nutrition Info: Calories: 154.6 Cal ;Fat: 3.1 g ;Carbs: 8.4 g ;Protein: 28.8 g ;Fiber: 0.4 g

Savory-sweet Turkey Legs

Servings: 4
Cooking Time: 4 To 5 Hours
Ingredients:
- 1 gallon hot water
- 1 cup curing salt (such as Morton Tender Quick)
- ¼ cup packed light brown sugar
- 1 teaspoon freshly ground black pepper
- 1 teaspoon ground cloves
- 1 bay leaf
- 2 teaspoons liquid smoke
- 4 turkey legs
- Mandarin Glaze, for serving

Directions:
1. In a large container with a lid, stir together the water, curing salt, brown sugar, pepper, cloves, bay leaf, and liquid smoke until the salt and sugar are dissolved; let come to room temperature.
2. Submerge the turkey legs in the seasoned brine, cover, and refrigerate overnight.
3. When ready to smoke, remove the turkey legs from the brine and rinse them; discard the brine.
4. Supply your smoker with wood pellets and follow the manufacturer's specific start-up procedure. Preheat, with the lid closed, to 225°F.
5. Arrange the turkey legs on the grill, close the lid, and smoke for 4 to 5 hours, or until dark brown and a meat thermometer inserted in the thickest part of the meat reads 165°F.

6. Serve with Mandarin Glaze on the side or drizzled over the turkey legs.

Smoked Chicken Thighs

Servings: 6
Cooking Time: 24 Minutes.
Ingredients:
- 6 chicken thighs
- ½ cup commercial BBQ sauce of your choice
- 1 ½ tablespoon poultry spice
- 4 tablespoons butter

Directions:
1. Place all ingredients in a bowl except for the butter. Massage the chicken to make sure that the chicken is coated with the marinade.
2. Place in the fridge to marinate for 4 hours.
3. Fire the Grill to 350F. Use hickory wood pellets. Close the lid and preheat for 15 minutes.
4. When ready to cook, place the chicken on the grill grate and cook for 12 minutes on each side.
5. Before serving the chicken, brush with butter on top.
Nutrition Info: Calories per serving: 504; Protein: 32.4g; Carbs: 2.7g; Fat: 39.9g Sugar: 0.9g

Paprika Chicken

Servings: 7
Cooking Time: 2 – 4 Hours
Ingredients:
- 4-6 chicken breast
- 4 tablespoons olive oil
- 2tablespoons smoked paprika
- ½ tablespoon salt
- ¼ teaspoon pepper
- 2teaspoons garlic powder
- 2teaspoons garlic salt
- 2teaspoons pepper
- 1teaspoon cayenne pepper
- 1teaspoon rosemary

Directions:
1. Preheat your smoker to 220 degrees Fahrenheit using your favorite wood Pellets
2. Prepare your chicken breast according to your desired shapes and transfer to a greased baking dish
3. Take a medium bowl and add spices, stir well
4. Press the spice mix over chicken and transfer the chicken to smoker
5. Smoke for 1-1 and a ½ hours
6. Turn-over and cook for 30 minutes more
7. Once the internal temperature reaches 165 degrees Fahrenheit
8. Remove from the smoker and cover with foil

9. Allow it to rest for 15 minutes
10. Enjoy!
Nutrition Info: Calories: 237 Fats: 6.1g Carbs: 14g Fiber: 3g

Spatchcocked Turkey

Servings: 10 To 14
Cooking Time: 2 Hours
Ingredients:
- 1 whole turkey
- 2 tablespoons olive oil
- 1 batch Chicken Rub

Directions:
1. Supply your smoker with wood pellets and follow the manufacturer's specific start-up procedure. Preheat the grill, with the lid closed, to 350°F.
2. To remove the turkey's backbone, place the turkey on a work surface, on its breast. Using kitchen shears, cut along one side of the turkey's backbone and then the other. Pull out the bone.
3. Once the backbone is removed, turn the turkey breast-side up and flatten it.
4. Coat the turkey with olive oil and season it on both sides with the rub. Using your hands, work the rub into the meat and skin.
5. Place the turkey directly on the grill grate, breast-side up, and cook until its internal temperature reaches 170°F.
6. Remove the turkey from the grill and let it rest for 10 minutes, before carving and serving.

Wood Pellet Chicken Breasts

Servings: 6
Cooking Time: 15 Minutes
Ingredients:
- 3 chicken breasts
- 1 tbsp avocado oil
- 1/4 tbsp garlic powder
- 1/4 tbsp onion powder
- 3/4 tbsp salt
- 1/4 tbsp pepper

Directions:
1. Preheat your pellet to 375°F.
2. Half the chicken breasts lengthwise then coat with avocado oil.
3. With the spices, drizzle it on all sides to season
4. Drizzle spices to season the chicken. Put the chicken on top of the grill and begin to cook until its internal temperature approaches 165 degrees Fahrenheit. Put the chicken on top of the grill and begin to cook until it rises to a temperature of 165 degrees Fahrenheit
5. Serve and enjoy.

Nutrition Info: Calories: 120 Cal Fat: 4 g
Carbohydrates: 0 g Protein: 19 g Fiber: 0 g

Nutrition Info: Calories per serving: 907;
Carbohydrates: 23.5g; Protein: 5.6g; Fat: 60.3g; Sugar:
19.9g; Sodium: 8000mg; Fiber: 1.1g

Christmas Dinner Goose

Servings: 12
Cooking Time: 3 Hours
Ingredients:
- 1½ C. kosher salt
- 1 C. brown sugar
- 20 C. water
- 1 (12-lb.) whole goose, giblets removed
- 1 naval orange, cut into 6 wedges
- 1 large onion, cut into 8 wedges
- 2 bay leaves
- ¼ C. juniper berries, crushed
- 12 black peppercorns
- Salt and freshly ground black pepper, to taste
- 1 apple, cut into 6 wedges
- 2-3 fresh parsley sprigs

Directions:
1. Trim off any loose neck skin.
2. Then, trim the first two joints off the wings.
3. Wash the goose under cold running water and with paper towels, pat dry it.
4. With the tip of a paring knife, prick the goose all over the skin.
5. In a large pitcher, dissolve kosher salt and brown sugar in water.
6. Squeeze 3 orange wedges into brine.
7. Add goose, 4 onion wedges, bay leaves, juniper berries and peppercorns in brine and refrigerate for 24 hours.
8. Set the temperature of Grill to 350 degrees F and preheat with closed lid for 15 minutes.
9. Remove the goose from brine and with paper towels, pat dry completely.
10. Season the in and outside of goose with salt and black pepper evenly.
11. Stuff the cavity with apple wedges, herbs, remaining orange and onion wedges.
12. With kitchen strings, tie the legs together loosely.
13. Place the goose onto a rack arranged in a shallow roasting pan.
14. Arrange the goose on grill and cook for about 1 hour.
15. With a basting bulb, remove some of the fat from the pan and cook for about 1 hour.
16. Again, remove excess fat from the pan and cook for about ½-1 hour more.
17. Remove goose from grill and place onto a cutting board for about 20 minutes before carving.
18. With a sharp knife, cut the goose into desired-sized pieces and serve.

Smoked Cornish Chicken In Wood Pellets

Servings: 6
Cooking Time: 1 Hour 10 Minutes
Ingredients:
- Cornish hens - 6
- Canola or avocado oil - 2-3 tbsp
- Spice mix - 6 tbsp

Directions:
1. Preheat your wood pellet grill to 275 degrees.
2. Rub the whole hen with oil and the spice mix. Use both of these ingredients liberally.
3. Place the breast area of the hen on the grill and smoke for 30 minutes.
4. Flip the hen, so the breast side is facing up. Increase the temperature to 400 degrees.
5. Cook until the temperature goes down to 165 degrees.
6. Pull it out and leave it for 10 minutes.
7. Serve warm with a side dish of your choice.

Nutrition Info: Carbohydrates: 1 g Protein: 57 g Fat: 50 g Sodium: 165 mg Cholesterol: 337 mg

Smoking Duck With Mandarin Glaze

Servings: 4
Cooking Time: 4 Hours
Ingredients:
- 1 quart buttermilk
- 1 (5-pound) whole duck
- ¾ cup soy sauce
- ½ cup hoisin sauce
- ½ cup rice wine vinegar
- 2 tablespoons sesame oil
- 1 tablespoon freshly ground black pepper
- 1 tablespoon minced garlic
- Mandarin Glaze, for drizzling

Directions:
1. With a very sharp knife, remove as much fat from the duck as you can. Refrigerate or freeze the fat for later use.
2. Pour the buttermilk into a large container with a lid and submerge the whole duck in it. Cover and let brine in the refrigerator for 4 to 6 hours.
3. Supply your smoker with wood pellets and follow the manufacturer's specific start-up procedure. Preheat, with the lid closed, to 250°F.
4. Remove the duck from the buttermilk brine, then rinse it and pat dry with paper towels.

5. In a bowl, combine the soy sauce, hoisin sauce, vinegar, sesame oil, pepper, and garlic to form a paste. Reserve ¼ cup for basting.
6. Poke holes in the skin of the duck and rub the remaining paste all over and inside the cavity.
7. Place the duck on the grill breast-side down, close the lid, and smoke for about 4 hours, basting every hour with the reserved paste, until a meat thermometer inserted in the thickest part of the meat reads 165°F. Use aluminum foil to tent the duck in the last 30 minutes or so if it starts to brown too quickly.
8. To finish, drizzle with glaze.

Rustic Maple Smoked Chicken Wings

Servings: 16
Cooking Time: 35 Minutes
Ingredients:
- 16 chicken wings
- 1 tablespoon olive oil
- 1 tablespoon Chicken Rub
- 1 cup 'Que BBQ Sauce or other commercial BBQ sauce of choice

Directions:
1. Place all ingredients in a bowl except for the BBQ sauce. Massage the chicken breasts so that it is coated with the marinade.
2. Place in the fridge to marinate for at least 4 hours.
3. Fire the Grill to 350F. Use maple wood pellets. Close the grill lid and preheat for 15 minutes.
4. Place the wings on the grill grate and cook for 12 minutes on each side with the lid closed.
5. Once the chicken wings are done, place in a clean bowl.
6. Pour over the BBQ sauce and toss to coat with the sauce.
Nutrition Info: Calories per serving: 230 ; Protein: 37.5g; Carbs: 2.2g; Fat: 7g Sugar: 1.3g

Chili Barbecue Chicken

Servings: 4
Cooking Time: 2 Hours And 10 Minutes
Ingredients:
- 1 tablespoon brown sugar
- 1 tablespoon lime zest
- 1 tablespoon chili powder
- 1/2 teaspoon ground cumin
- 1/2 tablespoon ground espresso
- Salt to taste
- 2 tablespoons olive oil
- 8 chicken legs
- 1/2 cup barbecue sauce

Directions:
1. Combine sugar, lime zest, chili powder, cumin, ground espresso and salt.
2. Drizzle the chicken legs with oil.
3. Sprinkle sugar mixture all over the chicken.
4. Cover with foil and refrigerate for 5 hours.
5. Set the wood pellet grill to 180 degrees F.
6. Preheat it for 15 minutes while the lid is closed.
7. Smoke the chicken legs for 1 hour.
8. Increase temperature to 350 degrees F.
9. Grill the chicken legs for another 1 hour, flipping once.
10. Brush the chicken with barbecue sauce and grill for another 10 minutes.
11. Tips: You can also add chili powder to the barbecue sauce.

Trager Smoked Spatchcock Turkey

Servings: 8
Cooking Time: 1 Hour 15 Minutes;
Ingredients:
- 1 turkey
- 1/2 cup melted butter
- 1/4 cup chicken rub
- 1 tbsp onion powder
- 1 tbsp garlic powder
- 1 tbsp rubbed sage

Directions:
1. Preheat your to high temperature.
2. Place the turkey on a chopping board with the breast side down and the legs pointing towards you.
3. Cut either side of the turkey backbone, to remove the spine. Flip the turkey and place it on a pan
4. Season both sides with the seasonings and place it on the grill skin side up on the grill.
5. Cook for 30 minutes, reduce temperature, and cook for 45 more minutes or until the internal temperature reaches 165F.
6. Remove from the and let rest for 15 minutes before slicing and serving.
Nutrition Info: Calories 156, Total fat 16g, Saturated fat 2g, Total carbs 1g, Net carbs 1g Protein 2g, Sugars 0g, Fiber 0g, Sodium 19mg

Buffalo Chicken Flatbread

Servings: 6
Cooking Time: 30 Minutes
Ingredients:
- 6 mini pita bread
- 1-1/2 cups buffalo sauce
- 4 cups chicken breasts, cooked and cubed
- 3 cups mozzarella cheese

- Blue cheese for drizzling

Directions:
1. Preheat the wood pellet grill to 375-400°F.
2. Place the breads on a flat surface and evenly spread sauce over all of them.
3. Toss the chicken with the remaining buffalo sauce and place it on the pita breads.
4. Top with cheese then place the breads on the grill but indirectly from the heat. Close the grill lid.
5. Cook for 7 minutes or until the cheese has melted and the edges are toasty.
6. Remove from grill and drizzle with blue cheese. Serve and enjoy.

Nutrition Info: Calories: 254 Cal Fat: 13 g Carbohydrates: 4 g Protein: 33 g Fiber: 3 g

Korean Chicken Wings

Servings: 6
Cooking Time: 1 Hour
Ingredients:
- 3 pounds of chicken wings
- 2 tablespoons olive oil
- For the Brine:
- 1 head garlic, halved
- 1 lemon, halved
- 1/2 cup sugar
- 1 cup of sea salt
- 4 sprigs of thyme
- 10 peppercorns
- 16 cups of water
- For the Sauce:
- 2 teaspoons minced garlic
- 1/2 cup gochujang hot pepper paste
- 1 tablespoon grated ginger
- 2 tablespoons of rice wine vinegar
- 1/3 cup honey
- 1/4 cup soy sauce
- 2 tablespoons lime juice
- 2 tablespoons toasted sesame oil
- 1/4 cup melted butter

Directions:
1. Prepare the brine and for this, take a large stockpot, place it over high heat, pour in water, stir in salt and sugar until dissolved, and bring to a boil.
2. Then remove the pot from heat, add remaining ingredients for the brine, and bring the brine to room temperature.
3. Add chicken wings, submerge them completely, cover the pot and let wings soak for a minimum of 4 hours in the refrigerator.
4. When ready to cook, switch on the grill, fill the grill hopper with flavored wood pellets, power the grill on by using the control panel, select 'smoke' on the temperature dial, or set the temperature to 375

degrees F and let it preheat for a minimum of 15 minutes.
5. Meanwhile, remove chicken wings from the brine, pat dry with paper towels, place them in a large bowl, drizzle with oil and toss until well coated.
6. When the grill has preheated, open the lid, place chicken wings on the grill grate, shut the grill, and smoke for 1 hour until the internal temperature reaches 165 degrees F.
7. Meanwhile, prepare the sauce and for this, take a medium bowl, place all of the sauce ingredients in it and whisk until smooth.
8. When done, transfer chicken wings to a dish, top with prepared sauce, toss until coated, and then serve.

Nutrition Info: Calories: 137 Cal ;Fat: 9 g ;Carbs: 4 g ;Protein: 8 g ;Fiber: 1 g

Smoked Turkey Wings

Servings: 2
Cooking Time: 1 Hour
Ingredients:
- 4 turkey wings
- 1 batch Sweet and Spicy Cinnamon Rub

Directions:
1. Supply your smoker with wood pellets and follow the manufacturer's specific start-up procedure. Preheat the grill, with the lid closed, to 180°F.
2. Using your hands, work the rub into the turkey wings, coating them completely.
3. Place the wings directly on the grill grate and cook for 30 minutes.
4. Increase the grill's temperature to 325°F and continue to cook until the turkey's internal temperature reaches 170°F. Remove the wings from the grill and serve immediately.

Hickory Smoked Chicken Leg And Thigh Quarters

Servings: 6
Cooking Time: 2 Hours
Ingredients:
- 6 chicken legs (with thigh and drumsticks)
- 2 tablespoons olive oil
- Poultry Rub to taste

Directions:
1. Place all ingredients in a bowl and mix until the chicken pieces are coated in oil and rub. Allow to marinate for at least 2 hours.
2. Fire the Grill to 180F. Close the lid and allow to preheat for 10 minutes. Use hickory wood pellets to smoke your chicken.

3. Arrange the chicken on the grill grate and smoke for one hour. Increase the temperature to 350F and continue cooking for another hour until the chicken is golden and the juices run clean.
4. To check if the meat is cooked, insert a meat thermometer, and make sure that the temperature on the thickest part of the chicken registers at 165F.
5. Remove the chicken and serve.
Nutrition Info: Calories per serving: 358 ; Protein: 50.8g; Carbs: 0g; Fat: 15.7g Sugar:0 g

Maple And Bacon Chicken

Servings: 7
Cooking Time: 1 And ½ Hours
Ingredients:
- 4 boneless and skinless chicken breast
- Salt as needed
- Fresh pepper
- 12 slices bacon, uncooked
- 1cup maple syrup
- ½ cup melted butter
- 1teaspoon liquid smoke

Directions:
1. Preheat your smoker to 250 degrees Fahrenheit
2. Season the chicken with pepper and salt
3. Wrap the breast with 3 bacon slices and cover the entire surface
4. Secure the bacon with toothpicks
5. Take a medium-sized bowl and stir in maple syrup, butter, liquid smoke, and mix well
6. Reserve 1/3rd of this mixture for later use
7. Submerge the chicken breast into the butter mix and coat them well
8. Place a pan in your smoker and transfer the chicken to your smoker
9. Smoker for 1 to 1 and a ½ hours
10. Brush the chicken with reserved butter and smoke for 30 minutes more until the internal temperature reaches 165 degrees Fahrenheit
11. Enjoy!
Nutrition Info: Calories: 458 Fats: 20g Carbs: 65g Fiber: 1g

Roasted Whole Chicken

Servings: 6 To 8
Cooking Time: 1 To 2 Hours
Ingredients:
- 1 whole chicken
- 2 tablespoons olive oil
- 1 batch Chicken Rub

Directions:

1. Supply your smoker with wood pellets and follow the manufacturer's specific start-up procedure. Preheat the grill, with the lid closed, to 375°F.
2. Coat the chicken all over with olive oil and season it with the rub. Using your hands, work the rub into the meat.
3. Place the chicken directly on the grill grate and smoke until its internal temperature reaches 170°F.
4. Remove the chicken from the grill and let it rest for 10 minutes, before carving and serving.

Smoked Whole Duck

Servings: 6
Cooking Time: 2 Hours 30 Minutes
Ingredients:
- 5 pounds whole duck (trimmed of any excess fat)
- 1small onion (quartered)
- 1apple (wedged)
- 1orange (quartered)
- 1tbsp freshly chopped parsley
- 1tbsp freshly chopped sage
- ½ tsp onion powder
- 2tsp smoked paprika
- 1tsp dried Italian seasoning
- 1tbsp dried Greek seasoning
- 1tsp pepper or to taste
- 1tsp sea salt or to taste

Directions:
1. Remove giblets and rinse duck, inside and pour, under cold running water.
2. Pat dry with paper towels.
3. Use the tip of a sharp knife to cut the duck skin all over. Be careful not to cut through the meat. Tie the duck legs together with butcher's string.
4. To make a rub, combine the onion powder, pepper, salt, Italian seasoning, Greek seasoning, and paprika in a mixing bowl.
5. Insert the orange, onion, and apple to the duck cavity. Stuff the duck with freshly chopped parsley and sage.
6. Season all sides of the duck generously with rub mixture.
7. Start your pellet grill on smoke mode, leaving the lip open or until the fire starts.
8. Close the lid and preheat the grill to 325°F for 10 minutes.
9. Place the duck on the grill grate.
10. Roast for 2 to 21/2 hours, or until the duck skin is brown and the internal temperature of the thigh reaches 160°F.
11. Remove the duck from heat and let it rest for a few minutes.
12. Cut into sizes and serve.

Nutrition Info: Calories: 809 Total Fat: 42.9 g Saturated Fat: 15.8 g Cholesterol: 337 mg Sodium: 638 mg Total Carbohydrate: 11.7 g Dietary Fiber: 2.4 g Total Sugars: 7.5 g Protein: 89.6 g

Chile Lime Chicken

Servings: 1
Cooking Time: 15 Minutes
Ingredients:
- 1 chicken breast
- 1 tbsp oil
- 1 tbsp spiceology Chile Lime Seasoning

Directions:
1. Preheat your to 400F.
2. Brush the chicken breast with oil then sprinkle the chile-lime seasoning and salt.
3. Place the chicken breast on the grill and cook for 7 minutes on each side or until the internal temperature reaches 165F.
4. Serve when hot and enjoy.
Nutrition Info: Calories 131, Total fat 5g, Saturated fat 1g, Total carbs 4g, Net carbs 3g Protein 19g, Sugars 1g, Fiber 1g, Sodium 235mg

Smoked Chicken With Apricot Bbq Glaze

Servings: 6
Cooking Time: 30 Minutes
Ingredients:
- 2 whole chicken, halved
- 4 tablespoon Chicken Rub
- 1 cup Trager Apricot BBQ Sauce

Directions:
1. Massage the chicken with the chicken rub. Allow to marinate for 2 hours in the fridge.
2. When ready to cook, fire the Grill to 350F. Use preferred wood pellets. Close the grill lid and preheat for 15 minutes.
3. Place the chicken on the grill grate and grill for 15 minutes on each side. Baste the chicken with Apricot BBQ glaze.
4. Once cooked, allow to rest for 10 minutes before slicing.
Nutrition Info: Calories per serving: 304; Protein: 49g; Carbs: 10.2g; Fat: 6.5g Sugar: 8.7g

Grilled Buffalo Chicken

Servings: 6
Cooking Time: 20 Minutes
Ingredients:
- 5 chicken breasts, boneless and skinless
- 2 tbsp homemade BBQ rub

- 1 cup homemade Cholula Buffalo sauce
Directions:
1. Preheat the to 400F.
2. Slice the chicken breast lengthwise into strips. Season the slices with BBQ rub.
3. Place the chicken slices on the grill and paint both sides with buffalo sauce.
4. Cook for 4 minutes with the lid closed. Flip the breasts, paint again with sauce and cook until the internal temperature reaches 165F.
5. Remove the chicken from the and serve when warm.
Nutrition Info: Calories 176, Total fat 4g, Saturated fat 1g, Total carbs 1g, Net carbs 1g Protein 32g, Sugars 1g, Fiber 0g, Sodium 631mg

Wood Pellet Sheet Pan Chicken Fajitas

Servings: 10
Cooking Time: 10 Minutes
Ingredients:
- 2 tbsp oil
- 2 tbsp chile margarita seasoning
- 1 tbsp salt
- 1/2 tbsp onion powder
- 1/2 tbsp garlic, granulated
- 2-pound chicken breast, thinly sliced
- 1 red bell pepper, seeded and sliced
- 1 orange bell pepper
- 1 onion, sliced

Directions:
1. Preheat the wood pellet to 450°F. Meanwhile, mix oil and seasoning then toss the chicken and the peppers. Line a sheet pan with foil then place it in the preheated grill. Let it heat for 10 minutes with the grill's lid closed. Open the grill and place the chicken with the veggies on the pan in a single layer. Cook for 10 minutes or until the chicken is cooked and no longer pink. Remove from grill and serve with tortilla or your favorite fixings.
Nutrition Info: Calories: 211 Cal Fat: 6 g Carbohydrates: 5 g Protein: 29 g Fiber: 1 g

Serrano Chicken Wings

Servings: 4
Cooking Time: 40 Minutes
Ingredients:
- 4 lb. chicken wings
- 2 cups beer
- 2 teaspoons crushed red pepper
- Cajun seasoning powder
- 1 lb. Serrano chili peppers
- 1 teaspoon fresh basil

- 1 teaspoon dried oregano
- 4 cloves garlic
- 1 cup vinegar
- Salt and pepper to taste

Directions:
1. Soak the chicken wings in beer.
2. Sprinkle with crushed red pepper.
3. Cover and refrigerate for 12 hours.
4. Remove chicken from brine.
5. Season with Cajun seasoning.
6. Preheat your wood pellet grill to 325 degrees F for 15 minutes while the lid is closed.
7. Add the chicken wings and Serrano chili peppers on the grill.
8. Grill for 5 minutes per side.
9. Remove chili peppers and place in a food processor.
10. Grill the chicken for another 20 minutes.
11. Add the rest of the ingredients to the food processor.
12. Pulse until smooth.
13. Dip the chicken wings in the sauce.
14. Grill for 5 minutes and serve.
15. Tips: You can also use prepared pepper sauce to save time.

Lemon Rosemary And Beer Marinated Chicken

Servings: 6
Cooking Time: 55 Minutes
Ingredients:
- 1 whole chicken
- 1 lemon, zested and juiced
- 1 teaspoon salt
- 1 teaspoon ground black pepper
- 1 teaspoon rosemary, chopped
- 12-ounce beer, apple-flavored

Directions:
1. Place all ingredients in a bowl and allow the chicken to marinate for at least 12 hours in the fridge.
2. When ready to cook, fire the Grill to 350F. Use preferred wood pellets. Close the grill lid and preheat for 15 minutes.
3. Place the chicken on the grill grate and cook for 55 minutes.
4. Cook until the internal temperature reads at 165F.
5. Take the chicken out and allow to rest before carving.
Nutrition Info: Calories per serving: 288; Protein: 36.1g; Carbs: 4.4g; Fat: 13.1g Sugar: 0.7g

Jamaican Jerk Chicken Quarters

Servings: 4
Cooking Time: 1 To 2 Hours
Ingredients:
- 4 chicken leg quarters, scored
- ¼ cup canola oil
- ½ cup Jamaican Jerk Paste
- 1 tablespoon whole allspice (pimento) berries

Directions:
1. Supply your smoker with wood pellets and follow the manufacturer's specific start-up procedure. Preheat, with the lid closed, to 275°F.
2. Brush the chicken with canola oil, then brush 6 tablespoons of the Jerk paste on and under the skin. Reserve the remaining 2 tablespoons of paste for basting.
3. Throw the whole allspice berries in with the wood pellets for added smoke flavor.
4. Arrange the chicken on the grill, close the lid, and smoke for 1 hour to 1 hour 30 minutes, or until a meat thermometer inserted in the thickest part of the thigh reads 165°F.
5. Let the meat rest for 5 minutes and baste with the reserved jerk paste prior to serving.

Smoked Whole Chicken

Servings: 6 To 8
Cooking Time: 4 Hours
Ingredients:
- 1 whole chicken
- 2 cups Tea Injectable (using Not-Just-for-Pork Rub)
- 2 tablespoons olive oil
- 1 batch Chicken Rub
- 2 tablespoons butter, melted

Directions:
1. Supply your smoker with wood pellets and follow the manufacturer's specific start-up procedure. Preheat the grill, with the lid closed, to 180°F.
2. Inject the chicken throughout with the tea injectable.
3. Coat the chicken all over with olive oil and season it with the rub. Using your hands, work the rub into the meat.
4. Place the chicken directly on the grill grate and smoke for 3 hours.
5. Baste the chicken with the butter and increase the grill's temperature to 375°F. Continue to cook the chicken until its internal temperature reaches 170°F.
6. Remove the chicken from the grill and let it rest for 10 minutes, before carving and serving.

Chicken Tikka Masala

Servings: 4
Cooking Time: 1 Hour
Ingredients:
- 1 tablespoon garam masala
- 1 tablespoon smoked paprika
- 1 tablespoon ground coriander
- 1 tablespoon ground cumin
- 1 teaspoon ground cayenne pepper
- 1 teaspoon turmeric
- 1 onion, sliced
- 6 cloves garlic, minced
- 1/4 cup olive oil
- 1 tablespoon ginger, chopped
- 1 tablespoon lemon juice
- 1 1/2 cups Greek yogurt
- 1 tablespoon lime juice
- 1 tablespoon curry powder
- Salt to taste
- 1 tablespoon lime juice
- 12 chicken drumsticks
- Chopped cilantro

Directions:
1. Make the marinade by mixing all the spices, onion, garlic, olive oil, ginger, lemon juice, yogurt, lime juice, curry powder and salt.
2. Transfer to a food processor.
3. Pulse until smooth.
4. Divide the mixture into two.
5. Marinade the chicken in the first bowl.
6. Cover the bowl and refrigerate for 12 hours.
7. Set the wood pellet grill to high.
8. Preheat it for 15 minutes while the lid is closed.
9. Grill the chicken for 50 minutes.
10. Garnish with the chopped cilantro.
11. Tips: You can also smoke the chicken before grilling.

Smoked Fried Chicken

Servings: 6
Cooking Time: 3 Hours
Ingredients:
- 3.5 lb. chicken
- Vegetable oil
- Salt and pepper to taste
- 2 tablespoons hot sauce
- 1 quart buttermilk
- 2 tablespoons brown sugar
- 1 tablespoon poultry dry rub
- 2 tablespoons onion powder
- 2 tablespoons garlic powder
- 2 1/2 cups all-purpose flour
- Peanut oil

Directions:
1. Set the wood pellet grill to 200 degrees F.
2. Preheat it for 15 minutes while the lid is closed.
3. Drizzle chicken with vegetable oil and sprinkle with salt and pepper.
4. Smoke chicken for 2 hours and 30 minutes.
5. In a bowl, mix the hot sauce, buttermilk and sugar.
6. Soak the smoked chicken in the mixture.
7. Cover and refrigerate for 1 hour.
8. In another bowl, mix the dry rub, onion powder, garlic powder and flour.
9. Coat the chicken with the mixture.
10. Heat the peanut oil in a pan over medium heat.
11. Fry the chicken until golden and crispy.
12. Tips: Drain chicken on paper towels before serving.

Beer Can Chicken

Servings: 6
Cooking Time: 1 Hour And 15 Minutes
Ingredients:
- 5-pound chicken
- 1/2 cup dry chicken rub
- 1 can beer

Directions:
1. Preheat your wood pellet grill on smoke for 5 minutes with the lid open.
2. The lid must then be closed and then preheated up to 450 degrees Fahrenheit
3. Pour out half of the beer then shove the can in the chicken and use the legs like a tripod.
4. Place the chicken on the grill until the internal temperature reaches 165°F.
5. Remove from the grill and let rest for 20 minutes before serving. Enjoy.
Nutrition Info: Calories: 882 Cal Fat: 51 g
Carbohydrates: 2 g Protein: 94 g Fiber: 0 g

Rosemary Orange Chicken

Servings: 6
Cooking Time: 45 Minutes
Ingredients:
- 4 pounds chicken, backbone removed
- For the Marinade:
- 2 teaspoons salt
- 3 tablespoons chopped rosemary leaves
- 2 teaspoons Dijon mustard
- 1 orange, zested
- 1/4 cup olive oil
- ¼ cup of orange juice

Directions:

1. Prepare the chicken and for this, rinse the chicken, pat dry with paper towels and then place in a large baking dish.
2. Prepare the marinade and for this, take a medium bowl, place all of its ingredients in it and whisk until combined.
3. Cover chicken with the prepared marinade, cover with a plastic wrap, and then marinate for a minimum of 2 hours in the refrigerator, turning halfway.
4. When ready to cook, switch on the grill, fill the grill hopper with flavored wood pellets, power the grill on by using the control panel, select 'smoke' on the temperature dial, or set the temperature to 350 degrees F and let it preheat for a minimum of 5 minutes.
5. When the grill has preheated, open the lid, place chicken on the grill grate skin-side down, shut the grill and smoke for 45 minutes until well browned, and the internal temperature reaches 165 degrees F.
6. When done, transfer chicken to a cutting board, let it rest for 10 minutes, cut it into slices, and then serve.

Nutrition Info: Calories: 258 Cal ;Fat: 17.4 g ;Carbs: 5.2 g ;Protein: 19.3 g ;Fiber: 0.3 g

Bbq Sauce Smothered Chicken Breasts

Servings: 4
Cooking Time: 30 Minutes
Ingredients:
- 1 tsp. garlic, crushed
- ¼ C. olive oil
- 1 tbsp. Worcestershire sauce
- 1 tbsp. sweet mesquite seasoning
- 4 chicken breasts
- 2 tbsp. regular BBQ sauce
- 2 tbsp. spicy BBQ sauce
- 2 tbsp. honey bourbon BBQ sauce

Directions:
1. Set the temperature of Grill to 450 degrees F and preheat with closed lid for 15 minutes.
2. In a large bowl, mix together garlic, oil, Worcestershire sauce and mesquite seasoning.
3. Coat chicken breasts with seasoning mixture evenly.
4. Place the chicken breasts onto the grill and cook for about 20-30 minutes.
5. Meanwhile, in a bowl, mix together all 3 BBQ sauces.
6. In the last 4-5 minutes of cooking, coat breast with BBQ sauce mixture.
7. Serve hot.

Nutrition Info: Calories per serving: 421; Carbohydrates: 10.1g; Protein: 41,2g; Fat: 23.3g; Sugar: 6.9g; Sodium: 763mg; Fiber: 0.2g

Turkey With Apricot Barbecue Glaze

Servings: 4
Cooking Time: 30 Minutes
Ingredients:
- 4 turkey breast fillets
- 4 tablespoons chicken rub
- 1 cup apricot barbecue sauce

Directions:
1. Preheat the wood pellet grill to 365 degrees F for 15 minutes while the lid is closed.
2. Season the turkey fillets with the chicken run.
3. Grill the turkey fillets for 5 minutes per side.
4. Brush both sides with the barbecue sauce and grill for another 5 minutes per side.
5. Tips: You can sprinkle turkey with chili powder if you want your dish spicy.

Wood Pellet Grilled Buffalo Chicken Leg

Servings: 6
Cooking Time: 25 Minutes
Ingredients:
- 12 chicken legs
- 1/2 tbsp salt
- 1 tbsp buffalo seasoning
- 1 cup buffalo sauce

Directions:
1. Preheat your wood pellet grill to 325°F.
2. Toss the legs in salt and buffalo seasoning then place them on the preheated grill.
3. Grill for 40 minutes ensuring you turn them twice through the cooking.
4. Brush the legs with buffalo sauce and cook for an additional 10 minutes or until the internal temperature reaches 165°F.
5. Remove the legs from the grill, brush with more sauce, and serve when hot.

Nutrition Info: Calories: 956 Cal Fat: 47 g Carbohydrates: 1 g Protein: 124 g Fiber: 0 g

Hellfire Chicken Wings

Servings: 6
Cooking Time: 40 Minutes
Ingredients:
- 3 pounds chicken wings, tips removed
- 2 tablespoons olive oil
- For the Rub:
- 1 teaspoon onion powder
- 1 teaspoon salt
- 1 teaspoon garlic powder
- 1 tablespoon paprika

- 1 teaspoon ground black pepper
- 1 teaspoon celery seed
- 1 teaspoon cayenne pepper
- 2 teaspoons brown sugar
- For the Sauce:
- 4 jalapeno peppers, sliced crosswise
- 8 tablespoons butter, unsalted
- 1/2 cup hot sauce
- 1/2 cup cilantro leaves

Directions:
1. Switch on the grill, fill the grill hopper with hickory flavored wood pellets, power the grill on by using the control panel, select 'smoke' on the temperature dial, or set the temperature to 350 degrees F and let it preheat for a minimum of 15 minutes.
2. Prepare the chicken wings and for this, remove tips from the wings, cut each chicken wing through the joint into two pieces, and then place in a large bowl.
3. Prepare the rub and for this, take a small bowl, place all of its ingredients in it and then stir until combined.
4. Sprinkle prepared rub on the chicken wings and then toss until well coated.
5. Meanwhile,
6. When the grill has preheated, open the lid, place chicken wings on the grill grate, shut the grill and smoke for 40 minutes until golden brown and skin have turned crisp, turning halfway.
7. Meanwhile, prepare the sauce and for this, take a small saucepan, place it over medium-low heat, add butter in it and when it melts, add jalapeno and cook for 4 minutes.
8. Then stir in hot sauce and cilantro until mixed and remove the pan from heat.
9. When done, transfer chicken wings to a dish, top with prepared sauce, toss until coated, and then serve.

Nutrition Info: Calories: 250 Cal ;Fat: 15 g ;Carbs: 11 g ;Protein: 19 g ;Fiber: 1 g

Skinny Smoked Chicken Breasts

Servings: 4 To 6
Cooking Time: 1 Hour 25 Minutes
Ingredients:
- 2½ pounds boneless, skinless chicken breasts
- Salt
- Freshly ground black pepper

Directions:
1. Supply your smoker with wood pellets and follow the manufacturer's specific start-up procedure. Preheat the grill, with the lid closed, to 180°F.

2. Season the chicken breasts all over with salt and pepper.
3. Place the breasts directly on the grill grate and smoke for 1 hour.
4. Increase the grill's temperature to 325°F and continue to cook until the chicken's internal temperature reaches 170°F. Remove the breasts from the grill and serve immediately.

Cinco De Mayo Chicken Enchiladas

Servings: 6
Cooking Time: 45 Minutes
Ingredients:
- 6 cups diced cooked chicken
- 3 cups grated Monterey Jack cheese, divided
- 1 cup sour cream
- 1 (4-ounce) can chopped green chiles
- 2 (10-ounce) cans red or green enchilada sauce, divided
- 12 (8-inch) flour tortillas
- ½ cup chopped scallions
- ¼ cup chopped fresh cilantro

Directions:
1. Supply your smoker with wood pellets and follow the manufacturer's specific start-up procedure. Preheat, with the lid closed, to 350°F.
2. In a large bowl, combine the cooked chicken, 2 cups of cheese, the sour cream, and green chiles to make the filling.
3. Pour one can of enchilada sauce in the bottom of a 9-by-13-inch baking dish or aluminum pan.
4. Spoon ⅓ cup of the filling on each tortilla and roll up securely.
5. Transfer the tortillas seam-side down to the baking dish, then pour the remaining can of enchilada sauce over them, coating all exposed surfaces of the tortillas.
6. Sprinkle the remaining 1 cup of cheese over the enchiladas and cover tightly with aluminum foil.
7. Bake on the grill, with the lid closed, for 30 minutes, then remove the foil.
8. Continue baking with the lid closed for 15 minutes, or until bubbly.
9. Garnish the enchiladas with the chopped scallions and cilantro and serve immediately.

Crispy & Juicy Chicken

Servings: 6
Cooking Time: 5 Hours
Ingredients:
- ¾ C. dark brown sugar
- ½ C. ground espresso beans
- 1 tbsp. ground cumin

- 1 tbsp. ground cinnamon
- 1 tbsp. garlic powder
- 1 tbsp. cayenne pepper
- Salt and freshly ground black pepper, to taste
- 1 (4-lb.) whole chicken, neck and giblets removed

Directions:
1. Set the temperature of Grill to 200-225 degrees F and preheat with closed lid for 15 minutes.
2. In a bowl, mix together brown sugar, ground espresso, spices, salt and black pepper.
3. Rub the chicken with spice mixture generously.
4. Place the chicken onto the grill and cook for about 3-5 hours.
5. Remove chicken from grill and place onto a cutting board for about 10 minutes before carving.
6. With a sharp knife, cut the chicken into desired-sized pieces and serve.

Nutrition Info: Calories per serving: 540; Carbohydrates: 20.7g; Protein: 88.3g; Fat: 9.6g; Sugar: 18.1g; Sodium: 226mg; Fiber: 1.2g

Smoked Airline Chicken

Servings: 4
Cooking Time: 1 To 2 Hours
Ingredients:
- 2 boneless chicken breasts with drumettes attached
- ½ cup soy sauce
- ½ cup teriyaki sauce
- ¼ cup canola oil
- ¼ cup white vinegar
- 1 tablespoon minced garlic
- ¼ cup chopped scallions
- 2 teaspoons freshly ground black pepper
- 1 teaspoon ground mustard

Directions:
1. Place the chicken in a baking dish.
2. In a bowl, whisk together the soy sauce, teriyaki sauce, canola oil, vinegar, garlic, scallions, pepper and ground mustard, then pour this marinade over the chicken, coating both sides.
3. Refrigerate the chicken in marinade for 4 hours, turning over every hour.
4. When ready to smoke the chicken, supply your smoker with wood pellets and follow the manufacturer's specific start-up procedure. Preheat, with the lid closed, to 250°F.
5. Remove the chicken from the marinade but do not rinse. Discard the marinade.
6. Arrange the chicken directly on the grill, close the lid, and smoke for 1 hour 30 minutes to 2 hours, or until a meat thermometer inserted in the thickest part of the meat reads 165°F.

7. Let the meat rest for 3 minutes before serving.

Whole Smoked Chicken

Servings: 6
Cooking Time: 3 Hours
Ingredients:
- ½ cup salt
- 1 cup brown sugar
- 1 whole chicken (3 ½ pounds)
- 1 teaspoon minced garlic
- 1 lemon, halved
- 1 medium onion, quartered
- 3 whole cloves
- 5 sprigs of thyme

Directions:
1. Dissolve the salt and sugar in 4 liters of water. Once dissolved, place the chicken in the brine and allow to marinate for 24 hours.
2. When ready to cook, fire the Grill up to 250F and allow to preheat for 15 minutes with the lid closed. Use any wood pellet desired but we recommend using the maple wood pellet.
3. While the grill is preheating, remove the chicken from the brine and pat dry using paper towel. Rub the minced garlic all over the chicken. Stuff the cavity of the chicken with the remaining ingredients.
4. Tie the legs together with a natural string.
5. Place the stuffed chicken directly on the grill grate and smoke for 3 hours until the internal temperature of the chicken is 160F particularly in the breast part.
6. Take the chicken out and grill.

Nutrition Info: Calories per serving: 251; Protein: 32.6g; Carbs: 19g; Fat: 4.3g Sugar: 17.3g

Bbq Half Chickens

Servings: 4
Cooking Time: 75 Minutes
Ingredients:
- 3.5-pound whole chicken, cleaned, halved
- Summer rub as needed
- Apricot BBQ sauce as needed

Directions:
1. Switch on the grill, fill the grill hopper with apple-flavored wood pellets, power the grill on by using the control panel, select 'smoke' on the temperature dial, or set the temperature to 375 degrees F and let it preheat for a minimum of 15 minutes.
2. Meanwhile, cut chicken in half along with backbone and then season with summer rub.
3. When the grill has preheated, open the lid, place chicken halves on the grill grate skin-side up, shut

the grill, change the smoking temperature to 225 degrees F, and smoke for 1 hour and 30 minutes until the internal temperature reaches 160 degrees F.

4. Then brush chicken generously with apricot sauce and continue grilling for 10 minutes until glazed.

5. When done, transfer chicken to cutting to a dish, let it rest for 5 minutes, and then serve.

Nutrition Info: Calories: 435 Cal ;Fat: 20 g ;Carbs: 20 g ;Protein: 42 g ;Fiber: 1 g

Special Occasion's Dinner Cornish Hen

Servings: 4
Cooking Time: 1 Hour
Ingredients:
- 4 Cornish game hens
- 4 fresh rosemary sprigs
- 4 tbsp. butter, melted
- 4 tsp. chicken rub

Directions:
1. Set the temperature of Grill to 375 degrees F and preheat with closed lid for 15 minutes.
2. With paper towels, pat dry the hens.
3. Tuck the wings behind the backs and with kitchen strings, tie the legs together.
4. Coat the outside of each hen with melted butter and sprinkle with rub evenly.
5. Stuff the cavity of each hen with a rosemary sprig.
6. Place the hens onto the grill and cook for about 50-60 minutes.
7. Remove the hens from grill and place onto a platter for about 10 minutes.
8. Cut each hen into desired-sized pieces and serve.

Nutrition Info: Calories per serving: 430; Carbohydrates: 2.1g; Protein: 25.4g; Fat: 33g; Sugar: 0g; Sodium: 331mg; Fiber: 0.7g

Turkey Breast

Servings: 6
Cooking Time: 8 Hours
Ingredients:
- For the Brine:
- 2 pounds turkey breast, deboned
- 2 tablespoons ground black pepper
- 1/4 cup salt
- 1 cup brown sugar
- 4 cups cold water
- For the BBQ Rub:
- 2 tablespoons dried onions
- 2 tablespoons garlic powder
- 1/4 cup paprika

- 2 tablespoons ground black pepper
- 1 tablespoon salt
- 2 tablespoons brown sugar
- 2 tablespoons red chili powder
- 1 tablespoon cayenne pepper
- 2 tablespoons sugar
- 2 tablespoons ground cumin

Directions:
1. Prepare the brine and for this, take a large bowl, add salt, black pepper, and sugar in it, pour in water, and stir until sugar has dissolved.
2. Place turkey breast in it, submerge it completely and let it soak for a minimum of 12 hours in the refrigerator.
3. Meanwhile, prepare the BBQ rub and for this, take a small bowl, place all of its ingredients in it and then stir until combined, set aside until required.
4. Then remove turkey breast from the brine and season well with the prepared BBQ rub.
5. When ready to cook, switch on the grill, fill the grill hopper with apple-flavored wood pellets, power the grill on by using the control panel, select 'smoke' on the temperature dial, or set the temperature to 180 degrees F and let it preheat for a minimum of 15 minutes.
6. When the grill has preheated, open the lid, place turkey breast on the grill grate, shut the grill, change the smoking temperature to 225 degrees F, and smoke for 8 hours until the internal temperature reaches 160 degrees F.
7. When done, transfer turkey to a cutting board, let it rest for 10 minutes, then cut it into slices and serve.

Nutrition Info: Calories: 250 Cal ;Fat: 5 g ;Carbs: 31 g ;Protein: 18 g ;Fiber: 5 g

Lemon Chicken

Servings: 6
Cooking Time: 10 Minutes
Ingredients:
- 2 teaspoons honey
- 1 tablespoon lemon juice
- 1 teaspoon lemon zest
- 1 clove garlic, coarsely chopped
- 2 sprigs thyme
- Salt and pepper to taste
- ½ cup olive oil
- 6 chicken breast fillets

Directions:
1. Mix the honey, lemon juice, lemon zest, garlic, thyme, salt and pepper in a bowl.
2. Gradually add olive oil to the mixture.
3. Soak the chicken fillets in the mixture.
4. Cover and refrigerate for 4 hours.

5. Preheat the wood pellet grill to 400 degrees F for 15 minutes while the lid is closed.
6. Grill the chicken for 5 minutes per side.
7. Tips: You can also make additional marinade to be used for basting during grill time.

Garlic Parmesan Chicken Wings

Servings: 6
Cooking Time: 20 Minutes
Ingredients:
- 5 pounds of chicken wings
- 1/2 cup chicken rub
- 3 tablespoons chopped parsley
- 1 cup shredded parmesan cheese
- For the Sauce:
- 5 teaspoons minced garlic
- 2 tablespoons chicken rub
- 1 cup butter, unsalted

Directions:
1. Switch on the grill, fill the grill hopper with cherry flavored wood pellets, power the grill on by using the control panel, select 'smoke' on the temperature dial, or set the temperature to 450 degrees F and let it preheat for a minimum of 15 minutes.
2. Meanwhile, take a large bowl, place chicken wings in it, sprinkle with chicken rub and toss until well coated.
3. When the grill has preheated, open the lid, place chicken wings on the grill grate, shut the grill, and smoke for 10 minutes per side until the internal temperature reaches 165 degrees F.
4. Meanwhile, prepare the sauce and for this, take a medium saucepan, place it over medium heat, add all the ingredients for the sauce in it and cook for 10 minutes until smooth, set aside until required.
5. When done, transfer chicken wings to a dish, top with prepared sauce, toss until mixed, garnish with cheese and parsley and then serve.
Nutrition Info: Calories: 180 Cal ;Fat: 1 g ;Carbs: 8 g ;Protein: 0 g ;Fiber: 0 g

Easy Rapid-fire Roast Chicken

Servings: 4
Cooking Time: 1 To 2 Hours
Ingredients:
- 1 (4-pound) whole chicken, giblets removed
- Extra-virgin olive oil, for rubbing
- 3 tablespoons Greek seasoning
- Juice of 1 lemon
- Butcher's string

Directions:

1. Supply your smoker with wood pellets and follow the manufacturer's specific start-up procedure. Preheat, with the lid closed, to 450°F.
2. Rub the bird generously all over with oil, including inside the cavity.
3. Sprinkle the Greek seasoning all over and under the skin of the bird, and squeeze the lemon juice over the breast.
4. Tuck the chicken wings behind the back and tie the legs together with butcher's string or cooking twine.
5. Put the chicken directly on the grill, breast-side up, close the lid, and roast for 1 hour to 1 hour 30 minutes, or until a meat thermometer inserted in the thigh reads 165°F.
6. Let the meat rest for 10 minutes before carving.

Grilled Sweet And Sour Chicken

Servings: 6
Cooking Time: 35 Minutes
Ingredients:
- 6 cups water
- 1/3 cup salt
- ¼ cup brown sugar
- ¼ cup soy sauce
- 6 chicken breasts, boneless
- 1 cup granulated white sugar
- ½ cup ketchup
- 1 cup apple cider vinegar
- 2 tablespoons soy sauce
- 1 teaspoon garlic powder

Directions:
1. Place the water, salt, brown sugar, and soy sauce in a large bowl. Stir until well combined. Add in the chicken breasts into the brine and allow to soak for 24 hours in the refrigerator.
2. Fire the Grill to 350F. Use maple wood pellets. Close the grill lid and preheat for 15 minutes.
3. Place the breasts on the grill grate and cook for 35 minutes on each side with the lid closed. Flip the chicken halfway through the cooking time.
4. Meanwhile, place the remaining ingredients in a bowl and stir until combined.
5. Ten minutes before the chicken breasts are cooked, brush with the sauce.
6. Serve immediately.
Nutrition Info: Calories per serving: 675 ; Protein: 61.9g; Carbs: 35.8g; Fat: 29.7g Sugar: 32.7g

Wood Pellet Smoked Spatchcock Turkey

Servings: 6
Cooking Time: 1 Hour And 45 Minutes
Ingredients:

- 1 whole turkey
- 1/2 cup oil
- 1/4 cup chicken rub
- 1 tbsp onion powder
- 1 tbsp garlic powder
- 1 tbsp rubbed sage

Directions:
1. Preheat your wood pellet grill to high.
2. Meanwhile, place the turkey on a platter with the breast side down then cut on either side of the backbone to remove the spine.
3. Flip the turkey and season on both sides then place it on the preheated grill or on a pan if you want to catch the drippings. Grill on high for 30 minutes, reduce the temperature to 325°F, and grill for 45 more minutes or until the internal temperature reaches 165°F Remove from the grill and let rest for 20 minutes before slicing and serving. Enjoy.

Nutrition Info: Calories: 156 Cal Fat: 16 g Carbohydrates: 1 g Protein: 2 g Fiber: 0 g

Chicken Tenders

Servings: 2 To 4
Cooking Time: 1 Hour, 20 Minutes
Ingredients:
- 1 pound boneless, skinless chicken breast tenders
- 1 batch Chicken Rub

Directions:
1. Supply your smoker with wood pellets and follow the manufacturer's specific start-up procedure. Preheat the grill, with the lid closed, to 180°F.
2. Season the chicken tenders with the rub. Using your hands, work the rub into the meat.
3. Place the tenders directly on the grill grate and smoke for 1 hour.
4. Increase the grill's temperature to 300°F and continue to cook until the tenders' internal temperature reaches 170°F. Remove the tenders from the grill and serve immediately.

Beer Can-smoked Chicken

Servings: 3 To 4
Cooking Time: 3 To 4 Hours
Ingredients:
- 8 tablespoons (1 stick) unsalted butter, melted
- ½ cup apple cider vinegar
- ½ cup Cajun seasoning, divided
- 1 teaspoon garlic powder
- 1 teaspoon onion powder
- 1 (4-pound) whole chicken, giblets removed
- Extra-virgin olive oil, for rubbing

- 1 (12-ounce) can beer
- 1 cup apple juice
- ½ cup extra-virgin olive oil

Directions:
1. In a small bowl, whisk together the butter, vinegar, ¼ cup of Cajun seasoning, garlic powder, and onion powder.
2. Use a meat-injecting syringe to inject the liquid into various spots in the chicken. Inject about half of the mixture into the breasts and the other half throughout the rest of the chicken.
3. Rub the chicken all over with olive oil and apply the remaining ¼ cup of Cajun seasoning, being sure to rub under the skin as well.
4. Drink or discard half the beer and place the opened beer can on a stable surface.
5. Place the bird's cavity on top of the can and position the chicken so it will sit up by itself. Prop the legs forward to make the bird more stable, or buy an inexpensive, specially made stand to hold the beer can and chicken in place.
6. Supply your smoker with wood pellets and follow the manufacturer's specific start-up procedure. Preheat, with the lid closed, to 250°F.
7. In a clean 12-ounce spray bottle, combine the apple juice and olive oil. Cover and shake the mop sauce well before each use.
8. Carefully put the chicken on the grill. Close the lid and smoke the chicken for 3 to 4 hours, spraying with the mop sauce every hour, until golden brown and a meat thermometer inserted in the thickest part of the thigh reads 165°F. Keep a piece of aluminum foil handy to loosely cover the chicken if the skin begins to brown too quickly.
9. Let the meat rest for 5 minutes before carving.

Easy Smoked Chicken Breasts

Servings: 4
Cooking Time: 30 Minutes
Ingredients:
- 4 large chicken breasts, bones and skin removed
- 1 tablespoon olive oil
- 2 tablespoons brown sugar
- 2 tablespoons maple syrup
- 1 teaspoon celery seeds
- 2 tablespoons paprika
- 2 tablespoons salt
- 1 teaspoon black pepper
- 2 tablespoons garlic powder
- 2 tablespoons onion powder

Directions:
1. Place all ingredients in a bowl and massage the chicken with your hands. Place in the fridge to marinate for at least 4 hours.

2. Fire the Grill to 350F and use maple wood pellets. Close the lid and allow to preheat to 15 minutes.
3. Place the chicken on the grill a and cook for 15 minutes with the lid closed.
4. Turn the chicken over and cook for another 10 minutes.
5. Insert a thermometer into the thickest part of the chicken and make sure that the temperature reads to 165F.
6. Remove the chicken from the grill and allow to rest for 5 minutes before slicing.
Nutrition Info: Calories per serving: 327 ; Protein: 40 g; Carbs: 23g; Fat: 9g Sugar: 13g

Wood Pellet Grilled Buffalo Chicken

Servings: 6
Cooking Time: 20 Minutes
Ingredients:
- 5 chicken breasts, boneless and skinless
- 2 tbsp homemade barbeque rub
- 1 cup homemade Cholula buffalo sauce

Directions:
1. Preheat the wood pellet grill to 400°F.
2. Slice the chicken into long strips and season with barbeque rub.
3. Place the chicken on the grill and paint both sides with buffalo sauce.
4. Cook for 4 minutes with the grill closed. Cook while flipping and painting with buffalo sauce every 5 minutes until the internal temperature reaches 165°F.
5. Remove from the grill and serve when warm. Enjoy.
Nutrition Info: Calories: 176 Cal Fat: 4 g Carbohydrates: 1 g Protein: 32 g Fiber: 0 g

Wood Pellet Grilled Buffalo Chicken

Servings: 6
Cooking Time: 20 Minutes
Ingredients:
- 5 chicken breasts, boneless and skinless
- 2 tbsp homemade bbq rub
- 1 cup homemade Cholula buffalo sauce

Directions:
1. Preheat the wood pellet grill to 400°F.
2. Slice the chicken into long strips and season with bbq rub.
3. Place the chicken on the grill and paint both sides with buffalo sauce.
4. Cook for 4 minutes with the grill closed. Cook while flipping and painting with buffalo sauce every

5 minutes until the internal temperature reaches 165°F.
5. Remove from the grill and serve when warm. Enjoy.
Nutrition Info: Calories 176, Total fat 4g, Saturated fat 1g, Total carbs 1g, Net carbs 1g, Protein 32g, Sugar 1g, Fiber 0g, Sodium: 631mg

Barbecue Chicken Wings

Servings: 4
Cooking Time: 15 Minutes
Ingredients:
- Fresh chicken wings
- Salt to taste
- Pepper to taste
- Garlic powder
- Onion powder
- Cayenne
- Paprika
- Seasoning salt
- Bbq sauce to taste

Directions:
1. Preheat the wood pellet grill to low.
2. In a mixing bowl, mix all the seasoning ingredients then toss the chicken wings until well coated.
3. Place the wings on the grill and cook for 20 minutes or until the wings are fully cooked.
4. Let rest to cool for 5 minutes then toss with bbq sauce.
5. Serve with orzo and salad. Enjoy.
Nutrition Info: Calories 311, Total fat 22g, Saturated fat 4g, Total carbs 22g, Net carbs 19g, Protein 22g, Sugar 12g, Fiber 3g, Sodium: 1400mg

Cornish Game Hen

Servings: 4
Cooking Time: 2 To 3 Hours
Ingredients:
- 4 Cornish game hens
- Extra-virgin olive oil, for rubbing
- 2 teaspoons salt
- 1 teaspoon freshly ground black pepper
- 1 teaspoon celery seeds

Directions:
1. Supply your smoker with wood pellets and follow the manufacturer's specific start-up procedure. Preheat, with the lid closed, to 275°F.
2. Rub the game hens over and under the skin with olive oil and season all over with the salt, pepper, and celery seeds.

3.   Place the birds directly on the grill grate, close the lid, and smoke for 2 to 3 hours, or until a meat thermometer inserted in each bird reads 170°F.
4.   Serve the Cornish game hens hot.

Buffalo Wings

Servings: 2 To 3
Cooking Time: 35 Minutes
Ingredients:
- 1 pound chicken wings
- 1 batch Chicken Rub
- 1 cup Frank's Red-Hot Sauce, Buffalo wing sauce, or similar

Directions:
1.   Supply your smoker with wood pellets and follow the manufacturer's specific start-up procedure. Preheat the grill, with the lid closed, to 300°F.
2.   Season the chicken wings with the rub. Using your hands, work the rub into the meat.
3.   Place the wings directly on the grill grate and smoke until their internal temperature reaches 160°F.
4.   Baste the wings with the sauce and continue to smoke until the wings' internal temperature reaches 170°F.

Asian Miso Chicken Wings

Servings: 6
Cooking Time: 25 Minutes
Ingredients:
- 2 lb chicken wings
- 3/4 cup soy
- 1/2 cup pineapple juice
- 1 tbsp sriracha
- 1/8 cup miso
- 1/8 cup gochujang
- 1/2 cup water
- 1/2 cup oil
- Togarashi

Directions:
1.   Preheat the to 375F
2.   Combine all the ingredients except togarashi in a zip lock bag. Toss until the chicken wings are well coated. Refrigerate for 12 hours
3.   Pace the wings on the grill grates and close the lid. Cook for 25 minutes or until the internal temperature reaches 165F
4.   Remove the wings from the and sprinkle Togarashi.
5.   Serve when hot and enjoy.
Nutrition Info: Calories 703, Total fat 56g, Saturated fat 14g, Total carbs 24g, Net carbs 23g Protein 27g, Sugars 6g, Fiber 1g, Sodium 1156mg

Smoked Chicken And Potatoes

Servings: 4
Cooking Time: 1 Hour And 30 Minutes
Ingredients:
- 1 2.5-pounds rotisserie chicken
- 2 tablespoon coconut sugar
- 1 tablespoons onion powder
- 2 tablespoon garlic powder
- 1 teaspoon cayenne pepper powder
- 2 teaspoon kosher salt
- 4 tablespoons olive oil
- 2 pounds creamer potatoes, scrubbed and halved
- A dash of black pepper powder

Directions:
1.   Place the chicken in a bowl. In a smaller bowl, combine the coconut sugar, onion powder, garlic powder, cayenne pepper powder, and salt. Add in the olive oil. Rub the mixture into the chicken and allow to marinate for 4 hours in the fridge.
2.   Fire the Grill to 400F and close the lid. Preheat to 15 minutes.
3.   Place the seasoned chicken in a heat-proof dish and place the potatoes around the chicken. Season the potatoes with salt.
4.   Place in the grill and cook for 30 minutes. Lower the heat to 250F and cook for another hour.
5.   Insert a meat thermometer in the thickest part of the chicken and make sure that the temperature reads at 165F. Flip the chicken halfway through the cooking time for even browning.
Nutrition Info: Calories per serving: 991; Protein: 79.7g; Carbs: 49.8g; Fat: 73.6g Sugar: 6.5g

Wood Pellet Grilled Chicken

Servings: 6
Cooking Time: 1 Hour And 10 Minutes
Ingredients:
- 5 pounds whole chicken
- 1/2 cup oil
- Chicken rub

Directions:
1.   Preheat your wood pellet on smoke with the lid open for 5 minutes. Close the lid, increase the temperature to 450°F and preheat for 15 more minutes.
2.   Tie the chicken legs together with the baker's twine then rub the chicken with oil and coat with chicken rub.
3.   Place the chicken on the grill with the breast side up.

4. Grill the chicken for 70 minutes without opening it or until the internal temperature reaches 165°F.
5. Once the chicken is out of the grill let it cool down for 15 minutes
6. Enjoy.
Nutrition Info: Calories: 935 Cal Fat: 53 g Carbohydrates: 0 g Protein: 107 g Fiber: 0 g

Authentic Holiday Turkey Breast

Servings: 6
Cooking Time: 4 Hours
Ingredients:
- ½ C. honey
- ¼ C. dry sherry
- 1 tbsp. butter
- 2 tbsp. fresh lemon juice
- Salt, to taste
- 1 (3-3½-pound) skinless, boneless turkey breast

Directions:
1. In a small pan, place honey, sherry and butter over low heat and cook until the mixture becomes smooth, stirring continuously.
2. Remove from heat and stir in lemon juice and salt. Set aside to cool.
3. Transfer the honey mixture and turkey breast in a sealable bag.
4. Seal the bag and shake to coat well.
5. Refrigerate for about 6-10 hours.
6. Set the temperature of Grill to 225-250 degrees F and preheat with closed lid for 15 minutes.
7. Place the turkey breast onto the grill and cook for about 2½-4 hours or until desired doneness.
8. Remove turkey breast from grill and place onto a cutting board for about 15-20 minutes before slicing.
9. With a sharp knife, cut the turkey breast into desired-sized slices and serve.
Nutrition Info: Calories per serving: 443; Carbohydrates: 23.7g; Protein: 59.2g; Fat: 11.4g; Sugar: 23.4g; Sodium: 138mg; Fiber: 0.1g

Smoked Quarters

Servings: 2 To 4
Cooking Time: 2 Hours
Ingredients:
- 4 chicken quarters
- 2 tablespoons olive oil
- 1 batch Chicken Rub
- 2 tablespoons butter

Directions:
1. Supply your smoker with wood pellets and follow the manufacturer's specific start-up procedure. Preheat the grill, with the lid closed, to 180°F.

2. Coat the chicken quarters all over with olive oil and season them with the rub. Using your hands, work the rub into the meat.
3. Place the quarters directly on the grill grate and smoke for 1½ hours.
4. Baste the quarters with the butter and increase the grill's temperature to 375°F. Continue to cook until the chicken's internal temperature reaches 170°F.
5. Remove the quarters from the grill and let them rest for 10 minutes before serving.

Smo-fried Chicken

Servings: 4 To 6
Cooking Time: 55 Minutes
Ingredients:
- 1 egg, beaten
- ½ cup milk
- 1 cup all-purpose flour
- 2 tablespoons salt
- 1 tablespoon freshly ground black pepper
- 2 teaspoons freshly ground white pepper
- 2 teaspoons cayenne pepper
- 2 teaspoons garlic powder
- 2 teaspoons onion powder
- 1 teaspoon smoked paprika
- 8 tablespoons (1 stick) unsalted butter, melted
- 1 whole chicken, cut up into pieces

Directions:
1. Supply your smoker with wood pellets and follow the manufacturer's specific start-up procedure. Preheat, with the lid closed, to 375°F.
2. In a medium bowl, combine the beaten egg with the milk and set aside.
3. In a separate medium bowl, stir together the flour, salt, black pepper, white pepper, cayenne, garlic powder, onion powder, and smoked paprika.
4. Line the bottom and sides of a high-sided metal baking pan with aluminum foil to ease cleanup.
5. Pour the melted butter into the prepared pan.
6. Dip the chicken pieces one at a time in the egg mixture, and then coat well with the seasoned flour. Transfer to the baking pan.
7. Smoke the chicken in the pan of butter ("smo-fry") on the grill, with the lid closed, for 25 minutes, then reduce the heat to 325°F and turn the chicken pieces over.
8. Continue smoking with the lid closed for about 30 minutes, or until a meat thermometer inserted in the thickest part of each chicken piece reads 165°F.
9. Serve immediately.

Turkey Meatballs

Servings: 8
Cooking Time: 40 Minutes
Ingredients:
- 1 1/4 lb. ground turkey
- 1/2 cup breadcrumbs
- 1 egg, beaten
- 1/4 cup milk
- 1 teaspoon onion powder
- 1/4 cup Worcestershire sauce
- Pinch garlic salt
- Salt and pepper to taste
- 1 cup cranberry jam
- 1/2 cup orange marmalade
- 1/2 cup chicken broth

Directions:
1. In a large bowl, mix the ground turkey, breadcrumbs, egg, milk, onion powder, Worcestershire sauce, garlic salt, salt and pepper.
2. Form meatballs from the mixture.
3. Preheat the wood pellet grill to 350 degrees F for 15 minutes while the lid is closed.
4. Add the turkey meatballs to a baking pan.
5. Place the baking pan on the grill.
6. Cook for 20 minutes.
7. In a pan over medium heat, simmer the rest of the ingredients for 10 minutes.
8. Add the grilled meatballs to the pan.
9. Coat with the mixture.
10. Cook for 10 minutes.
11. Tips: You can add chili powder to the meatball mixture if you want spicy flavor.

Chile-lime Rubbed Chicken

Servings: 6
Cooking Time: 40 Minutes
Ingredients:
- 3 tablespoons chili powder
- 2 tablespoons extra virgin olive oil
- 2 teaspoons lime zest
- 3 tablespoons lime juice
- 1 tablespoon garlic, minced
- 1 teaspoon ground coriander
- 1 teaspoon ground cumin
- 1 teaspoon dried oregano
- 1 ½ teaspoons salt
- 1 teaspoon ground black pepper
- A pinch of cinnamon
- 1 chicken, spatchcocked

Directions:
1. In a bowl, place the chili powder, olive oil, lime zest, juice, garlic, coriander, cumin, oregano, salt, pepper, cinnamon, and cinnamon in a bowl. Mix to form a paste.
2. Place the chicken cut-side down on a chopping board and flatten using the heel of your hand. Carefully, break the breastbone to flatten the chicken.
3. Generously rub the spices all over the chicken and make sure to massage the chicken with the spice rub. Place in a baking dish and refrigerate for 24 hours in the fridge.
4. When ready to cook, fire the Grill to 400F. Use maple wood pellets. Close the grill lid and preheat for 15 minutes.
5. Place the chicken breastbone-side down on the grill grate and cook for 40 minutes or until a thermometer inserted in the thickest part reads at 165F.
6. Make sure to flip the chicken halfway through the cooking time.
7. Once cooked, transfer to a plate and allow to rest before carving the chicken.
Nutrition Info: Calories per serving: 213; Protein: 33.1g; Carbs: 3.8g; Fat: 7g Sugar: 0.5g

Buttered Thanksgiving Turkey

Servings: 12 To 14
Cooking Time: 5 To 6 Hours
Ingredients:
- 1 whole turkey (make sure the turkey is not pre-brined)
- 2 batches Garlic Butter Injectable
- 3 tablespoons olive oil
- 1 batch Chicken Rub
- 2 tablespoons butter

Directions:
1. Supply your smoker with wood pellets and follow the manufacturer's specific start-up procedure. Preheat the grill, with the lid closed, to 180°F.
2. Inject the turkey throughout with the garlic butter injectable. Coat the turkey with olive oil and season it with the rub. Using your hands, work the rub into the meat and skin.
3. Place the turkey directly on the grill grate and smoke for 3 or 4 hours (for an 8- to 12-pound turkey, cook for 3 hours; for a turkey over 12 pounds, cook for 4 hours), basting it with butter every hour.
4. Increase the grill's temperature to 375°F and continue to cook until the turkey's internal temperature reaches 170°F.
5. Remove the turkey from the grill and let it rest for 10 minutes, before carving and serving.

Succulent Duck Breast

Servings: 4
Cooking Time: 10 Minutes
Ingredients:

- 4 (6-oz.) boneless duck breasts
- 2 tbsp. chicken rub

Directions:
1. Set the temperature of Grill to 275 degrees F and preheat with closed lid for 15 minutes.
2. With a sharp knife, score the skin of the duck into ¼-inch diamond pattern.
3. Season the duck breast with rub evenly.
4. Place the duck breasts onto the grill, meat side down and cook for about 10 minutes.
5. Now, set the temperature of Grill to 400 degrees F.
6. Now, arrange the breasts, skin side down and cook for about 10 minutes, flipping once halfway through.
7. Remove from the grill and serve.

Nutrition Info: Calories per serving: 231; Carbohydrates: 1.5g; Protein: 37.4g; Fat: 6.8g; Sugar: 0g; Sodium: 233mg; Fiber: 0g

Smoked And Fried Chicken Wings

Servings: 6
Cooking Time: 2 Hours
Ingredients:
- 3 pounds chicken wings
- 1 tbsp Goya adobo all-purpose seasoning
- Sauce of your choice

Directions:
1. Fire up your wood pellet grill and set it to smoke.
2. Meanwhile, coat the chicken wings with adobo all-purpose seasoning. Place the chicken on the grill and smoke for 2 hours.
3. Remove the wings from the grill.
4. Preheat oil to 375°F in a frying pan. Drop the wings in batches and let fry for 5 minutes or until the skin is crispy.
5. Drain the oil and proceed with drizzling preferred sauce
6. Drain oil and drizzle preferred sauce
7. Enjoy.

Nutrition Info: Calories: 755 Cal Fat: 55 g Carbohydrates: 24 g Protein: 39 g Fiber: 1 g

Thanksgiving Dinner Turkey

Servings: 16
Cooking Time: 4 Hours
Ingredients:
- ½ lb. butter, softened
- 2 tbsp. fresh thyme, chopped
- 2 tbsp. fresh rosemary, chopped
- 6 garlic cloves, crushed
- 1 (20-lb.) whole turkey, neck and giblets removed

- Salt and freshly ground black pepper, to taste

Directions:
1. Set the temperature of Grill to 300 degrees F and preheat with closed lid for 15 minutes, using charcoal.
2. In a bowl, place butter, fresh herbs, garlic, salt and black pepper and mix well.
3. With your fingers, separate the turkey skin from breast to create a pocket.
4. Stuff the breast pocket with ¼-inch thick layer of butter mixture.
5. Season the turkey with salt and black pepper evenly.
6. Arrange the turkey onto the grill and cook for 3-4 hours.
7. Remove the turkey from grill and place onto a cutting board for about 15-20 minutes before carving.
8. With a sharp knife, cut the turkey into desired-sized pieces and serve.

Nutrition Info: Calories per serving: 965; Carbohydrates: 0.6g; Protein: 106.5g; Fat: 52g; Sugar: 0g; Sodium: 1916mg; Fiber: 0.2g

Ultimate Tasty Chicken

Servings: 5
Cooking Time: 3 Hours
Ingredients:
- For Brine:
- 1 C. brown sugar
- ½ C. kosher salt
- 16 C. water
- For Chicken:
- 1 (3-lb.) whole chicken
- 1 tbsp. garlic, crushed
- 1 tsp. onion powder
- Salt and freshly ground black pepper, to taste
- 1 medium yellow onion, quartered
- 3 whole garlic cloves, peeled
- 1 lemon, quartered
- 4-5 fresh thyme sprigs

Directions:
1. For brine: in a bucket, dissolve brown sugar and kosher salt in water.
2. Place the chicken in brine and refrigerate overnight.
3. Set the temperature of Grill to 225 degrees F and preheat with closed lid for 15 minutes.
4. Remove the chicken from brine and with paper towels, pat it dry.
5. In a small bowl, mix together crushed garlic, onion powder, salt and black pepper.
6. Rub the chicken with garlic mixture evenly.
7. Stuff the cavity of chicken with onion, garlic cloves, lemon and thyme.

8. With kitchen strings, tie the legs together.
9. Place the chicken onto grill and cook, covered for about 2½-3 hours.
10. Remove chicken from pallet grill and transfer onto a cutting board for about 10 minutes before carving.
11. With a sharp knife, cut the chicken in desired sized pieces and serve.
Nutrition Info: Calories per serving: 641; Carbohydrates: 31.7g; Protein: 79.2g; Fat: 20.2g; Sugar: 29.3g; Sodium: 11500mg; Fiber: 0.6g

Wood Pellet Smoked Cornish Hens

Servings: 6
Cooking Time: 1 Hour
Ingredients:
- 6 Cornish hens
- 3 tbsp avocado oil
- 6 tbsp rub of choice

Directions:
1. Fire up the wood pellet and preheat it to 275°F.
2. Rub the hens with oil then coat generously with rub. Place the hens on the grill with the chest breast side down.
3. Smoke for 30 minutes. Flip the hens and increase the grill temperature to 400°F. Cook until the internal temperature reaches 165°F.
4. Remove from the grill and let rest for 10 minutes before serving. Enjoy.
Nutrition Info: Calories: 696 Cal Fat: 50 g Carbohydrates: 1 g Protein: 57 g Fiber: 0 g

Cajun Chicken

Servings: 4
Cooking Time: 30 Minutes
Ingredients:
- 2 lb. chicken wings
- Poultry dry rub
- Cajun seasoning

Directions:
1. Season the chicken wings with the dry rub and Cajun seasoning.
2. Preheat the to 350 degrees F for 15 minutes while the lid is closed.
3. Grill for 30 minutes, flipping twice.
4. Tips: You can also smoke the chicken before grilling.

Smoked Lemon Chicken Breasts

Servings: 6
Cooking Time: 30 Minutes

Ingredients:
- 2 lemons, zested and juiced
- 1 clove of garlic, minced
- 2 teaspoons honey
- 2 teaspoons salt
- 1 teaspoon ground black pepper
- 2 sprigs fresh thyme
- ½ cup olive oil
- 6 boneless chicken breasts

Directions:
1. Place all ingredients in a bowl. Massage the chicken breasts so that it is coated with the marinade.
2. Place in the fridge to marinate for at least 4 hours.
3. Fire the Grill to 350F. Use apple wood pellets. Close the grill lid and preheat for 15 minutes.
4. Place the chicken breasts on the grill grate and cook for 15 minutes on both sides.
5. Serve immediately or drizzle with lemon juice.
Nutrition Info: Calories per serving: 671 ; Protein: 60.6 g; Carbs: 3.5 g; Fat: 44.9g Sugar: 2.3g

Hickory Smoked Chicken

Servings: 4
Cooking Time: 30 Minutes
Ingredients:
- 4 chicken breasts
- ¼ cup olive oil
- 1 teaspoon pressed garlic
- 1 tablespoon Worcestershire sauce
- Kirkland Sweet Mesquite Seasoning as needed
- 1 button Honey Bourbon Sauce

Directions:
1. Place all ingredients in a bowl except for the Bourbon sauce. Massage the chicken until all parts are coated with the seasoning.
2. Allow to marinate in the fridge for 4 hours.
3. Once ready to cook, fire the Grill to 350F. Use Hickory wood pellets and close the lid. Preheat for 15 minutes.
4. Place the chicken directly into the grill grate and cook for 30 minutes. Flip the chicken halfway through the cooking time.
5. Five minutes before the cooking time ends, brush all surfaces of the chicken with the Honey Bourbon Sauce.
6. Serve immediately.
Nutrition Info: Calories per serving: 622; Protein: 60.5g; Carbs: 1.1g; Fat: 40.3g Sugar: 0.4g

Lemon Chicken Breasts

Servings: 6

Cooking Time: 40 Minutes
Ingredients:
- 1 clove of garlic, minced
- 2 teaspoons honey
- 2 teaspoons salt
- 1 teaspoon black pepper, ground
- 2 sprigs fresh thyme leaves
- 1 lemon, zested and juiced
- ½ cup olive oil
- 6 boneless chicken breasts

Directions:
1. Make the marinade by combining the garlic, honey, salt, pepper, thyme, lemon zest, and juice in a bowl. Whisk until well-combined.
2. Place the chicken into the marinade and mix with hands to coat the meat with the marinade. Refrigerate for 4 hours.
3. When ready to grill, fire the Grill to 400F. Close the lid and preheat for 10 minutes.
4. Drain the chicken and discard the marinade.
5. Arrange the chicken breasts directly on to the grill grate and cook for 40 minutes or until the internal temperature of the thickest part of the chicken reaches to 165F.
6. Drizzle with more lemon juice before serving.
Nutrition Info: Calories per serving: 669; Protein: 60.6g; Carbs: 3g; Fat: 44.9g Sugar: 2.1g

Applewood-smoked Whole Turkey

Servings: 6 To 8
Cooking Time: 5 To 6 Hours
Ingredients:
- 1 (10- to 12-pound) turkey, giblets removed
- Extra-virgin olive oil, for rubbing
- ¼ cup poultry seasoning
- 8 tablespoons (1 stick) unsalted butter, melted
- ½ cup apple juice
- 2 teaspoons dried sage
- 2 teaspoons dried thyme

Directions:
1. Supply your smoker with wood pellets and follow the manufacturer's specific start-up procedure. Preheat, with the lid closed, to 250°F.
2. Rub the turkey with oil and season with the poultry seasoning inside and out, getting under the skin.
3. In a bowl, combine the melted butter, apple juice, sage, and thyme to use for basting.
4. Put the turkey in a roasting pan, place on the grill, close the lid, and grill for 5 to 6 hours, basting every hour, until the skin is brown and crispy, or until a meat thermometer inserted in the thickest part of the thigh reads 165°F.

5. Let the bird rest for 15 to 20 minutes before carving.

Honey Garlic Chicken Wings

Servings: 4
Cooking Time: 1 Hour And 15 Minutes
Ingredients:
- 2 1/2 lb. chicken wings
- Poultry dry rub
- 4 tablespoons butter
- 3 cloves garlic, minced
- 1/2 cup hot sauce
- 1/4 cup honey

Directions:
1. Sprinkle chicken wings with dry rub.
2. Place on a baking pan.
3. Set the wood pellet grill to 350 degrees F.
4. Preheat for 15 minutes while the lid is closed.
5. Place the baking pan on the grill.
6. Cook for 50 minutes.
7. Add butter to a pan over medium heat.
8. Sauté garlic for 3 minutes.
9. Stir in hot sauce and honey.
10. Cook for 5 minutes while stirring.
11. Coat the chicken wings with the mixture.
12. Grill for 10 more minutes.
13. Tips: You can make the sauce in advance to reduce preparation time.

Sweet And Spicy Smoked Wings

Servings: 2 To 4
Cooking Time: 1 Hour, 25 Minutes
Ingredients:
- 1 pound chicken wings
- 1 batch Sweet and Spicy Cinnamon Rub
- 1 cup barbecue sauce

Directions:
1. Supply your smoker with wood pellets and follow the manufacturer's specific start-up procedure. Preheat the grill, with the lid closed, to 325°F.
2. Season the chicken wings with the rub. Using your hands, work the rub into the meat.
3. Place the wings directly on the grill grate and cook until they reach an internal temperature of 165°F.
4. Transfer the wings into an aluminum pan. Add the barbecue sauce and stir to coat the wings.
5. Reduce the grill's temperature to 250°F and put the pan on the grill. Smoke the wings for 1 hour more, uncovered. Remove the wings from the grill and serve immediately.

Chicken Cordon Bleu

Servings: 6
Cooking Time: 40 Minutes
Ingredients:
- 6 boneless skinless chicken breasts
- 6 slices of ham
- 12 slices swiss cheese
- 1cup panko breadcrumbs
- ½ cup all-purpose flour
- 1tsp ground black pepper or to taste
- 1tsp salt or to taste
- 4tbsp grated parmesan cheese
- 2tbsp melted butter
- ½ tsp garlic powder
- ½ tsp thyme
- ¼ tsp parsley

Directions:
1. Butterfly the chicken breast with a pairing knife. Place the chicken breast in between 2 plastic wraps and pound with a mallet until the chicken breasts are ¼ inch thick.
2. Place a plastic wrap on a flat surface. Place one fat chicken breast on it.
3. Place one slice of swiss cheese on the chicken. Place one slice of ham over the cheese and place another cheese slice over the ham.
4. Roll the chicken breast tightly. Fold both ends of the roll tightly. Pin both ends of the rolled chicken breast with a toothpick.
5. Repeat step 3 and 4 for the remaining chicken breasts
6. In a mixing bowl, combine the all-purpose flour, ½ tsp salt, and ½ tsp pepper. Set aside.
7. In another mixing bowl, combine breadcrumbs, parmesan, butter, garlic, thyme, parsley, ½ tsp salt, and ½ tsp pepper. Set aside.
8. Break the eggs into another mixing bowl and whisk. Set aside.
9. Grease a baking sheet.
10. Bake one chicken breast roll. Dip into the flour mixture, brush with eggs and dip into breadcrumb mixture. The chicken breast should be coated.
11. Place it on the baking sheet.
12. Repeat steps 9 and 10 for the remaining breast rolls.
13. Preheat your grill to 375°F with the lid closed for 15 minutes.
14. Place the baking sheet on the grill and cook for about 40 minutes, or until the chicken is golden brown.
15. Remove the baking sheet from the grill and let the chicken rest for a few minutes.
16. Slice cordon bleu and serve.
Nutrition Info: Calories: 560 Total Fat: 27.4 g Saturated Fat: 15.9 g Cholesterol: 156mg Sodium: 1158 mg Total Carbohydrate: 23.2 g Dietary Fiber: 1.1 g Total Sugars: 1.2 g Protein: 54.3 g

Bacon-wrapped Chicken Tenders

Servings: 6
Cooking Time: 30 Minutes
Ingredients:
- 1-pound chicken tenders
- 10 strips bacon
- 1/2 tbsp Italian seasoning
- 1/2 tbsp black pepper
- 1/2 tbsp salt
- 1 tbsp paprika
- 1 tbsp onion powder
- 1 tbsp garlic powder
- 1/3 cup light brown sugar
- 1 tbsp chili powder

Directions:
1. Preheat your wood pellet smoker to 350°F.
2. Mix seasonings
3. Sprinkle the mixture on all sides of chicken tenders
4. Wrap each chicken tender with a strip of bacon
5. Mix sugar and chili then sprinkle the mixture on the bacon-wrapped chicken.
6. Place them on the smoker and smoker for 30 minutes with the lid closed or until the chicken is cooked.
7. Serve and enjoy.
Nutrition Info: Calories: 206 Cal Fat: 7.9 g Carbohydrates: 1.5 g Protein: 30.3 g Fiber: 0 g

Wood-fired Chicken Breasts

Servings: 2 To 4
Cooking Time: 45 Minutes
Ingredients:
- 2 (1-pound) bone-in, skin-on chicken breasts
- 1 batch Chicken Rub

Directions:
1. Supply your smoker with wood pellets and follow the manufacturer's specific start-up procedure. Preheat the grill, with the lid closed, to 350°F.
2. Season the chicken breasts all over with the rub. Using your hands, work the rub into the meat.
3. Place the breasts directly on the grill grate and smoke until their internal temperature reaches 170°F. Remove the breasts from the grill and serve immediately.

Sweet Sriracha Bbq Chicken

Servings: 5

Cooking Time: 1 And ½-2 Hours
Ingredients:
- 1cup sriracha
- ½ cup butter
- ½ cup molasses
- ½ cup ketchup
- ¼ cup firmly packed brown sugar
- 1teaspoon salt
- 1teaspoon fresh ground black pepper
- 1whole chicken, cut into pieces
- ½ teaspoon fresh parsley leaves, chopped

Directions:
1. Preheat your smoker to 250 degrees Fahrenheit using cherry wood
2. Take a medium saucepan and place it over low heat, stir in butter, sriracha, ketchup, molasses, brown sugar, mustard, pepper and salt and keep stirring until the sugar and salt dissolves
3. Divide the sauce into two portions
4. Brush the chicken half with the sauce and reserve the remaining for serving
5. Make sure to keep the sauce for serving on the side, and keep the other portion for basting
6. Transfer chicken to your smoker rack and smoke for about 1 and a ½ to 2 hours until the internal temperature reaches 165 degrees Fahrenheit
7. Sprinkle chicken with parsley and serve with reserved BBQ sauce
8. Enjoy!

Nutrition Info: Calories: 148 Fats: 0.6g Carbs: 10g Fiber: 1g

Chinese Inspired Duck Legs

Servings: 8
Cooking Time: 1 Hour 10 Minutes
Ingredients:
- For Glaze:
- ¼ C. fresh orange juice
- ¼ C. orange marmalade
- ¼ C. mirin
- 2 tbsp. hoisin sauce
- ½ tsp. red pepper flakes, crushed
- For Duck:
- 1 tsp. kosher salt
- ¾ tsp. freshly ground black pepper
- ¾ tsp. Chinese five-spice powder
- 8 (6-oz.) duck legs

Directions:
1. Set the temperature of Grill to 235 degrees F and preheat with closed lid for 15 minutes.
2. Forb glaze: in a small pan, add all ingredients over medium-high heat and bring to gentle boil, stirring continuously.

3. Remove from heat and set aside.
4. For rub: in a small bowl, mix together salt, black pepper and five-spice powder.
5. Rub the duck legs with spice rub evenly.
6. Place the duck legs onto the grill, skin side up and cook for about 50 minutes.
7. Coat the duck legs with glaze ad cook for about 20 minutes, flipping and coating with glaze after every 5 minutes.

Nutrition Info: Calories per serving: 303; Carbohydrates: 0.1g; Protein: 49.5g; Fat: 10.2g; Sugar: 0g; Sodium: 474mg; Fiber: 0.1g

Chicken Breast

Servings: 6
Cooking Time: 15 Minutes
Ingredients:
- 3 chicken breasts
- 1 tbsp avocado oil
- 1/4 tbsp garlic powder
- 1/4 tbsp onion powder
- 3/4 tbsp salt
- 1/4 tbsp pepper

Directions:
1. Preheat your to 375F
2. Cut the chicken breast into halves lengthwise then coat with avocado oil.
3. Season with garlic powder, onion powder, salt, and pepper.
4. Place the chicken on the grill and cook for 7 minutes on each side or until the internal temperature reaches 165F

Nutrition Info: Calories 120, Total fat 4g, Saturated fat 1g, Total carbs 0g, Net carbs 0g Protein 19g, Sugars 0g, Fiber 0g, Sodium 309mg

Smoke-roasted Chicken Thighs

Servings: 12 To 15
Cooking Time: 1 To 2 Hours
Ingredients:
- 3 pounds chicken thighs
- 2 teaspoons salt
- 2 teaspoons freshly ground black pepper
- 2 teaspoons garlic powder
- 2 teaspoons onion powder
- 2 cups prepared Italian dressing

Directions:
1. Place the chicken thighs in a shallow dish and sprinkle with the salt, pepper, garlic powder, and onion powder, being sure to get under the skin.
2. Cover with the Italian dressing, coating all sides, and refrigerate for 1 hour.

3. Supply your smoker with wood pellets and follow the manufacturer's specific start-up procedure. Preheat, with the lid closed, to 250°F.
4. Remove the chicken thighs from the marinade and place directly on the grill, skin-side down. Discard the marinade.
5. Close the lid and roast the chicken for 1 hour 30 minutes to 2 hours, or until a meat thermometer inserted in the thickest part of the thighs reads 165°F. Do not turn the thighs during the smoking process.

Smoked Cornish Hens

Servings: 6
Cooking Time: 1 Hour
Ingredients:
- 6 Cornish hens
- 3 tbsp canola oil
- 6 tbsp rub

Directions:
1. Preheat your to 275F.
2. Meanwhile, rub the hens with canola oil then with your favorite rub.
3. Place the hens on the grill with the breast side down. Smoke for 30 minutes.
4. Flip the hens and increase the temperature to 400F. Cook until the internal temperature reaches 165F.
5. Remove the hens from the grill and let rest for 10 minutes before serving.
Nutrition Info: Calories 696, Total fat 50g, Saturated fat 13g, Total carbs 1g, Net carbs 1g Protein 57g, Sugars 0g, Fiber 0g, Sodium 165mg

Smoked Drumsticks

Servings: 2 To 4
Cooking Time: 25 Minutes
Ingredients:
- 1 pound chicken drumsticks
- 2 tablespoons olive oil
- 1 batch Sweet and Spicy Cinnamon Rub

Directions:
1. Supply your smoker with wood pellets and follow the manufacturer's specific start-up procedure. Preheat the grill, with the lid closed, to 350°F.
2. Coat the drumsticks all over with olive oil and season with the rub. Using your hands, work the rub into the meat.
3. Place the drumsticks directly on the grill grate and smoke until their internal temperature reaches 170°F. Remove the drumsticks from the grill and serve immediately.

Cajun Chicken Breasts

Servings: 6
Cooking Time: 6 Hours
Ingredients:
- 2 lb. skinless, boneless chicken breasts
- 2 tbsp. Cajun seasoning
- 1 C. BBQ sauce

Directions:
1. Set the temperature of Grill to 225 degrees F and preheat with closed lid for 15 minutes.
2. Rub the chicken breasts with Cajun seasoning generously.
3. Place the chicken breasts onto the grill and cook for about 4-6 hours.
4. During last hour of cooking, coat the breasts with BBQ sauce twice.
5. Serve hot.
Nutrition Info: Calories per serving: 252; Carbohydrates: 15.1g; Protein: 33.8g; Fat: 5.5g; Sugar: 10.9g; Sodium: 570mg; Fiber: 0.3g

Traditional Bbq Chicken

Servings: 8
Cooking Time: 1 To 2 Hours
Ingredients:
- 8 boneless, skinless chicken breasts
- 2 teaspoons salt
- 2 teaspoons freshly ground black pepper
- 2 teaspoons garlic powder
- 2 cups The Ultimate BBQ Sauce or your preferred barbecue sauce, divided

Directions:
1. Supply your smoker with wood pellets and follow the manufacturer's specific start-up procedure. Preheat, with the lid closed, to 250°F.
2. Place the chicken breasts in a large pan and sprinkle both sides with the salt, pepper, and garlic powder, being sure to rub under the skin.
3. Place the roasting pan on the grill, close the lid, and smoke for 1 hour 30 minutes to 2 hours, or until a meat thermometer inserted in the thickest part of each breast reads 165°F. During the last 15 minutes of cooking, cover the chicken with 1 cup of barbecue sauce.
4. Serve the chicken warm with the remaining 1 cup of barbecue sauce.

Wood Pellet Grilled Chicken Kabobs

Servings: 6
Cooking Time: 12 Minutes
Ingredients:
- 1/2 cup olive oil

- 2 tbsp white vinegar
- 1 tbsp lemon juice
- 1-1/2 tbsp salt
- 1/2 tbsp pepper, coarsely ground
- 2 tbsp chives, freshly chopped
- 1-1/2 tbsp thyme, freshly chopped
- 2 tbsp Italian parsley freshly chopped
- 1 tbsp garlic, minced
- Kabobs
- 1 each orange, red, and yellow pepper
- 1-1/2 pounds chicken breast, boneless and skinless
- 12 mini mushrooms

Directions:
1. In a mixing bowl, add all the marinade ingredients and mix well. Toss the chicken and mushrooms in the marinade then refrigerate for 30 minutes.
2. Meanwhile, soak the skewers in hot water. Remove the chicken from the fridge and start assembling the kabobs.
3. Preheat your wood pellet to 450°F.
4. Grill the kabobs in the wood pellet for 6 minutes, flip them and grill for 6 more minutes.
5. Remove from the grill and let rest. Heat up the naan bread on the grill for 2 minutes.
6. Serve and enjoy.

Nutrition Info: Calories: 165 Cal Fat: 13 g Carbohydrates: 1 g Protein: 33 g Fiber: 0 g

Lemon Chicken Breast

Servings: 4
Cooking Time: 30 Minutes
Ingredients:
- 6 chicken breasts, skinless and boneless
- ½ cup oil
- 1-3 fresh thyme sprigs
- 1 teaspoon ground black pepper
- 2 teaspoon salt
- 2 teaspoons honey
- 1 garlic clove, chopped
- 1 lemon, juiced and zested
- Lemon wedges

Directions:
1. Take a bowl and prepare the marinade by mixing thyme, pepper, salt, honey, garlic, lemon zest, and juice. Mix well until dissolved
2. Add oil and whisk
3. Clean breasts and pat them dry, place in a bag alongside marinade and let them sit in the fridge for 4 hours
4. Preheat your smoker to 400 degrees F

5. Drain chicken and smoke until the internal temperature reaches 165 degrees, for about 15 minutes
6. Serve and enjoy!
Nutrition Info: Calories: 230 Fats: 7g Carbs: 1g Fiber: 2g

Grill Bbq Chicken Breasts

Servings: 4
Cooking Time: 30 Minutes
Ingredients:
- 4 whole chicken breasts, deboned
- ¼ cup olive oil
- 1 teaspoon pressed garlic
- 1 teaspoon Worcestershire sauce
- 1 teaspoon cayenne pepper powder
- ½ cup 'Que BBQ Sauce

Directions:
1. In a bowl, combine all ingredients except for the 'Que BBQ Sauce and make sure to rub the chicken breasts until coated with the mixture. Allow to marinate in the fridge for at least overnight.
2. Place the preferred wood pellets into the Grill and fire the grill. Allow the temperature to rise to 500F and preheat for 5 minutes. Reduce the temperature to 165F.
3. Place the chicken on the grill grate and cook for 30 minutes.
4. Five minutes before the chicken is done, glaze the chicken with Traeger's BBQ sauce.
5. Serve immediately.
Nutrition Info: Calories per serving: 631; Protein: 61g; Carbs: 2.9g; Fat: 40.5g Sugar: 1.5g

Budget Friendly Chicken Legs

Servings: 6
Cooking Time: 1½ Hours
Ingredients:
- For Brine:
- 1 C. kosher salt
- ¾ C. light brown sugar
- 16 C. water
- 6 chicken leg quarters
- For Glaze:
- ½ C. mayonnaise
- 2 tbsp. BBQ rub
- 2 tbsp. fresh chives, minced
- 1 tbsp. garlic, minced

Directions:
1. For brine: in a bucket, dissolve salt and brown sugar in water.

2. Place the chicken quarters in brine and refrigerate, covered for about 4 hours.
3. Set the temperature of Grill to 275 degrees F and preheat with closed lid for 15 minutes.
4. Remove chicken quarters from brine and rinse under cold running water.
5. With paper towels, pat dry chicken quarters.
6. For glaze: in a bowl, add all ingredients and mix till ell combined.
7. Coat chicken quarters with glaze evenly.
8. Place the chicken leg quarters onto grill and cook for about 1-1½ hours.
9. Serve immediately.

Nutrition Info: Calories per serving: 399; Carbohydrates: 17.2g; Protein: 29.1g; Fat: 24.7g; Sugar: 14.2g; Sodium: 15000mg; Fiber: 0g

Chicken Fajitas On A Wood Pellet Grill

Servings: 10
Cooking Time: 20 Minutes
Ingredients:
- Chicken breast - 2 lbs, thin sliced
- Red bell pepper - 1 large
- Onion - 1 large
- Orange bell pepper - 1 large
- Seasoning mix
- Oil - 2 tbsp
- Onion powder - ½ tbsp
- Granulated garlic - ½ tbsp
- Salt - 1 tbsp

Directions:
1. Preheat the grill to 450 degrees.
2. Mix the seasonings and oil.
3. Add the chicken slices to the mix.
4. Line a large pan with a non-stick baking sheet.
5. Let the pan heat for 10 minutes.
6. Place the chicken, peppers, and other vegetables in the grill.
7. Grill for 10 minutes or until the chicken is cooked.
8. Remove it from the grill and serve with warm tortillas and vegetables.

Nutrition Info: Carbohydrates: 5 g Protein: 29 g Fat: 6 g Sodium: 360 mg Cholesterol: 77 mg

Peach And Basil Grilled Chicken

Servings: 4
Cooking Time: 35 Minutes
Ingredients:
- 4 boneless chicken breasts
- ½ cup peach preserves, unsweetened
- ½ cup olive oil
- ¼ cup apple cider vinegar

- 3 tablespoons lemon juice
- 2 tablespoons Dijon mustard
- 1 garlic clove, crushed
- ½ teaspoon red hot sauce
- ½ cup fresh basil leaves, chopped
- Salt to taste
- 4 peaches, halved, pit removed

Directions:
1. Place chicken in a bowl and stir in the peach preserves, olive oil, vinegar, lemon juice, Dijon mustard, garlic, red hot sauce, and basil leaves.
2. Massage the chicken until all surfaces are coated with the marinade. Marinate in the fridge for 4 hours.
3. Once ready to cook, fire the Grill to 400F. Use apple wood pellets. Close the lid and preheat for 15 minutes.
4. Place the chicken directly on the grill grate and cook for 35 minutes.
5. Flip the chicken halfway through the cooking time.
6. Ten minutes before the cooking time ends, place the peach halves and grill.
7. Serve with the chicken.

Nutrition Info: Calories per serving: 777; Protein: 61g; Carbs: 9.8g; Fat: 54.2g Sugar: 8g

Roasted Chicken With Pimenton Potatoes

Servings: 16
Cooking Time: 1 Hour
Ingredients:
- 2 whole chicken
- 6 clove garlic, minced
- 2 tablespoons salt
- 3 tablespoons pimento (smoked paprika)
- 3 tablespoons extra virgin olive oil
- 2 bunch fresh thyme
- 3 pounds Yukon gold potatoes

Directions:
1. Season the whole chicken with garlic, salt, paprika, olive oil, and thyme. Massage the chicken to coat all surface of the chicken with the spices. Tie the legs together with a string. Place in a baking dish and place the potatoes on the side. Season the potatoes with salt and olive oil.
2. Allow the chicken to rest in the fridge for 4 hours.
3. When ready to cook, fire the Grill to 300F. Use preferred wood pellets. Close the grill lid and preheat for 15 minutes.
4. Place the chicken and potatoes in the grill and cook for 1 hour until a thermometer inserted in the thickest part of the chicken comes out clean.
5. Remove from the grill and allow to rest before carving.

Nutrition Info: Calories per serving: 210; Protein: 26.1g; Carbs: 15.3g; Fat: 4.4g Sugar: 0.7g

Grilled Buffalo Chicken Legs

Servings: 8
Cooking Time: 1 Hour 15 Minutes;
Ingredients:
- 12 chicken legs
- 1/2 tbsp salt
- 1 tbsp buffalo seasoning
- 1 cup Buffalo sauce

Directions:
1. Preheat your to 325F.
2. Toss the chicken legs in salt and seasoning then place them on the preheated grill.
3. Grill for 40 minutes turning twice through the cooking.
4. Increase the heat and cook for 10 more minutes. Brush the chicken legs and brush with buffalo sauce. Cook for an additional 10 minutes or until the internal temperature reaches 165F.
5. Remove from the and brush with more buffalo sauce.
6. Serve with blue cheese, celery, and hot ranch.
Nutrition Info: Calories 956, Total fat 47g, Saturated fat 13g, Total carbs 1g, Net carbs 1g Protein 124g, Sugars 0g, Fiber 0g, Sodium 1750mg

Wood Pellet Chicken Wings With Spicy Miso

Servings: 6
Cooking Time: 25 Minutes
Ingredients:
- 2-pound chicken wings
- 3/4 cup soy
- 1/2 cup pineapple juice
- 1 tbsp sriracha
- 1/8 cup miso
- 1/8 cup gochujang
- 1/2 cup water
- 1/2 cup oil
- Togarashi

Directions:
1. Mix all ingredients then toss the chicken wings until well coated. Refrigerate for 12 minutes.
2. Preheat your wood pellet grill to 375°F. Place the chicken wings on the grill grates and close the lid. Cook until the internal temperature reaches 165°F. Remove the wings from the grill and sprinkle with togarashi. Serve when hot and enjoy.
Nutrition Info: Calories: 704 Cal Fat: 56 g Carbohydrates: 24 g Protein: 27 g Fiber: 1 g

BEEF,PORK & LAMB RECIPES

Smoked Spare Ribs

Servings: 4 To 8
Cooking Time: 4 To 6 Hours
Ingredients:
- 2 (2- or 3-pound) racks spare ribs
- 2 tablespoons yellow mustard
- 1 batch Sweet Brown Sugar Rub
- ¼ cup The Ultimate BBQ Sauce

Directions:
1. Supply your smoker with wood pellets and follow the manufacturer's specific start-up procedure. Preheat the grill, with the lid closed, to 225°F.
2. Remove the membrane from the backside of the ribs. This can be done by cutting just through the membrane in an X pattern and working a paper towel between the membrane and the ribs to pull it off.
3. Coat the ribs on both sides with mustard and season with the rub. Using your hands, work the rub into the meat.
4. Place the ribs directly on the grill grate and smoke until their internal temperature reaches between 190°F and 200°F.
5. Baste both sides of the ribs with barbecue sauce.
6. Increase the grill's temperature to 300°F and continue to cook the ribs for 15 minutes more.
7. Remove the racks from the grill, cut them into individual ribs, and serve immediately.

Teriyaki Beef Jerky

Servings: 9
Cooking Time: 5 Hours
Ingredients:
- 3 lb. sirloin steaks, cut into ¼-inch thick slices
- 2 C. soy sauce
- ½ C. brown sugar
- 1 C. pineapple juice
- 2 tbsp. rice wine vinegar
- 2 tbsp. hoisin sauce
- 2 tbsp. Sriracha
- 2 tbsp. garlic, minced
- 2 tbsp. red pepper flakes, crushed
- 2 tsp. onion powder

Directions:
1. In a large zip lock bag, place all ingredients.
2. Seal the bag, squeezing out the air and then shake to coat well.
3. Refrigerate to marinate for 6-24 hours.
4. Remove the bag from the refrigerator and set aside at room temperature for about 1 hour before cooking.

5. Set the temperature of Grill to 180-190 degrees F and preheat with closed lid for 15 minutes.
6. Remove the steak slices from the bag and discard the marinade.
7. With paper towels, pat dry the steak slices.
8. Arrange the steak slices onto the grill in a single layer and cook for about 4-5 hours, flipping once after 2-2½ hours.
Nutrition Info: Calories per serving: 378; Carbohydrates: 19.8g; Protein: 50g; Fat: 9.8g; Sugar: 12.9g; Sodium: 3379mg; Fiber: 1g

Bbq Brisket

Servings: 8
Cooking Time: 10 Hours
Ingredients:
- 1 beef brisket, about 12 pounds
- Beef rub as needed

Directions:
1. Season beef brisket with beef rub until well coated, place it in a large plastic bag, seal it and let it marinate for a minimum of 12 hours in the refrigerator.
2. When ready to cook, switch on the grill, fill the grill hopper with hickory flavored wood pellets, power the grill on by using the control panel, select 'smoke' on the temperature dial, or set the temperature to 225 degrees F and let it preheat for a minimum of 15 minutes.
3. When the grill has preheated, open the lid, place marinated brisket on the grill grate fat-side down, shut the grill, and smoke for 6 hours until the internal temperature reaches 160 degrees F.
4. Then wrap the brisket in foil, return it back to the grill grate and cook for 4 hours until the internal temperature reaches 204 degrees F.
5. When done, transfer brisket to a cutting board, let it rest for 30 minutes, then cut it into slices and serve.
Nutrition Info: Calories: 328 Cal ;Fat: 21 g ;Carbs: 0 g ;Protein: 32 g ;Fiber: - g

Lamb Chops With Rosemary And Olive Oil

Servings: 4
Cooking Time: 50 Minutes
Ingredients:
- 12 Lamb loin chops, fat trimmed
- 1 tablespoon chopped rosemary leaves
- Salt as needed for dry brining
- Jeff's original rub as needed
- ¼ cup olive oil

Directions:
1.   Take a cookie sheet, place lamb chops on it, sprinkle with salt, and then refrigerate for 2 hours. Meanwhile, take a small bowl, place rosemary leaves in it, stir in oil and let the mixture stand for 1 hour.
2.   When ready to cook, switch on the grill, fill the grill hopper with apple-flavored wood pellets, power the grill on by using the control panel, select 'smoke' on the temperature dial, or set the temperature to 225 degrees F and let it preheat for a minimum of 5 minutes.
3.   Meanwhile, brush rosemary-oil mixture on all sides of lamb chops and then sprinkle with Jeff's original rub.
4.   When the grill has preheated, open the lid, place lamb chops on the grill grate, shut the grill and smoke for 50 minutes until the internal temperature of lamb chops reach to 138 degrees F.
5.   When done, wrap lamb chops in foil, let them rest for 7 minutes and then serve.
Nutrition Info: Calories: 171.5 Cal ;Fat: 7.8 g ;Carbs: 0.4 g ;Protein: 23.2 g ;Fiber: 0.1 g

Texas Smoked Brisket

Servings: 12 To 15
Cooking Time: 16 To 20 Hours
Ingredients:
- 1 (12-pound) full packer brisket
- 2 tablespoons yellow mustard
- 1 batch Espresso Brisket Rub
- Worcestershire Mop and Spritz, for spritzing

Directions:
1.   Supply your with wood pellets and follow the start-up procedure. Preheat the grill, with the lid closed, to 225°F.
2.   Using a boning knife, carefully remove all but about ½ inch of the large layer of fat covering one side of your brisket.
3.   Coat the brisket all over with mustard and season it with the rub. Using your hands, work the rub into the meat. Pour the mop into a spray bottle.
4.   Place the brisket directly on the grill grate and smoke until its internal temperature reaches 195°F, spritzing it every hour with the mop.
5.   Pull the brisket from the grill and wrap it completely in aluminum foil or butcher paper. Place the wrapped brisket in a cooler, cover the cooler, and let it rest for 1 or 2 hours.
6.   Remove the brisket from the cooler and unwrap it.
7.   Separate the brisket point from the flat by cutting along the fat layer and slice the flat. The point can be saved for burnt ends (see Sweet Heat Burnt Ends), or sliced and served as well.

Bacon-swiss Cheesesteak Meatloaf

Servings: 4
Cooking Time: 2 Hours
Ingredients:
- 1 tablespoon canola oil
- 2 garlic cloves, finely chopped
- 1 medium onion, finely chopped
- 1 poblano chile, stemmed, seeded, and finely chopped
- 2 pounds extra-lean ground beef
- 2 tablespoons Montreal steak seasoning
- 1 tablespoon A.Steak Sauce
- ½ pound bacon, cooked and crumbled
- 2 cups shredded Swiss cheese
- 1 egg, beaten
- 2 cups breadcrumbs
- ½ cup Tiger Sauce

Directions:
1.   On your stove top, heat the canola oil in a medium sauté pan over medium-high heat. Add the garlic, onion, and poblano, and sauté for 3 to 5 minutes, or until the onion is just barely translucent
2.   Supply your smoker with wood pellets and follow the manufacturer's specific start-up procedure. Preheat, with the lid closed, to 225°F.
3.   In a large bowl, combine the sautéed vegetables, ground beef, steak seasoning, steak sauce, bacon, Swiss cheese, egg, and breadcrumbs. Mix with your hands until well incorporated, then shape into a loaf.
4.   Put the meatloaf in a cast iron skillet and place it on the grill. Close the lid and smoke for 2 hours, or until a meat thermometer inserted in the loaf reads 165°F.
5.   Top with the meatloaf with the Tiger Sauce, remove from the grill, and let rest for about 10 minutes before serving.

Smoked Pork Sausages

Servings: 6
Cooking Time: 1 Hour
Ingredients:
- 3 pounds ground pork
- ½ tablespoon ground mustard
- 1 tablespoon onion powder
- 1 tablespoon garlic powder
- 1 teaspoon pink curing salt
- 1 teaspoon salt
- 1 teaspoon black pepper
- ¼ cup ice water
- Hog casings, soaked and rinsed in cold water

Directions:
1.   Mix all ingredients except for the hog casings in a bowl. Using your hands, mix until all ingredients are well-combined.

2. Using a sausage stuffer, stuff the hog casings with the pork mixture.

3. Measure 4 inches of the stuffed hog casing and twist to form into a sausage. Repeat the process until you create sausage links.

4. When ready to cook, fire the Grill to 225F. Use apple wood pellets when cooking the ribs. Close the lid and preheat for 15 minutes.

5. Place the sausage links on the grill grate and cook for 1 hour or until the internal temperature of the sausage reads at 155F.

6. Allow to rest before slicing.

Nutrition Info: Calories per serving: 688; Protein: 58.9g; Carbs: 2.7g; Fat: 47.3g Sugar: 0.2g

Smoked Lamb Shoulder

Servings: 6
Cooking Time: 4 Hours
Ingredients:
- 8 pounds lamb shoulder, fat trimmed
- 2 tablespoons olive oil
- Salt as needed
- For the Rub:
- 1 tablespoon dried oregano
- 2 tablespoons salt
- 1 tablespoon crushed dried bay leaf
- 1 tablespoon sugar
- 2 tablespoons dried crushed sage
- 1 tablespoon dried thyme
- 1 tablespoon ground black pepper
- 1 tablespoon dried basil
- 1 tablespoon dried rosemary
- 1 tablespoon dried parsley

Directions:
1. Switch on the grill, fill the grill hopper with cherry flavored wood pellets, power the grill on by using the control panel, select 'smoke' on the temperature dial, or set the temperature to 250 degrees F and let it preheat for a minimum of 5 minutes.

2. Meanwhile, prepare the rub and for this, take a small bowl, place all of its ingredients in it and stir until mixed.

3. Brush lamb with oil and then sprinkle with prepared rub until evenly coated.

4. When the grill has preheated, open the lid, place lamb should on the grill grate fat-side up, shut the grill and smoke for 3 hours.

5. Then change the smoking temperature to 325 degrees F and continue smoking to 1 hour until fat renders, and the internal temperature reaches 195 degrees F.

6. When done, wrap lamb should in aluminum foil and let it rest for 20 minutes.

7. Pull lamb shoulder by using two forks and then serve.

Nutrition Info: Calories: 300 Cal ;Fat: 24 g ;Carbs: 0 g ;Protein: 19 g ;Fiber: 0 g

Braised Pork Chile Verde

Servings: 6
Cooking Time: 40 Minutes
Ingredients:
- 3 pounds pork shoulder, bone removed and cut into ½ inch cubes
- 1 tablespoon all-purpose flour
- Salt and pepper to taste
- 1-pound tomatillos, husked and washed
- 2 jalapenos, chopped
- 1 medium yellow onion, peeled and cut into chunks
- 4 cloves of garlic
- 4 tablespoons extra virgin olive oil
- 2 cup chicken stock
- 2 cans green chilies
- 1 tablespoon cumin
- 1 tablespoon oregano
- ½ lime, juiced
- ¼ cup cilantro

Directions:
1. Place the pork shoulder chunks in a bowl and toss with flour. Season with salt and pepper to taste.

2. When ready to cook, fire the Grill to 500F. Use desired wood pellets when cooking. Place a large cast iron skillet on the bottom rack of the grill. Close the lid and preheat for 15 minutes.

3. Place the tomatillos, jalapeno, onion, and garlic on a sheet tray lined with foil and drizzle with 2 tablespoon olive oil. Season with salt and pepper to taste.

4. Place the remaining olive oil in the heated cast iron skillet and cook the pork shoulder. Spread the meat evenly then close.

5. Before closing the lid, place the vegetables in the tray on the grill rack. Close the lid of the grill.

6. Cook for 20 minutes without opening the lid or stirring the pork. After 20 minutes, remove the vegetables from the grill and transfer to a blender. Pulse until smooth and pour into the pan with the pork.

7. Stir in the chicken stock, green chilies, cumin, oregano, and lime juice. Season with salt and pepper to taste.

8. Close the grill lid and cook for another 20 minutes.

9. Once cooked, stir in the cilantro.

Nutrition Info: Calories per serving: 389; Protein: 28.5g; Carbs: 4.5g; Fat: 24.3g Sugar: 2.1g

Beef Jerky

Servings: 10
Cooking Time: 5 Hours
Ingredients:
- 3 pounds sirloin steaks
- 2 cups soy sauce
- 1 cup pineapple juice
- 1/2 cup brown sugar
- 2 tbsp sriracha
- 2 tbsp hoisin
- 2 tbsp red pepper flake
- 2 tbsp rice wine vinegar
- 2 tbsp onion powder

Directions:
1. Mix the marinade in a zip lock bag and add the beef. Mix until well coated and remove as much air as possible.
2. Place the bag in a fridge and let marinate overnight or for 6 hours. Remove the bag from the fridge an hour prior to cooking
3. Startup the and set it on the smoking settings or at 190F.
4. Lay the meat on the grill leaving a half-inch space between the pieces. Let cool for 5 hours and turn after 2 hours.
5. Remove from the grill and let cool. Serve or refrigerate

Nutrition Info: Calories: 309 Cal Fat: 7 g Carbohydrates: 20 g Protein: 34 g Fiber: 1 g

Bbq Baby Back Ribs

Servings: 8
Cooking Time: 6 Hours
Ingredients:
- 2 racks of baby back pork ribs, membrane removed
- Pork and poultry rub as needed
- 1/2 cup brown sugar
- 1/3 cup honey, warmed
- 1/3 cup yellow mustard
- 1 tablespoon Worcestershire sauce
- 1 cup BBQ sauce
- 1/2 cup apple juice, divided

Directions:
1. Switch on the grill, fill the grill hopper with hickory flavored wood pellets, power the grill on by using the control panel, select 'smoke' on the temperature dial, or set the temperature to 180 degrees F and let it preheat for a minimum of 15 minutes.

2. Meanwhile, take a small bowl, place mustard, and Worcestershire sauce in it, pour in ¼ cup apple juice and whisk until combined and smooth paste comes together.
3. Brush this paste on all sides of ribs and then season with pork and poultry rub until coated.
4. When the grill has preheated, open the lid, place ribs on the grill grate meat-side up, shut the grill and smoke for 3 hours.
5. After 3 hours, transfer ribs to a rimmed baking dish, let rest for 15 minutes, and meanwhile, change the smoking temperature of the grill to 225 degrees F and let it preheat for a minimum of 10 minutes.
6. Then return pork into the rimmed baking sheet to the grill grate and cook for 3 minutes per side until slightly charred.
7. When done, remove the baking sheet from the grill and work on one rib at a time, sprinkle half of the sugar over the rib, drizzle with half of the honey and half of the remaining apple juice, cover with aluminum foil to seal completely.
8. Repeat with the remaining ribs, return foiled ribs on the grill grate, shut with lid, and then smoke for 2 hours.
9. After 2 hours, uncover the grill, brush them with BBQ sauce generously, arrange them on the grill grate and grill for 1 hour until glazed.
10. When done, transfer ribs to a cutting board, let it rest for 15 minutes, slice into pieces and then serve.
Nutrition Info: Calories: 334 Cal ;Fat: 22.5 g ;Carbs: 6.5 g ;Protein: 24 g ;Fiber: 0.1 g

Apricot Pork Tenderloin

Servings: 4
Cooking Time: 1 ½ Hours
Ingredients:
- 2 pounds pork tenderloin
- 3 ounces Big Game Rub
- 1 cup Apricot BBQ Sauce

Directions:
1. Place the pork tenderloin in a bowl and massage with the Big Game Rub. Allow to rest in the fridge for 2 hours.
2. When ready to cook, fire the Grill to 355F. Use desired wood pellets when cooking. Close the lid and preheat for 15 minutes.
3. Place the seasoned pork tenderloin on the grill grate and close the lid. Cook for 1 ½ hours. Make sure to flip the pork tenderloin halfway through the cooking time.
4. 10 minutes before the cooking time ends, baste the meat with the apricot BBQ sauce.
5. Allow to rest for 10 minutes before slicing.
Nutrition Info: Calories per serving: 426; Protein: 65.3g; Carbs: 20.4g; Fat: 8.4g Sugar: 17.8g

Braised Short Ribs

Servings: 2 To 4
Cooking Time: 4 Hours
Ingredients:
- 4 beef short ribs
- Salt
- Freshly ground black pepper
- ½ cup beef broth

Directions:
1. Supply your with wood pellets and follow the start-up procedure. Preheat the grill, with the lid closed, to 180°F.
2. Season the ribs on both sides with salt and pepper.
3. Place the ribs directly on the grill grate and smoke for 3 hours.
4. Pull the ribs from the grill and place them on enough aluminum foil to wrap them completely.
5. Increase the grill's temperature to 375°F.
6. Fold in three sides of the foil around the ribs and add the beef broth. Fold in the last side, completely enclosing the ribs and liquid. Return the wrapped ribs to the grill and cook for 45 minutes more. Remove the short ribs from the grill, unwrap them, and serve immediately.

Drunken Beef Jerky

Servings: 6
Cooking Time: 5 Hours
Ingredients:
- 1 (12-oz.) bottle dark beer
- 1 C. soy sauce
- ¼ C. Worcestershire sauce
- 2 tbsp. hot sauce
- 3 tbsp. brown sugar
- 2 tbsp. coarse ground black pepper, divided
- 1 tbsp. curing salt
- ½ tsp. garlic salt
- 2 lb. flank steak, trimmed and cut into ¼-inch thick slices

Directions:
1. In a bowl, add the beer, soy sauce, Worcestershire sauce, brown sugar, 2 tbsp. of black pepper, curing salt and garlic salt and mix well.
2. In a large resealable plastic bag, place the steak slices and marinade mixture.
3. Seal the bag, squeezing out the air and then shake to coat well.
4. Refrigerate to marinate overnight.
5. Set the temperature of Grill to 180 degrees F and preheat with closed lid for 15 minutes.

6. Remove the steak slices from the bag and discard the marinade.
7. With paper towels, pat dry the steak slices.
8. Sprinkle the steak slices with remaining black pepper generously.
9. Arrange the steak slices onto the grill in a single layer and cook for about 4-5 hours.
Nutrition Info: Calories per serving: 374; Carbohydrates: 13.3g; Protein: 45.3g; Fat: 12.7g; Sugar: 7.2g; Sodium: 2700mg; Fiber: 0.9g

Kalbi Beef Short Ribs

Servings: 6
Cooking Time: 6 Hours
Ingredients:
- 1/2 cup soy sauce
- 1/2 cup brown sugar
- 1/8 cup rice wine
- 2 tbsp minced garlic
- 1 tbsp sesame oil
- 1/8 cup onion, finely grated
- 2-1/2 pound beef short ribs, thinly sliced

Directions:
1. Mix soy sauce, sugar, rice wine, garlic, sesame oil and onion in a medium mixing bowl.
2. Add the beef in the bowl and cover it in the marinade. Cover the bowl with a plastic wrap and refrigerate for 6 hours.
3. Heat your to high and ensure the grill is well heated.
4. Place on grill and close the lid ensuring you don't lose any heat.
5. Cook for 4 minutes, flip, and cook for 4 more minutes on the other side.
6. Remove the meat and serve with rice and veggies of choice. Enjoy.
Nutrition Info: Calories: 355 Cal Fat: 10 g Carbohydrates: 22 g Protein: 28 g Fiber: 0 g

Baked Venison Meatloaf

Servings: 6
Cooking Time: 1 Hour And 30 Minutes
Ingredients:
- 2 pounds venison, ground
- 1-pound pork, ground
- 1 cup breadcrumbs
- 1 cup milk
- 2 tablespoons onion, diced
- 3 tablespoons salt
- 1 tablespoon black pepper
- ½ tablespoon thyme
- 1 ½ pounds parsnips, chopped

- 1 ½ pounds russet potatoes, chopped
- ¼ cup butter

Directions:
1. Fire the Grill to 500F. Use desired wood pellets when cooking. Close the lid and preheat for 15 minutes.
2. Combine all ingredients in a bowl. Place the mixture in a greased loaf pan.
3. Place in the Grill and cook for 1 hour and 30 minutes or until the internal temperature reads at 160F.

Nutrition Info: Calories per serving: 668 ; Protein: 70.4g; Carbs: 45.7 g; Fat: 22g Sugar: 8.7g

Teriyaki Pineapple Pork Tenderloin Sliders

Servings: 6
Cooking Time: 2 Hours
Ingredients:
- 1-1/2 lb. pork tenderloin
- 1 can pineapple rings
- 1 pack Kings Hawaiian rolls
- 8 oz. teriyaki sauce
- 1-1/2 tbsp. salt
- 1 tbsp. onion powder
- 1 tbsp. paprika
- 1/2 tbsp. garlic powder
- 1/2 tbsp. cayenne pepper

Directions:
1. Preheat your to 325F.
2. Add all the rub ingredients and evenly apply on the pork tenderloin.
3. Place the pork on the preheated and cook while turning every 4 minutes. Cook until the internal temperature of the meat is 145F.
4. Meanwhile, place the pineapple rings on the grill and cook them until nicely browned.
5. As the pineapples are cooking cut the Hawaiin rolls into halves and place them on the grill until toasty brown.
6. Remove the pork from the and let rest for 5 minutes.
7. Assemble the sliders by put a bottom roll, followed by pork tenderloin, pineapple ring, some teriyaki sauce, and the top roll.
8. enjoy

Nutrition Info: Calories 243, Total fat 5g, Saturated fat 2g, Total carbs 15g, Net carbs 14g Protein 33g, Sugars 10g, Fiber 1g, Sodium 2447mg

Wood Pellet Grill Deli-style Roast Beef

Servings: 2

Cooking Time: 4 Hours
Ingredients:
- 4lb round-bottomed roast
- 1 tbsp coconut oil
- 1/4 tbsp garlic powder
- 1/4 tbsp onion powder
- 1/4 tbsp thyme
- 1/4 tbsp oregano
- 1/2 tbsp paprika
- 1/2 tbsp salt
- 1/2 tbsp black pepper

Directions:
1. Combine all the dry hubs to get a dry rub.
2. Roll the roast in oil then coat with the rub.
3. Set your grill to 185°F and place the roast on the grill.
4. Smoke for 4 hours or until the internal temperature reaches 140°F.
5. Remove the roast from the grill and let rest for 10 minutes.
6. Slice thinly and serve.

Nutrition Info: Calories 90, Total fat 3g, Saturated fat 1g, Total Carbs 0g, Net Carbs 0g, Protein 14g, Sugar 0g, Fiber 0g, Sodium: 420mg

Simple Grilled Lamb Chops

Servings: 6
Cooking Time: 20 Minutes
Ingredients:
- 1/4 cup white vinegar, distilled
- 2 tbsp olive oil
- 2 tbsp salt
- 1/2 tbsp black pepper
- 1 tbsp minced garlic
- 1 onion, thinly sliced
- 2 lb lamb chops

Directions:
1. In a resealable bag, mix vinegar, oil, salt, black pepper, garlic, and sliced onions until all salt has dissolved.
2. Add the lamb and toss until evenly coated. Place in a fridge to marinate for 2 hours.
3. Preheat your Traeger.
4. Remove the lamb from the resealable bag and leave any onion that is stuck on the meat. Use an aluminum foil to cover any exposed bone ends.
5. Grill until the desired doneness is achieved. Serve and enjoy when hot.

Nutrition Info: Calories 519, Total fat 44.8g, Saturated fat 18.4g, Total carbs 2.3g, Net carbs 1.9g Protein 25g, Sugars 0.8g, Fiber 0.4g, Sodium 861mg, Potassium 358.6mg

Favorite American Short Ribs

Servings: 6
Cooking Time: 3 Hours
Ingredients:
- For Mustard Sauce:
- 1 C. prepared yellow mustard
- ¼ C. red wine vinegar
- ¼ C. dill pickle juice
- 2 tbsp. soy sauce
- 2 tbsp. Worcestershire sauce
- 1 tsp. ground ginger
- 1 tsp. granulated garlic
- For Spice Rub:
- 2 tbsp. salt
- 2 tbsp. freshly ground black pepper
- 1 tbsp. white cane sugar
- 1 tbsp. granulated garlic
- For Ribs:
- 6 (14-oz.) (4-5-inch long) beef short ribs

Directions:
1. Set the temperature of Grill to 230-250 degrees F and preheat with closed lid for 15 minutes, using charcoal.
2. For sauce: in a bowl, add all the ingredients and with a wire whisk, bet until well combined.
3. For rub: in a small bowl, mix together all ingredients.
4. Coat the ribs with sauce generously and then sprinkle with spice rub evenly.
5. Place the ribs onto the grill over indirect heat, bone side down and cook for about 1-1½ hours.
6. Flip the side and cook for about 45 minutes.
7. Flip the side and cook for about 45 minutes more.
8. Remove the ribs from grill and place onto a cutting board for about 10 minutes before serving.
9. With a sharp knife, cut the ribs into equal-sized individual pieces and serve.

Nutrition Info: Calories per serving: 867; Carbohydrates: 7.7g; Protein: 117.1g; Fat: 37.5g; Sugar: 3.6g; Sodium: 3400mg; Fiber: 2.1g

Beef Short Rib Lollipop

Servings: 4
Cooking Time: 3 Hours
Ingredients:
- 4 beef short rib lollipops
- BBQ Rub
- BBQ Sauce

Directions:
1. Preheat your to 275F.
2. Season the short ribs with BBQ rub and place them on the grill.

3. Cook for 4 hours while turning occasionally until the meat is tender.
4. Apply the sauce on the meat in the last 30 minutes of cooking.
5. Serve and enjoy.

Nutrition Info: Calories 265, Total fat 19g, Saturated fat 9g, Total carbs 1g, Net carbs 0g Protein 22g, Sugars 1g, Fiber 0g, Sodium 60mmg

Cowboy Cut Steak

Servings: 4
Cooking Time: 1 Hour And 15 Minutes
Ingredients:
- 2 cowboy cut steak, each about 2 ½ pounds
- Salt as needed
- Beef rub as needed
- For the Gremolata:
- 2 tablespoons chopped mint
- 1 bunch of parsley, leaves separated
- 1 lemon, juiced
- 1 tablespoon lemon zest
- ½ teaspoon minced garlic
- ¼ teaspoon salt
- 1/8 teaspoon ground black pepper
- 1/4 cup olive oil

Directions:
1. Switch on the grill, fill the grill hopper with mesquite flavored wood pellets, power the grill on by using the control panel, select 'smoke' on the temperature dial, or set the temperature to 225 degrees F and let it preheat for a minimum of 5 minutes.
2. Meanwhile, prepare the steaks, and for this, season them with salt and BBQ rub until well coated.
3. When the grill has preheated, open the lid, place steaks on the grill grate, shut the grill and smoke for 45 minutes to 1 hour until thoroughly cooked, and internal temperature reaches 115 degrees F.
4. Meanwhile, prepare gremolata and for this, take a medium bowl, place all of its ingredients in it and then stir well until combined, set aside until combined.
5. When done, transfer steaks to a dish, let rest for 15 minutes, and meanwhile, change the smoking temperature of the grill to 450 degrees F and let it preheat for a minimum of 10 minutes.
6. Then return steaks to the grill grate and cook for 7 minutes per side until the internal temperature reaches 130 degrees F.

Nutrition Info: Calories: 361 Cal ;Fat: 31 g ;Carbs: 1 g ;Protein: 19 g ;Fiber: 0.2 g

Smoked Ham

Servings: 12 To 15
Cooking Time: 5 Or 6 Hours
Ingredients:
- 1 (10-pound) fresh ham, skin removed
- 2 tablespoons olive oil
- 1 batch Rosemary-Garlic Lamb Seasoning

Directions:
1. Supply your smoker with wood pellets and follow the manufacturer's specific start-up procedure. Preheat the grill, with the lid closed, to 180°F.
2. Rub the ham all over with olive oil and sprinkle it with the seasoning.
3. Place the ham directly on the grill grate and smoke for 3 hours.
4. Increase the grill's temperature to 375°F and continue to smoke the ham until its internal temperature reaches 170°F.
5. Remove the ham from the grill and let it rest for 10 minutes, before carving and serving.

Traditional Tomahawk Steak

Servings: 4 To 6
Cooking Time: 1 Or 2 Hours
Ingredients:
- 1 tomahawk ribeye steak (2 1/2 to 3 1/2 lbs)
- 5 garlic cloves, minced
- 2 tbsp kosher salt
- 1 bundle fresh thyme
- 2 tbsp ground black pepper
- 8 oz butter stick
- 1 tbsp garlic powder
- 1/8 cup olive oil

Directions:
1. Mix rub ingredients (salt, black pepper, and garlic powder) in a small bowl. Use this mixture to season all sides of the ribeye steak generously. You can also substitute your favorite steak seasoning. After applying seasoning, let the steak rest at room temperature for at least 30 minutes.
2. While the steak rests, preheat your pellet grill to 450°F - 550°F for searing
3. Sear the steak for 5 minutes on each side. Halfway through each side (so after 2 1/2 minutes), rotate the steak 90° to form grill marks on the tomahawk
4. After the tomahawk steak has seared for 5 minutes on each side (10 minutes total), move the steak to a raised rack
5. Adjust your pellet grill's temperature to 250°F and turn up smoke setting if applicable. Leave the lid open for a moment to help allow some heat to escape

6. Stick your probe meat thermometer into the very center of the cut to measure internal temperature.
7. Place butter stick, garlic cloves, olive oil, and thyme in the aluminum pan. Then place the aluminum pan under the steak to catch drippings. After a few minutes, the steak drippings and ingredients will mix together
8. Baste the steak with the aluminum pan mixture every 10 minutes until the tomahawk steak reaches your desired doneness
9. Once the steak reaches its desired doneness, remove from the grill and place on a cutting board or serving dish. The steak should rest for 10-15 minutes before cutting/serving.

Grilled Filet Mignon

Servings: 3
Cooking Time: 20 Minutes
Ingredients:
- Salt
- Pepper
- Filet mignon - 3

Directions:
1. Preheat your grill to 450 degrees.
2. Season the steak with a good amount of salt and pepper to enhance its flavor.
3. Place on the grill and flip after 5 minutes.
4. Grill both sides for 5 minutes each.
5. Take it out when it looks cooked and serve with your favorite side dish.

Nutrition Info: Carbohydrates: 0 g Protein: 23 g Fat: 15 g Sodium: 240 mg Cholesterol: 82 mg

Trager New York Strip

Servings: 6
Cooking Time: 15 Minutes
Ingredients:
- 3 New York strips
- Salt and pepper

Directions:
1. If the steak is in the fridge, remove it 30 minutes prior to cooking.
2. Preheat the to 450F.
3. Meanwhile, season the steak generously with salt and pepper. Place it on the grill and let it cook for 5 minutes per side or until the internal temperature reaches 1280F.
4. Remove the steak from the grill and let it rest for 10 minutes.

Nutrition Info: Calories 198, Total fat 14g, Saturated fat 6g, Total carbs 0g, Net carbs 0g Protein 17g, Sugars 0g, Fiber 0g, Sodium 115mg

Competition Style Bbq Pork Ribs

Servings: 6
Cooking Time: 2 Hours
Ingredients:

- 2 racks of St. Louis-style ribs
- 1 cup Pork and Poultry Rub
- 1/8 cup brown sugar
- 4 tablespoons butter
- 4 tablespoons agave
- 1 bottle Sweet and Heat BBQ Sauce

Directions:
1. Place the ribs in working surface and remove the thin film of connective tissues covering it. In a smaller bowl, combine the Pork and Poultry Rub, brown sugar, butter, and agave. Mix until well combined.
2. Massage the rub onto the ribs and allow to rest in the fridge for at least 2 hours.
3. When ready to cook, fire the Grill to 225F. Use desired wood pellets when cooking the ribs. Close the lid and preheat for 15 minutes.
4. Place the ribs on the grill grate and close the lid. Smoke for 1 hour and 30 minutes. Make sure to flip the ribs halfway through the cooking time.
5. Ten minutes before the cooking time ends, brush the ribs with BBQ sauce.
6. Remove from the grill and allow to rest before slicing.
Nutrition Info: Calories per serving: 399 ; Protein: 47.2g; Carbs: 3.5g; Fat: 20.5g Sugar: 2.3g

Smoked Apple Bbq Ribs

Servings: 6
Cooking Time: 2 Hours
Ingredients:

- 2 racks St. Louis-style ribs
- ¼ cup Big Game Rub
- 1 cup apple juice
- A bottle of BBQ Sauce

Directions:
1. Place the ribs on a working surface and remove the film of connective tissues covering it.
2. In another bowl, mix the Game Rub and apple juice until well-combined.
3. Massage the rub on to the ribs and allow to rest in the fridge for at least 2 hours.
4. When ready to cook, fire the Grill to 225F. Use apple wood pellets when cooking the ribs. Close the lid and preheat for 15 minutes.
5. Place the ribs on the grill grate and close the lid. Smoke for 1 hour and 30 minutes. Make sure to flip the ribs halfway through the cooking time.

6. Ten minutes before the cooking time ends, brush the ribs with BBQ sauce.
7. Remove from the grill and allow to rest before slicing.
Nutrition Info: Calories per serving: 337 ; Protein: 47.1g; Carbs: 4.7 g; Fat: 12.9g Sugar: 4g

St. Patrick Day's Corned Beef

Servings: 14
Cooking Time: 7 Hours
Ingredients:

- 6 lb. corned beef brisket, drained, rinsed and pat dried
- Freshly ground black pepper, to taste
- 8 oz. light beer

Directions:
1. Set the temperature of Grill to 275 degrees F and preheat with closed lid for 15 minutes.
2. Sprinkle the beef brisket with spice packet evenly.
3. Now, sprinkle the brisket with black pepper lightly.
4. Place the brisket onto the grill and cook for about 3-4 hours.
5. Remove from grill and transfer briskets into an aluminum pan.
6. Add enough beer just to cover the bottom of pan.
7. With a piece of foil, cover the pan, leaving one corner open to let out steam.
8. Cook for about 2-3 hours.
9. Remove the brisket from grill and place onto a cutting board for about 10-15 minutes before slicing.
10. With a sharp knife, cut the brisket in desired sized slices and serve.
11. Remove the brisket from grill and place onto a cutting board for about 25-30 minutes before slicing.
12. With a sharp knife, cut the brisket in desired sized slices and serve.
Nutrition Info: Calories per serving: 337; Carbohydrates: 0.6g; Protein: 26.1g; Fat: 24.3g; Sugar: 0g; Sodium: 1719mg; Fiber: 0g

Simple Wood Pellet Smoked Pork Ribs

Servings: 7
Cooking Time: 5 Hours
Ingredients:

- 3 rack baby back ribs
- 3/4 cup pork and poultry rub
- 3/4 cup Que BBQ Sauce

Directions:
1. Peel the membrane from the backside of the ribs and trim any fat.
2. Season the pork generously with the rub.

3. Set the wood pellet grill to 180°F and preheat for 15 minutes with the lid closed.
4. Place the pork ribs on the grill and smoke them for 5 hours.
5. Remove the pork from the grill and wrap them in a foil with the BBQ sauce.
6. Place back the pork and increase the temperature to 350°F. Cook for 45 more minutes.
7. Remove the pork from the grill and let it rest for 20 minutes before serving. Enjoy.
Nutrition Info: Calories 762, Total fat 57g, Saturated fat 17g, Total Carbs 23g, Net Carbs 22.7g, Protein 39g, Sugar 18g, Fiber 0.5g, Sodium: 737mg, Potassium 618mg

Simple Grilled Lamb Chops

Servings: 6
Cooking Time: 6 Minutes
Ingredients:
- 1/4 cup distilled white vinegar
- 2 tbsp salt
- 1/2 tbsp black pepper
- 1 tbsp garlic, minced
- 1 onion, thinly sliced
- 2 tbsp olive oil
- 2lb lamb chops

Directions:
1. In a resealable bag, mix vinegar, salt, black pepper, garlic, sliced onion, and oil until all salt has dissolved.
2. Add the lamb chops and toss until well coated. Place in the fridge to marinate for 2 hours.
3. Preheat the wood pellet grill to high heat.
4. Remove the lamb from the fridge and discard the marinade. Wrap any exposed bones with foil.
5. Grill the lamb for 3 minutes per side. You can also broil in a broiler for more crispness.
6. Serve and enjoy.
Nutrition Info: Calories 519, Total fat 44.8g, Saturated fat 18g, Total Carbs 2.3g, Net Carbs 1.9g, Protein 25g, Sugar1g, Fiber 0.4g, Sodium: 861mg, Potassium 359mg

Restaurant-style Rib-eye Steak

Servings: 2
Cooking Time: 20 Minutes
Ingredients:
- 2 (1 3/8-inch thick) rib-eye steaks, trimmed
- 1 tbsp. olive oil
- 1 tbsp. steak seasoning

Directions:
1. Coat both sides of each steak with oil and season with steak seasoning.

2. Set aside at room temperature for about 15 minutes.
3. Set the temperature of Grill to 325 degrees F and preheat with closed lid for 15 minutes.
4. Place the steaks onto the grill and cook for about 15-20 minutes, flipping after every 6 minutes.
5. Remove from grill and serve immediately.
Nutrition Info: Calories per serving: 527; Carbohydrates: 0g; Protein: 30.1g; Fat: 44.6; Sugar: 0g; Sodium: 98mg; Fiber: 0g

Smoked Porchetta With Italian Salsa Verde

Servings: 8 To 12
Cooking Time: 3 Hours
Ingredients:
- 3 Tablespoon dried fennel seed
- 2 Tablespoon red pepper flakes
- 2 Tablespoon sage, minced
- 1 Tablespoon rosemary, minced
- 3 Clove garlic, minced
- As Needed lemon zest
- As Needed orange zest
- To Taste salt and pepper
- 6 Pound Pork Belly, skin on
- As Needed salt and pepper
- 1 Whole shallot, thinly sliced
- 6 Tablespoon parsley, minced
- 2 Tablespoon freshly minced chives
- 1 Tablespoon Oregano, fresh
- 3 Tablespoon white wine vinegar
- 1/2 Teaspoon kosher salt
- 3/4 Cup olive oil
- 1/2 Teaspoon Dijon mustard
- As Needed fresh lemon juice

Directions:
1. Prepare herb mixture: In a medium bowl, mix together fennel seeds, red pepper flakes, sage, rosemary, garlic, citrus zest, salt and pepper.
2. Place pork belly skin side up on a clean work surface and score in a crosshatch pattern. Flip the pork belly over and season flesh side with salt, pepper and half of the herb mixture.
3. Place trimmed pork loin in the center of the belly and rub with remaining herb mixture. Season with salt and pepper.
4. Roll the pork belly around the loin to form a cylindrical shape and tie tightly with kitchen twine at 1" intervals.
5. Season the outside with salt and pepper and transfer to refrigerator, uncovered and let air dry overnight.
6. When ready to cook, start the grill and set to Smoke.

7. Fit a rimmed baking sheet with a rack and place the pork on the rack seam side down.
8. Place the pan directly on the grill grate and smoke for 1 hour.
9. Increase the grill temperature to 325 degrees F and roast until the internal temperature of the meat reaches 135 degrees, about 2 1/2 hours. If the exterior begins to burn before the desired internal temperature is reached, tent with foil.
10. Remove from grill and let stand 30 minutes before slicing.
11. 1To make the Italian salsa verde: Combine shallot, parsley, chives, vinegar, oregano and salt in a medium bowl. Whisk in olive oil then stir in mustard and lemon juice.

Sweet Smoked Country Ribs

Servings: 12 To 15
Cooking Time: 4 Hours
Ingredients:
- 2 pounds country-style ribs
- 1 batch Sweet Brown Sugar Rub
- 2 tablespoons light brown sugar
- 1 cup Pepsi or other cola
- ¼ cup The Ultimate BBQ Sauce

Directions:
1. Supply your smoker with wood pellets and follow the manufacturer's specific start-up procedure. Preheat the grill, with the lid closed, to 180°F.
2. Sprinkle the ribs with the rub and use your hands to work the rub into the meat.
3. Place the ribs directly on the grill grate and smoke for 3 hours.
4. Remove the ribs from the grill and place them on enough aluminum foil to wrap them completely. Dust the brown sugar over the ribs.
5. Increase the grill's temperature to 300°F.
6. Fold in three sides of the foil around the ribs and add the cola. Fold in the last side, completely enclosing the ribs and liquid. Return the ribs to the grill and cook for 45 minutes.
7. Remove the ribs from the foil and place them on the grill grate. Baste all sides of the ribs with barbecue sauce. Cook for 15 minutes more to caramelize the sauce.
8. Remove the ribs from the grill and serve immediately.

Wood Pellet Grill Pork Crown Roast

Servings: 5
Cooking Time: 1 Hour
Ingredients:
- 13 ribs pork
- 1/4 cup favorite rub
- 1cup apple juice
- 1 cup Apricot BBQ sauce

Directions:
1. Set the wood pellet temperature to 375°F to preheat for 15 minutes with the lid closed.
2. Meanwhile, season the pork with the rub then let sit for 30 minutes.
3. Wrap the tips of each crown roast with foil to prevent the borns from turning black.
4. Place the meat on the grill grate and cook for 90 minutes. Spray apple juice every 30 minutes.
5. When the meat has reached an internal temperature of 125°F remove the foils.
6. Spray the roast with apple juice again and let cook until the internal temperature has reached 135°F.
7. In the last 10 minutes of cooking, baste the roast with BBQ sauce.
8. Remove from the grill and wrap with foil. Let rest for 15 minutes before serving. Enjoy.
Nutrition Info: Calories 240, Total fat 16g, Saturated fat 6g, Total Carbs 0g, Net Carbs 0g, Protein 23g, Sugar 0g, Fiber 0g, Sodium: 50mg

Wood Pellet Smoked Brisket

Servings: 10
Cooking Time: 9 Hours
Ingredients:
- 2 tbsp garlic powder
- 2 tbsp onion powder
- 2 tbsp paprika
- 2 tbsp chili powder
- 1/3 cup salt
- 1/3 cup black pepper
- 12 lb whole packer brisket, trimmed
- 1-1/2 cup beef broth

Directions:
1. Set your wood pellet temperature to 225°F. Let preheat for 15 minutes with the lid closed.
2. Meanwhile, mix garlic, onion, paprika, chili, salt, and pepper in a mixing bowl.
3. Season the brisket generously on all sides.
4. Place the meat on the grill with the fat side down and let it cool until the internal temperature reaches 160°F.
5. Remove the meat from the grill and double wrap it with foil. Return it to the grill and cook until the internal temperature reaches 204°F.
6. Remove from grill, unwrap the brisket and let est for 15 minutes.
7. Slice and serve.
Nutrition Info: Calories 270, Total fat 20g, Saturated fat 8g, Total Carbs 3g, Net Carbs 3g, Protein 20g, Sugar 1g, Fiber 0g, Sodium: 1220mg

Spicy Pork Chops

Servings: 4
Cooking Time: 10-15 Minutes
Ingredients:
- 1 tbsp. olive oil
- 2 cloves garlic, crushed and minced
- 1 tbsp. cayenne pepper
- ½ tsp. hot sauce
- ¼ cup lime juice
- 2 tsp. ground cumin
- 1 tsp. ground cinnamon
- 4 pork chops
- Lettuce

Directions:
1.   Mix the olive oil, garlic, cayenne pepper, hot sauce, lime juice, cumin and cinnamon.
2.   Pour the mixture into a re-sealable plastic bag. Place the pork chops inside. Seal and turn to coat evenly. Chill in the refrigerator for 4 hours. Grill for 10 to 15 minutes, flipping occasionally.
Nutrition Info: Calories: 196 Cal Fat: 9 g Carbohydrates: 3 g Protein: 25 g Fiber: 1 g

Easy-to-prepare Lamb Chops

Servings: 6
Cooking Time: 12 Minutes
Ingredients:
- 6 (6-oz.) lamb chops
- 3 tbsp. olive oil
- Salt and freshly ground black pepper, to taste

Directions:
1.   Set the temperature of Grill to 450 degrees F and preheat with closed lid for 15 minutes.
2.   Coat the lamb chops with oil and then, season with salt and black pepper evenly.
3.   Arrange the chops onto the grill and cook for about 4-6 minutes per side.
4.   Remove the chops from grill and serve hot.
Nutrition Info: Calories per serving: 376; Carbohydrates: 0g; Protein: 47.8g; Fat: 19.5g; Sugar: 0g; Sodium: 156mg; Fiber: 0g

Smoked Rack Of Lamb

Servings: 4
Cooking Time: 1 Hour And 15 Minutes
Ingredients:
- 1rack of lamb rib, membrane removed
- For the Marinade:
- 1lemon, juiced

- 2teaspoons minced garlic
- 1teaspoon salt
- 1teaspoon ground black pepper
- 1teaspoon dried thyme
- ¼ cup balsamic vinegar
- 1teaspoon dried basil
- For the Glaze:
- 2tablespoons soy sauce
- ¼ cup Dijon mustard
- 2tablespoons Worcestershire sauce
- ¼ cup red wine

Directions:
1.   Prepare the marinade and for this, take a small bowl, place all the ingredients in it and whisk until combined.
2.   Place the rack of lamb into a large plastic bag, pour in marinade, seal it, turn it upside down to coat lamb with the marinade and let it marinate for a minimum of 8 hours in the refrigerator.
3.   When ready to cook, switch on the grill, fill the grill hopper with flavored wood pellets, power the grill on by using the control panel, select 'smoke' on the temperature dial, or set the temperature to 300 degrees F and let it preheat for a minimum of 5 minutes.
4.   Meanwhile, prepare the glaze and for this, take a small bowl, place all of its ingredients in it and whisk until combined.
5.   When the grill has preheated, open the lid, place lamb rack on the grill grate, shut the grill and smoke for 15 minutes.
6.   Brush with glaze, flip the lamb and then continue smoking for 1 hour and 15 minutes until the internal temperature reaches 145 degrees F, basting with the glaze every 30 minutes.
7.   When done, transfer lamb rack to a cutting board, let it rest for 15 minutes, cut it into slices, and then serve.
Nutrition Info: Calories: 323 Cal Fat: 18 g Carbs: 13 g Protein: 25 g Fiber: 1 g

Sweetheart Steak

Servings: 1
Cooking Time: 14 Minutes
Ingredients:
- 20 ounces boneless strip steak, butterflied
- 2 ounces pure sea salt
- 2 teaspoons black pepper
- 2 tablespoons raw dark chocolate, finely chopped
- ½ tablespoon extra-virgin olive oil

Directions:
1.   On a cutting board, trim the meat into heart shape using a sharp knife. Set aside.

2. In a smaller bowl, combine the rest of the ingredients to create a spice rub mix.
3. Rub onto the steak and massage until well-seasoned.
4. When ready to cook, fire the Grill to 450F. Use desired wood pellets when cooking. Close the lid and preheat for 15 minutes.
5. Grill the steak for 7 minutes on each side.
6. Allow to rest for 5 minutes before slicing.
Nutrition Info: Calories per serving: 727 ; Protein: 132.7g; Carbs: 8.8 g; Fat: 18.5g Sugar: 5.2g

Fall-of-the-bones Short Ribs

Servings: 4
Cooking Time: 5½ Hours
Ingredients:
- 2½ lb. beef short ribs, trimmed
- 4 tbsp. extra-virgin olive oil
- 4 tbsp. beef rub
- 1 C. apple juice
- 1 C. apple cider vinegar
- 1 C. red wine
- 1 C. beef broth
- 2 tbsp. butter
- 2 tbsp. Worcestershire sauce
- Salt and freshly ground black pepper, to taste

Directions:
1. Set the temperature of Grill to 225 degrees F and preheat with closed lid for 15 minutes.
2. Coat the ribs with olive oil and season with rub evenly.
3. Arrange the ribs onto the grill and cook for about 1 hour.
4. In a food-safe spray bottle, mix together apple juice and vinegar.
5. After 1 hour spray the ribs with vinegar mixture evenly.
6. Cook for about 2 hours, spraying with vinegar mixture after every 15 minutes.
7. In a bowl, mix together remaining ingredients.
8. Transfer the ribs in a baking dish with wine mixture.
9. With a piece of foil, cover the baking dish tightly and cook for about 2-2½ hours.
10. Remove the ribs from grill and place onto a cutting board for about 10-15 minutes before slicing.
11. With a sharp knife, cut the ribs into equal-sized individual ribs and serve.
Nutrition Info: Calories per serving: 859; Carbohydrates: 10.9g; Protein: 83.2g; Fat: 45.7g; Sugar: 8.4g; Sodium: 532mg; Fiber: 0.1g

Strip Steak With Onion Sauce

Servings: 4
Cooking Time: 1 Hour
Ingredients:
- 2 New York strip steaks
- Prime rib rub
- ½ lb. bacon, chopped
- 1 onion, sliced
- 1/4 cup brown sugar
- 1/2 tablespoon balsamic vinegar
- 3 tablespoons brewed coffee
- 1/4 cup apple juice

Directions:
1. Sprinkle both sides of steaks with prime rib rub.
2. Set the wood pellet grill to 350 degrees F.
3. Preheat for 15 minutes while the lid is closed.
4. Place a pan over the grill.
5. Cook the bacon until crispy.
6. Transfer to a plate.
7. Cook the onion in the bacon drippings for 10 minutes.
8. Stir in brown sugar and cook for 20 minutes.
9. Add the rest of the ingredients and cook for 20 minutes.
10. Grill the steaks for 5 minutes per side.
11. Serve with the onion and bacon mixture.
12. Tips: Ensure steak is in room temperature before seasoning.

Smoked Prime Rib

Servings: 12
Cooking Time: 5 Hours
Ingredients:
- 10 lb. rib eye roast
- Salt to taste
- Barbecue rub
- Garlic and herb seasoning
- Worcestershire sauce
- Beef stock
- 3 tablespoons butter

Directions:
1. Preheat the wood pellet grill to 275 degrees F for 15 minutes while the lid is closed.
2. Sprinkle the roast with salt, rub, and garlic and herb seasoning.
3. Marinate for 20 minutes.
4. Add the rib roast to the grill.
5. Smoke for 5 hours, basting with a mixture of Worcestershire sauce and beef stock every 45 minutes.
6. Transfer to a plate.
7. Add the butter to the roast and let it melt.
8. Serve after 5 minutes.
9. Tips: Use boneless rib-eye roast for this recipe.

Thai Beef Salad

Servings: 4
Cooking Time: 10 Minutes
Ingredients:
- 1 ½ pound skirt steak
- 1 ½ teaspoon salt
- 1 teaspoon ground white pepper
- For the Dressing:
- 4 jalapeño peppers, minced
- ½ teaspoon minced garlic
- 4 tablespoons Thai fish sauce
- 4 tablespoons lime juice
- 1 tablespoon brown sugar
- For the Salad:
- 1 small red onion, peeled, thinly sliced
- 6 cherry tomatoes, halved
- 2 green onions, ¼-inch diced
- 1 cucumber, deseeded, thinly sliced
- 1 heart of romaine lettuce, chopped
- ½ cup chopped mint
- 2 tablespoons cilantro
- ½ teaspoon red pepper flakes
- 1 tablespoon lime juice
- 2 tablespoons fish sauce

Directions:
1. Switch on the grill, fill the grill hopper with cherry flavored wood pellets, power the grill on by using the control panel, select 'smoke' on the temperature dial, or set the temperature to 450 degrees F and let it preheat for a minimum of 15 minutes.
2. Meanwhile, prepare the steak, and for this, season it with salt and black pepper until well coated.
3. When the grill has preheated, open the lid, place steak on the grill grate, shut the grill and smoke for 10 minutes until internal temperature reaches 130 degrees F.
4. Meanwhile, prepare the dressing and for this, take a medium bowl, place all of its ingredients in it and then stir until combined.
5. Take a large salad, place all the ingredients for the salad in it, drizzle with dressing and toss until well coated and mixed.
6. When done, transfer steak to a cutting board, let it rest for 10 minutes and then cut it into slices.
7. Add steak slices into the salad, toss until mixed, and then serve.

Nutrition Info: Calories: 128 Cal ;Fat: 6 g ;Carbs: 6 g ;Protein: 12 g ;Fiber: 1 g

Pork Belly Burnt Ends

Servings: 8 To 10
Cooking Time: 6 Hours
Ingredients:
- 1 (3-pound) skinless pork belly (if not already skinned, use a sharp boning knife to remove the skin from the belly), cut into 1½- to 2-inch cubes
- 1 batch Sweet Brown Sugar Rub
- ½ cup honey
- 1 cup The Ultimate BBQ Sauce
- 2 tablespoons light brown sugar

Directions:
1. Supply your smoker with wood pellets and follow the manufacturer's specific start-up procedure. Preheat the grill, with the lid closed, to 250°F.
2. Generously season the pork belly cubes with the rub. Using your hands, work the rub into the meat.
3. Place the pork cubes directly on the grill grate and smoke until their internal temperature reaches 195°F.
4. Transfer the cubes from the grill to an aluminum pan. Add the honey, barbecue sauce, and brown sugar. Stir to combine and coat the pork.
5. Place the pan in the grill and smoke the pork for 1 hour, uncovered. Remove the pork from the grill and serve immediately.

Wood Pellet Grilled Tenderloin With Fresh Herb Sauce

Servings: 4
Cooking Time: 15 Minutes
Ingredients:
- Pork
- 1 pork tenderloin, silver skin removed and dried
- BBQ seasoning
- Fresh herb sauce
- 1 handful basil, fresh
- 1/4 tbsp garlic powder
- 1/3 cup olive oil
- 1/2 tbsp kosher salt

Directions:
1. Preheat the wood pellet grill to medium heat.
2. Coat the pork with BBQ seasoning then cook on semi-direct heat of the grill. Turn the pork regularly to ensure even cooking.
3. Cook until the internal temperature is 145°F. Remove from the grill and let it rest for 10 minutes.
4. Meanwhile, make the herb sauce by pulsing all the sauce ingredients in a food processor. Pulse for a few times or until well chopped.
5. Slice the pork diagonally and spoon the sauce on top. Serve and enjoy.

Nutrition Info: Calories 300, Total fat 22g, Saturated fat 4g, Total Carbs 13g, Net Carbs 12g, Protein 14g, Sugar 10g, Fiber 1g, Sodium: 791mg

Delish Beef Brisket

Servings: 10
Cooking Time: 7 Hours
Ingredients:
- 1 C. paprika
- ¾ C. sugar
- 3 tbsp. garlic salt
- 3 tbsp. onion powder
- 1 tbsp. celery salt
- 1 tbsp. lemon pepper
- 1 tbsp. ground black pepper
- 1 tsp. cayenne pepper
- 1 tsp. mustard powder
- ½ tsp. dried thyme, crushed
- 1 (5-6-lb.) beef brisket, trimmed

Directions:
1. In a bowl, place all ingredients except for beef brisket and mix well.
2. Rub the brisket with spice mixture generously.
3. With a plastic wrap, cover the brisket and refrigerate overnight.
4. Set the temperature of Grill to 250 degrees F and preheat with closed lid for 15 minutes.
5. Place the brisket onto grill over indirect heat and cook for about 3-3½ hours.
6. Flip and cook for about 3-3½ hours more.
7. Remove the brisket from grill and place onto a cutting board for about 10-15 minutes before slicing.
8. With a sharp knife, cut the brisket in desired sized slices and serve.

Nutrition Info: Calories per serving: 536; Carbohydrates: 24.8g; Protein: 71.1g; Fat: 15.6g; Sugar: 17.4g; Sodium: 158mg; Fiber: 4.5g

Stuffed Peppers

Servings: 6
Cooking Time: 5 Minutes
Ingredients:
- 3 bell peppers, sliced in halves
- 1 pound ground beef, lean
- 1 onion, chopped
- 1/2 tbsp red pepper flakes
- 1/2 tbsp salt
- 1/4 tbsp pepper
- 1/2 tbsp garlic powder
- 1/2 tbsp onion powder
- 1/2 cup white rice
- 15 oz stewed tomatoes

- 8 oz tomato sauce
- 6 cups cabbage, shredded
- 1-1/2 cup water
- 2 cups cheddar cheese

Directions:
1. Arrange the pepper halves on a baking tray and set aside.
2. Preheat your grill to 325F.
3. Brown the meat in a large skillet. Add onions, pepper flakes, salt, pepper garlic, and onion and cook until the meat is well cooked.
4. Add rice, stewed tomatoes, tomato sauce, cabbage, and water. Cover and simmer until the rice is well cooked, the cabbage is tender and there is no water in the rice.
5. Place the cooked beef mixture in the pepper halves and top with cheese.
6. Place in the grill and cook for 30 minutes.
7. Serve immediately and enjoy it.

Nutrition Info: Calories: 422 Cal Fat: 22 g Carbohydrates: 24 g Protein: 34 g Fiber: 5 g

Smoked Ham Recipe

Servings: 4
Cooking Time: 12-15 Minutes
Ingredients:
- 4 ounces of smoked ham, scored
- 1/2 cup of butter
- 2 tablespoons of brown sugar
- 1tablespoon of honey
- 2tablespoons of pineapple cane syrup

Directions:
1. Place the grill rack inside and pour a cup of water in it, then close the unit.
2. Let it preheat for 20 minutes at high.
3. Meanwhile, melt butter in a cooking pot and add two tablespoons of brown sugar.
4. Melt it down and add a tablespoon of honey and pineapple cane syrup.
5. Mix well, and let it get simmer until thickened.
6. Turn off the grill and open the unit.
7. Then brush the ham with glaze.
8. Close the unit and cook for 7 minutes.
9. After 5 minutes, open the unit by turning it off and glazed the ham again.
10. Cook for remaining 2 minutes
11. Sprinkle the ham with any favorite spice blend.
12. Slice and serve.

Nutrition Info: Calories: 291 Total Fat: 25.5gSaturated Fat: 15.4gCholesterol: 77mg Sodium: 535mg Total Carbohydrate: 12g Dietary Fiber 0.5g Total Sugars: 10.7g Protein: 5g

Bbq Spareribs With Mandarin Glaze

Servings: 6
Cooking Time: 60 Minutes
Ingredients:
- 3 large spareribs, membrane removed
- 3 tablespoons yellow mustard
- 1 tablespoons Worcestershire sauce
- 1 cup honey
- 1 ½ cup brown sugar
- 13 ounces Mandarin Glaze
- 1 teaspoon sesame oil
- 1 teaspoon soy sauce
- 1 teaspoon garlic powder

Directions:
1. Place the spareribs on a working surface and carefully remove the connective tissue membrane that covers the ribs.
2. In another bowl, mix together the rest of the ingredients until well combined. Massage the spice mixture on to the spareribs. Allow to rest in the fridge for at least 3 hours.
3. When ready to cook, fire the Grill to 300F. Use hickory wood pellets when cooking the ribs. Close the lid and preheat for 15 minutes.
4. Place the seasoned ribs on the grill grate and cover the lid. Cook for 60 minutes.
5. Once cooked, allow to rest before slicing.

Nutrition Info: Calories per serving: 1263 ; Protein: 36.9g; Carbs: 110.3g; Fat: 76.8g Sugar: 107g

Holiday Dinner Leg Of Lamb

Servings: 8
Cooking Time: 5 Hours
Ingredients:
- ½ C. olive oil
- ½ C. red wine vinegar
- ½ C. dry white wine
- 1 tbsp. garlic, minced
- 1 tsp. dried marjoram, crushed
- 1 tsp. dried rosemary, crushed
- Salt and freshly ground black pepper, to taste
- 1 (5-lb.) leg of lamb

Directions:
1. In a bowl, add all ingredients except for leg of lamb and mix until well combined.
2. In a large resealable bag, add marinade and leg of lamb.
3. Seal the bag and shake to coat completely.
4. Refrigerate for about 4-6 hours, flipping occasionally.
5. Set the temperature of Grill to 225 degrees F and preheat with closed lid for 15 minutes.
6. Place the leg of lamb onto the grill and cook for about 4-5 hours.

7. Remove the leg of lamb from grill and place onto a cutting board for about 20 minutes before slicing.
8. With a sharp knife, cut the leg of lamb into desired-sized slices and serve.

Nutrition Info: Calories per serving: 653; Carbohydrates: 1g; Protein: 79.7g; Fat: 33.4g; Sugar: 0.2g; Sodium: 237mg; Fiber: 0.1g

Grilled Lamb With Sugar Glaze

Servings: 4
Cooking Time: 20 Minutes
Ingredients:
- 1/4 cup sugar
- 2 tbsp ground ginger
- 2 tbsp dried tarragon
- 1/2 tbsp salt
- 1 tbsp black pepper, ground
- 1 tbsp ground cinnamon
- 1 tbsp garlic powder
- 4 lamb chops

Directions:
1. In a mixing bowl, mix sugar, ground ginger, tarragon, salt, pepper, cinnamon, and garlic.
2. Rub the lamb chops with the mixture and refrigerate for an hour.
3. Meanwhile, preheat your Traeger.
4. Brush the grill grates with oil and place the marinated lamb chops on it. Cook for 5 minutes on each side.
5. Serve and enjoy.

Nutrition Info: Calories 241, Total fat 13.1g, Saturated fat 5.6g, Total carbs 15.8g, Net carbs 15.1g Protein 14.6g, Sugars 13.6g, Fiber 0.7g, Sodium 339.2mg, Potassium 256.7mg

Bloody Mary Flank Steak

Servings: 3
Cooking Time: 14 Minutes
Ingredients:
- 2 cups Smoked Bloody Mary Mix or V8 Juice
- ½ cup vodka
- 1 whole lemon, juiced
- 3 cloves garlic, minced
- 1 tablespoon Worcestershire sauce
- 1 teaspoon ground black pepper
- 1 teaspoon celery salt
- ½ cup vegetable oil
- 1 ½ pound flank steak

Directions:
1. Place all ingredients except for the flank steak in a bowl. Mix until well-combined.

2. Put the flank steak in a plastic bag and pour half of the marinade over. Marinate for at least 24 hours in the fridge.
3. When ready to cook, fire the Grill to 500F. Use desired wood pellets when cooking. Close the lid and preheat for 15 minutes.
4. Drain the flank steak and pat dry using a paper towel.
5. Place on the grill grate and cook for 7 minutes on each side.
6. Meanwhile, place the remaining marinade (unused) in a saucepan and heat until the sauce thickens.
7. Once the steak is cooked, remove from the grill, and allow to rest for 5 minutes before slicing.
8. Pour over the sauce.
Nutrition Info: Calories per serving: 719 ; Protein: 51.9g; Carbs: 15.4g; Fat: 51g Sugar: 6.9g

Grilled Lamb Sandwiches

Servings: 6
Cooking Time: 50 Minutes
Ingredients:
- 1 (4 pounds) boneless lamb.
- 1 cup of raspberry vinegar.
- 2 tablespoons of olive oil.
- 1 tablespoon of chopped fresh thyme.
- 2 pressed garlic cloves.
- 1/4 teaspoon of salt to taste.
- 1/4 teaspoon of ground pepper.
- Sliced bread.

Directions:
1. Using a large mixing bowl, add in the raspberry vinegar, oil, and thyme then mix properly to combine. Add in the lamb, toss to combine then let it sit in the refrigerator for about eight hours or overnight. Next, discard the marinade the season the lamb with salt and pepper to taste. Preheat a Wood Pellet Smoker and grill t0 400-500 degrees F, add in the seasoned lamb and grill for about thirty to forty minutes until it attains a temperature of 150 degrees F. Once cooked, let the lamb cool for a few minutes, slice as desired then serve on the bread with your favorite topping.
Nutrition Info: Calories: 407 Cal Fat: 23 g Carbohydrates: 26 g Protein: 72 g Fiber: 2.3 g

Beautiful Christmas Ham

Servings: 16
Cooking Time: 1 Hour 20 Minutes
Ingredients:
- 1 C. honey
- ¼ C. dark corn syrup

- 1 (7-lb.) ready-to-eat ham
- ¼ C. whole cloves
- ½ C. butter, softened

Directions:
1. Set the temperature of Grill to 325 degrees F and preheat with closed lid for 15 minutes, using charcoal.
2. In a small pan, add honey and corn syrup and cook until heated slightly, stirring continuously.
3. Remove the pan of glaze from heat and set aside.
4. With a sharp knife, score the ham in a cross pattern.
5. Insert whole cloves at the crossings.
6. Coat the ham with butter evenly.
7. Arrange ham in foil-lined roasting pan and top with ¾ of glaze evenly.
8. Place the pan onto the grill and cook for about 1¼ hours, coating with remain glaze after every 10-15 minutes.
9. Remove the ham from grill and place onto a cutting board for about 20-25 minutes before serving.
10. With a sharp knife, cut the ham into desired-sized slices and serve.
Nutrition Info: Calories per serving: 457; Carbohydrates: 29.7g; Protein: 33.2g; Fat: 23.1g; Sugar: 18.7g; Sodium: 2633mg; Fiber: 3.2g

Corned Beef And Cabbage

Servings: 6-8
Cooking Time: 4-5 Hours
Ingredients:
- 1-gallon water
- 1 (3- to 4-pound) point cut corned beef brisket with pickling spice packet
- 1 tablespoon freshly ground black pepper
- 1 tablespoon garlic powder
- ½ cup molasses
- 1 teaspoon ground mustard
- 1 head green cabbage
- 4 tablespoons (½ stick) butter
- 2 tablespoons rendered bacon fat
- 1 chicken bouillon cube, crushed

Directions:
1. Refrigerate overnight, changing the water as often as you remember to do so—ideally, every 3 hours while you're awake—to soak out some of the curing salt initially added.
2. Supply your smoker with wood pellets and follow the manufacturer's specific start-up procedure. Preheat, with the lid closed, to 275°F.
3. Remove the meat from the brining liquid, pat it dry, and generously rub with the black pepper and garlic powder.

4. Put the seasoned corned beef directly on the grill, fat-side up, close the lid, and grill for 2 hours. Remove from the grill when done.
5. In a small bowl, combine the molasses and ground mustard and pour half of this mixture into the bottom of a disposable aluminum pan.
6. Transfer the meat to the pan, fat-side up, and pour the remaining molasses mixture on top, spreading it evenly over the meat. Cover tightly with aluminum foil.
7. Transfer the pan to the grill, close the lid, and continue smoking the corned beef for 2 to 3 hours, or until a meat thermometer inserted in the thickest part reads 185°F.
8. Rest meat
9. Serve.
Nutrition Info: Calories: 295 Cal Fat: 17 g Carbohydrates: 19 g Protein: 18 g Fiber: 6 g

Wood Pellet Grilled Pork Chops

Servings: 6
Cooking Time: 10 Minutes
Ingredients:
- 6 pork chops, thickly cut
- BBQ rub

Directions:
1. Preheat the wood pellet to 450°F.
2. Season the pork chops generously with the bbq rub. Place the pork chops on the grill and cook for 6 minutes or until the internal temperature reaches 145°F.
3. Remove from the grill and let sit for 10 minutes before serving.
4. Enjoy.
Nutrition Info: Calories 264, Total fat 13g, Saturated fat 6g, Total Carbs 4g, Net Carbs 1g, Protein 33g, Sugar 0g, Fiber 3g, Sodium: 66mg

Wood Pellet Grill Teriyaki Beef Jerky

Servings: 10
Cooking Time: 5 Hours
Ingredients:
- 3 cups soy sauce
- 2 cups brown sugar
- 3 garlic cloves
- 2-inch ginger knob, peeled and chopped
- 1 tbsp sesame oil
- 4 lb beef, skirt steak

Directions:
1. Place all the ingredients except the meat in a food processor. Pulse until well mixed.
2. Trim any excess fat from the meat and slice into 1/4 inch slices. Add the steak with the marinade into

a zip lock bag and let marinate for 12-24 hours in a fridge.
3. Set the wood pellet grill to smoke and let preheat for 5 minutes.
4. Arrange the steaks on the grill leaving a space between each. Let smoke for 5 hours.
5. Remove the steak from grill and serve when warm.
Nutrition Info: Calories 80, Total fat 1g, Saturated fat 0g, Total Carbs 7g, Net Carbs 0g, Protein 11g, Sugar 6g, Fiber 0g, Sodium: 390mg

Apple Bourbon Glazed Ham

Servings: 6
Cooking Time: 60 Minutes
Ingredients:
- 1 cup apple jelly
- 2 tablespoons Dijon mustard
- 2 tablespoons bourbon
- 2 tablespoons lemon juice
- ½ teaspoon ground cloves
- 2 cups apple juice
- 1 large ham

Directions:
1. Fire the Grill to 500F. Use maple wood pellets when cooking. Close the lid and preheat for 15 minutes.
2. In a small saucepan, combine the apple jelly, mustard, bourbon, lemon juice, cloves, and apple juice. Cook on low heat to melt the apple jelly. Cook for 5 minutes and set aside.
3. Place the ham in a baking tray and glaze with the reserved mixture.
4. Place on the grill rack and cook for 60 minutes.
5. Once the ham is cooked, remove from the grill, and allow to rest for 20 minutes before slicing.
6. Pour over the remaining glaze.
Nutrition Info: Calories per serving: 283; Protein: 38.7 g; Carbs: 14.7g; Fat: 8g Sugar: 10g

Herby Lamb Chops

Servings: 4
Cooking Time: 2 Hours
Ingredients:
- 8 lamb chops, each about ¾-inch thick, fat trimmed
- For the Marinade:
- 1 teaspoon minced garlic
- Salt as needed
- 1 tablespoon dried rosemary
- Ground black pepper as needed
- ½ tablespoon dried thyme

- 3 tablespoons balsamic vinegar
- 1 tablespoon Dijon mustard
- ½ cup olive oil

Directions:

1. Prepare the marinade and for this, take a small bowl, place all of its ingredients in it and stir until well combined.
2. Place lamb chops in a large plastic bag, pour in marinade, seal the bag, turn it upside down to coat lamb chops with the marinade and let it marinate for a minimum of 4 hours in the refrigerator.
3. When ready to cook, switch on the grill, fill the grill hopper with flavored wood pellets, power the grill on by using the control panel, select 'smoke' on the temperature dial, or set the temperature to 450 degrees F and let it preheat for a minimum of 5 minutes.
4. Meanwhile, remove lamb chops from the refrigerator and bring them to room temperature.
5. When the grill has preheated, open the lid, place lamb chops on the grill grate, shut the grill and smoke for 5 minutes per side until seared.
6. When done, transfer lamb chops to a dish, let them rest for 5 minutes and then serve.

Nutrition Info: Calories: 280 Cal ;Fat: 12.3 g ;Carbs: 8.3 g ;Protein: 32.7 g ;Fiber: 1.2 g

Cheeseburger Hand Pies

Servings: 4
Cooking Time: 10 Minutes

Ingredients:

- ½ pound lean ground beef
- 1 tablespoon minced onion
- 1 tablespoon steak seasoning
- 1 cup shredded Monterey Jack and Colby cheese blend
- 8 slices white American cheese, divided
- 2 (14-ounce) refrigerated prepared pizza dough sheets, divided
- 2 eggs, beaten with 2 tablespoons water (egg wash), divided
- 24 hamburger dill pickle chips
- 2 tablespoons sesame seeds
- 6 slices tomato, for garnish
- Ketchup and mustard, for serving

Directions:

1. Supply your smoker with wood pellets and follow the manufacturer's specific start-up procedure. Preheat, with the lid closed, to 325°F.
2. On your stove top, in a medium sauté pan over medium-high heat, brown the ground beef for 4 to 5 minutes, or until cooked through. Add the minced onion and steak seasoning.

3. Toss in the shredded cheese blend and 2 slices of American cheese, and stir until melted and fully incorporated.
4. Remove the cheeseburger mixture from the heat and set aside.
5. Make sure the dough is well chilled for easier handling. Working quickly, roll out one prepared pizza crust on parchment paper and brush with half of the egg wash.
6. Arrange the remaining 6 slices of American cheese on the dough to outline 6 hand pies.
7. Top each cheese slice with ¼ cup of the cheeseburger mixture, spreading slightly inside the imaginary lines of the hand pies.
8. Place 4 pickle slices on top of the filling for each pie.
9. Top the whole thing with the other prepared pizza crust and cut between the cheese slices to create 6 hand pies.
10. Using kitchen scissors, cut the parchment to further separate the pies, but leave them on the paper.
11. 1Using a fork dipped in egg wash, seal the edges of the pies on all sides. Baste the tops of the pies with the remaining egg wash and sprinkle with the sesame seeds.
12. 1Remove the pies from the parchment paper and gently place on the grill grate. Close the lid and smoke for 5 minutes, then carefully flip and smoke with the lid closed for 5 more minutes, or until browned.
13. 1Top with the sliced tomato and serve with ketchup and mustard.

Bbq Sweet Pepper Meatloaf

Servings: 8
Cooking Time: 3 Hours And 15 Minutes

Ingredients:

- 1 cup chopped red sweet peppers
- 5 pounds ground beef
- 1 cup chopped green onion
- 1 tablespoon salt
- 1 tablespoon ground black pepper
- 1 cup panko bread crumbs
- 2 tablespoon BBQ rub and more as needed
- 1 cup ketchup
- 2 eggs

Directions:

1. Switch on the grill, fill the grill hopper with Texas beef blend flavored wood pellets, power the grill on by using the control panel, select 'smoke' on the temperature dial, or set the temperature to 225 degrees F and let it preheat for a minimum of 5 minutes.

2. Meanwhile, take a large bowl, place all the ingredients in it except for ketchup and then stir until well combined.

3. Shape the mixture into meatloaf and then sprinkle with some BBQ rub.

4. When the grill has preheated, open the lid, place meatloaf on the grill grate, shut the grill, and smoke for 2 hours and 15 minutes.

5. Then change the smoking temperature to 375 degrees F, insert a food thermometer into the meatloaf and cook for 45 minutes or more until the internal temperature of meatloaf reaches 155 degrees F.

6. Brush the top of meatloaf with ketchup and then continue cooking for 15 minutes until glazed. When done, transfer food to a dish, let it rest for 10 minutes, then cut it into slices and serve.

Nutrition Info: Calories: 160.5 Cal ;Fat: 2.8 g ;Carbs: 13.2 g ;Protein: 17.2 g ;Fiber: 1 g

Cowboy Steak

Servings: 4
Cooking Time: 1 Hour
Ingredients:
- 2.5 lb. cowboy cut steaks
- Salt to taste
- Beef rub
- 1/4 cup olive oil
- 2 tablespoons fresh mint leaves, chopped
- ½ cup parsley, chopped
- 1 clove garlic, crushed and minced
- 1 tablespoon lemon juice
- 1 tablespoon lemon zest
- Salt and pepper to taste

Directions:
1. Season the steak with the salt and dry rub.
2. Preheat the wood pellet grill to 225 degrees F for 10 minutes while the lid is closed.
3. Grill the steaks for 45 minutes, flipping once or twice.
4. Increase temperature to 450 degrees F.
5. Put the steaks back to the grill. Cook for 5 minutes per side.
6. In a bowl, mix the remaining ingredients.
7. Serve steaks with the parsley mixture.
8. Tips: Let steak rest for 10 minutes before putting it back to the grill for the second round of cooking.

Roasted Venison Tenderloin

Servings: 4
Cooking Time: 20 Minutes
Ingredients:

- 2 pounds venison
- ¼ cup dry red wine
- 2 cloves garlic, minced
- 2 tablespoons soy sauce
- 1 ½ tablespoons red wine vinegar
- 1 tablespoon rosemary
- 1 teaspoon black pepper
- ½ cup olive oil
- Salt to taste

Directions:
1. Remove the membrane covering the venison. Set aside.
2. Mix the rest of the ingredients in a bowl. Place the venison in the bowl and allow to marinate for at least 5 hours in the fridge.
3. Fire the Grill to 500F. Use desired wood pellets when cooking. Close the lid and preheat for 15 minutes.
4. Remove the venison from the marinade and pat dry using a paper towel.
5. Place on the grill grate and cook for 10 minutes on each side for medium rare.

Nutrition Info: Calories per serving: 611 ; Protein: 68.4g; Carbs: 3.1g; Fat: 34.4g Sugar: 1.6g

Smoked Sausages

Servings: 4
Cooking Time: 3 Hours
Ingredients:
- 3 pounds ground pork
- 1 tablespoon onion powder
- 1 tablespoon garlic powder
- 1 teaspoon curing salt
- 4 teaspoon black pepper
- 1/2 tablespoon salt
- 1/2 tablespoon ground mustard
- Hog casings, soaked
- 1/2 cup ice water

Directions:
1. Switch on the grill, fill the grill hopper with flavored wood pellets, power the grill on by using the control panel, select 'smoke' on the temperature dial, or set the temperature to 225 degrees F and let it preheat for a minimum of 15 minutes.
2. Meanwhile, take a medium bowl, place all the ingredients in it except for water and hog casings, and stir until well mixed.
3. Pour in water, stir until incorporated, place the mixture in a sausage stuffer, then stuff the hog casings and tie the link to the desired length.
4. When the grill has preheated, open the lid, place the sausage links on the grill grate, shut the grill, and smoke for 2 to 3 hours until the internal temperature reaches 155 degrees F.

5. When done, transfer sausages to a dish, let them rest for 5 minutes, then slice and serve.
Nutrition Info: Calories: 230 Cal ;Fat: 22 g ;Carbs: 2 g ;Protein: 14 g ;Fiber: 0 g

Grilled Lamb Kabobs

Servings: 7
Cooking Time: 16 Minutes
Ingredients:
- ½ cup olive oil
- ½ tablespoon salt
- 2 teaspoons black pepper
- 2 tablespoons chopped mint
- ½ tablespoon cilantro, chopped
- 1 teaspoon cumin
- ½ cup lemon juice
- 3 pounds boneless leg of lamb, cut into 2-inch cubes
- 15 apricots, halved and seeded
- 5 onions, cut into wedges

Directions:
1. In a bowl, combine the oil, salt, pepper, mint, cilantro, cumin, and lemon juice.
2. Massage the mixture on to the lamb shoulder and allow to marinate in the fridge for at least 2 hours.
3. Remove the lamb from the marinade and thread the lamb, apricots, and red onion alternatingly on a skewer.
4. When ready to cook, fire the Grill to 400F. Use desired wood pellets when cooking. Close the lid and preheat for 15 minutes.
5. Place the skewers on the grill grate and cook for 8 minutes on each side.
6. Remove from the grill.
Nutrition Info: Calories per serving: 652; Protein: 53.9g; Carbs: 38.1g; Fat: 31.8g Sugar: 29.4g

Reverse-seared Steaks

Servings: 4
Cooking Time: 1 Or 2 Hours
Ingredients:
- 4 (4-ounce) sirloin steaks
- 2 tablespoons olive oil
- Salt
- Freshly ground black pepper
- 4 tablespoons butter

Directions:
1. Supply your with wood pellets and follow the start-up procedure. Preheat the grill, with the lid closed, to 180°F.
2. Rub the steaks all over with olive oil and season both sides with salt and pepper.
3. Place the steaks directly on the grill grate and smoke until their internal temperature reaches 135°F. Remove the steaks from the grill.
4. Place a cast-iron skillet on the grill grate and increase the grill's temperature to 450°F.
5. Place the steaks in the skillet and top each with 1 tablespoon of butter. Cook the steaks until their internal temperature reaches 145°F, flipping once after 2 or 3 minutes. (I recommend reverse-searing over an open flame rather than in the cast-iron skillet, if your grill has that option.) Remove the steaks and serve immediately.

Asian Steak Skewers

Servings: 6
Cooking Time: 1 Hour And 20 Minutes
Ingredients:
- 1 1/2 lbs top sirloin steak
- 6 garlic cloves, minced
- 1 red onion
- 1/3 cup sugar
- 3/4 cup soy sauce
- 1 tbsp ground ginger
- 1/4 cup sesame oil
- 3 tbsp sesame seeds
- 1/4 cup vegetable oil
- Bamboo skewers

Directions:
1. Cut sirloin steak into cubes, about 1 inch.
2. Cut red onion into chunks similar in size to the sirloin steak cubes.
3. In a bowl, combine and whisk soy sauce, sesame oil, vegetable oil, minced garlic, sugar, ginger, and sesame seeds.
4. Add steak to sauce bowl and toss to coat until steak is covered in the sauce.
5. Marinate for at least 1 hour in a refrigerator (if you are in a rush it's ok to skip this part, but you'll sacrifice a little bit of flavor).
6. Preheat pellet grill to 350°F.
7. Thread marinated beef and red onion pieces onto bamboo skewers.
8. Grill the skewers, turning after about 4 minutes. Cook for 8 minutes total or until meat reaches your desired doneness.

Grilled Lamb Chops With Rosemary

Servings: 4
Cooking Time: 12 Minutes
Ingredients:
- ½ cup extra virgin olive oil

- ¼ cup coarsely chopped onion
- 2 cloves of garlic, minced
- 2 tablespoons soy sauce
- 2 tablespoons balsamic vinegar
- 1 tablespoon fresh rosemary
- 2 teaspoons Dijon mustard
- 1 teaspoon Worcestershire sauce
- Salt and pepper to taste
- 4 lamb chops (8 ounce each)

Directions:
1. Heat oil in a saucepan over medium flame and sauté the onion and garlic until fragrant. Place in food processor together with the soy sauce, vinegar, rosemary, mustard, Worcestershire sauce, salt, and pepper. Pulse until smooth. Set aside.
2. Fire the Grill to 500F. Use desired wood pellets when cooking. Close the lid and preheat for 15 minutes.
3. Brush the lamb chops on both sides with the paste.
4. Place on the grill grates and cook for 6 minutes per side or until the internal temperature reaches 135F for medium rare.
5. Serve with the paste if you have leftover.

Nutrition Info: Calories per serving: 442; Protein: 16.7g; Carbs: 6.1g; Fat:38.5 g Sugar: 3.7g

Braised Elk Shank

Servings: 6
Cooking Time: 4 Hours And 10 Minutes
Ingredients:
- 3 elk shanks
- Salt and pepper to taste
- 3 tablespoons canola oil
- 2 whole onions, halved
- 4 cloves of garlic, minced
- 2 dried bay leaves
- 2 cups red wine
- 1 sprig of rosemary
- 2 carrots, peeled and halved lengthwise
- 1 bunch fresh thyme
- 3 quarts beef stock

Directions:
1. Fire the Grill to 500F. Use desired wood pellets when cooking. Place a cast-iron pan on the grill grate. Close the lid and preheat for 15 minutes.
2. Season the shanks with salt and pepper. Place canola oil in the heated cast iron and place the shanks. Close the grill lid and cook for five minutes on each side.
3. Add the onions and garlic and sauté for 1 minute.
4. Stir in the rest of the ingredients.
5. Close the grill lid and cook for 4 hours until soft.

Nutrition Info: Calories per serving: 331 ; Protein: 47.2g; Carbs: 11.5g; Fat: 11.2g Sugar: 5.4g

Wood Pellet Smoked Ribeye Steaks

Servings: 1
Cooking Time: 35 Minutes
Ingredients:
- 2-inch thick ribeye steaks
- Steak rub of choice

Directions:
1. Preheat your pellet grill to low smoke.
2. Sprinkle the steak with your favorite steak rub and place it on the grill. Let it smoke for 25 minutes.
3. Remove the steak from the grill and set the temperature to 400°F.
4. Return the steak to the grill and sear it for 5 minutes on each side.
5. Cook until the desired temperature is achieved; 125°F-rare, 145°F-Medium, and 165°F.-Well done.
6. Wrap the steak with foil and let rest for 10 minutes before serving. Enjoy.

Nutrition Info: Calories 225, Total fat 10.4g, Saturated fat 3.6g, Total Carbs 0.2g, Net Carbs 0.2g, Protein 32.5g, Sugar 0g, Fiber 0g, Sodium: 63mg, Potassium 463mg

Grilled Lambchops

Servings: 3
Cooking Time: 8 Minutes
Ingredients:
- 2 garlic cloves, crushed
- 1 tbsp rosemary leaves, fresh chopped
- 2 tbsp olive oil
- 1 tbsp lemon juice, fresh
- 1 tbsp thyme leaves, fresh
- 1 tbsp salt
- 9 lamb loin chops

Directions:
1. Add the garlic, rosemary, oil, juice, salt, and thyme in a food processor. Pulse until smooth.
2. Rub the marinade on the lamb chops both sides and let marinate for 1 hour in a fridge. Remove from the fridge and let sit at room temperature for 20 minutes before cooking.
3. Preheat your wood pellet smoker to high heat. smoke the lamb chops for 5 minutes on each side.
4. Sear the lamb chops for 3 minutes on each side. Remove from the grill and serve with a green salad.

Nutrition Info: Calories 1140, Total fat 99g, Saturated fat 41g, Total Carbs 1g, Net Carbs 1g, Protein 55g, Sugar0g, Fiber 0g, Sodium: 965mg, Potassium 739mg

Bbq Beef Short Ribs

Servings: 8
Cooking Time: 10 Hours
Ingredients:
- 4 beef short rib racks, membrane removed, containing 4 bones
- 1/2 cup beef rub
- 1 cup apple juice

Directions:
1. Switch on the grill, fill the grill hopper with apple-flavored wood pellets, power the grill on by using the control panel, select 'smoke' on the temperature dial, or set the temperature to 225 degrees F and let it preheat for a minimum of 15 minutes.
2. Meanwhile, prepare the ribs, and for this, sprinkle beef rub on both sides until well coated.
3. When the grill has preheated, open the lid, place ribs on the grill grate bone-side down, shut the grill, and smoke for 10 hours until internal temperature reaches 205 degrees F, spritzing with apple juice every hour.
4. When done, transfer ribs to a cutting board, let rest for 10 minutes, then cut into slices and serve.
Nutrition Info: Calories: 280 Cal ;Fat: 15 g ;Carbs: 17 g ;Protein: 20 g ;Fiber: 1 g

Apple-smoked Pork Tenderloin

Servings: 4 To 6
Cooking Time: 4 To 5 Hours
Ingredients:
- 2 (1-pound) pork tenderloins
- 1 batch Pork Rub

Directions:
1. Supply your smoker with wood pellets and follow the manufacturer's specific start-up procedure. Preheat the grill, with the lid closed, to 180°F.
2. Generously season the tenderloins with the rub. Using your hands, work the rub into the meat.
3. Place the tenderloins directly on the grill grate and smoke for 4 or 5 hours, until their internal temperature reaches 145°F.
4. Remove the tenderloins from the grill and let them rest for 5 to 10 minutes before thinly slicing and serving.

Wet-rubbed St. Louis Ribs

Servings: 3
Cooking Time: 4 Hours
Ingredients:

- 1/2 cup brown sugar
- 1 tbsp cumin, ground
- 1 tbsp Ancho Chile powder
- 1 tbsp smoked paprika
- 1 tbsp garlic salt
- 3 tbsp balsamic vinegar
- 1 Rack St. Louis style ribs
- 2 cup apple juice

Directions:
1. Add all the ingredients except ribs in a mixing bowl and mix until well mixed. Place the rub on both sides of the ribs and let sit for 10 minutes.
2. Set the wood pellet temperature to 180°F and preheat for 15 minutes. Smoke the ribs for 2 hours.
3. Increase the temperature to 250°F and wrap the ribs and apple juice with foil or in tinfoil.
4. Place back the pork and cook for an additional 2 hours.
5. Remove from the grill and let rest for 10 minutes before serving. Enjoy.
Nutrition Info: Calories 210, Total fat 13g, Saturated fat 4g, Total Carbs 0g, Net Carbs 0g, Protein 24g, Sugar 0g, Fiber 0g, Sodium: 85mg

Peppered Beef Tenderloin

Servings: 6
Cooking Time: 1 Hour And 15 Minutes
Ingredients:
- 2 1/2 lb center cut beef tenderloin, trimmed and tied if uneven
- 2 tbsp unsalted butter, room temperature
- 6 tbsp peppercorns, mixed colors
- 1 tbsp kosher salt
- 1 cup parsley, chopped
- Horseradish sauce, on the side
- 4 tbsp Dijon mustard

Directions:
1. Coarsely grind peppercorn mixture into a bowl. Add parsley, mustard, butter, and salt. Mix until thoroughly combined
2. Rub spiced butter mixture generously and thoroughly on all sides of the tenderloin. Coat completely and roll tenderloin in bowl if necessary to soak up as much seasoning as possible.
3. Preheat pellet grill to 450°F4. Place tenderloin on an elevated rack (important) and roast. Use a probe meat thermometer to measure internal temperature. Cook until the center of the tenderloin reaches a temperature of 130°F. This typically takes 30-45 minutes but could be more or less depending on the size of your tenderloin
4. Once tenderloin reaches desired doneness, remove from grill and allow to rest for at least 15 minutes6. Move tenderloin to a cutting board and

slice. Try to catch as many juices as possible. Garnish with additional parsley

Wood Pellet Smoked Lamb Shoulder

Servings: 7
Cooking Time: 1hour 30 Minutes;
Ingredients:
- For Smoked Lamb Shoulder
- 5 lb lamb shoulder, boneless and excess fat trimmed
- 2 tbsp kosher salt
- 2 tbsp black pepper
- 1 tbsp rosemary, dried
- The Injection
- 1 cup apple cider vinegar
- The Spritz
- 1 cup apple cider vinegar
- 1 cup apple juice

Directions:
1. Preheat the wood pellet smoker with a water pan to 225 F.
2. Rinse the lamb in cold water then pat it dry with a paper towel. Inject vinegar to the lamb.
3. Pat the lamb dry again and rub with oil, salt black pepper and rosemary. Tie with kitchen twine.
4. Smoke uncovered for 1 hour then spritz after every 15 minutes until the internal temperature reaches 195 F.
5. Remove the lamb from the grill and place it on a platter. Let cool before shredding it and enjoying it with your favorite side.

Nutrition Info: Calories 243, Total fat 19g, Saturated fat 8g, Total Carbs 0g, Net Carbs 0g, Protein 17g, Sugar 0g, Fiber 1g, Sodium: 63mg, Potassium 234mg

Maple Baby Backs

Servings: 4 To 6
Cooking Time: 4 Hours
Ingredients:
- 2 (2- or 3-pound) racks baby back ribs
- 2 tablespoons yellow mustard
- 1 batch Sweet Brown Sugar Rub
- ½ cup plus 2 tablespoons maple syrup, divided
- 2 tablespoons light brown sugar
- 1 cup Pepsi or other non-diet cola
- ¼ cup The Ultimate BBQ Sauce

Directions:
1. Supply your smoker with wood pellets and follow the manufacturer's specific start-up procedure. Preheat the grill, with the lid closed, to 180°F.
2. Remove the membrane from the backside of the ribs. This can be done by cutting just through the membrane in an X pattern and working a paper towel between the membrane and the ribs to pull it off.
3. Coat the ribs on both sides with mustard and season them with the rub. Using your hands, work the rub into the meat.
4. Place the ribs directly on the grill grate and smoke for 3 hours.
5. Remove the ribs from the grill and place them, bone-side up, on enough aluminum foil to wrap the ribs completely. Drizzle 2 tablespoons of maple syrup over the ribs and sprinkle them with 1 tablespoon of brown sugar. Flip the ribs and repeat the maple syrup and brown sugar application on the meat side.
6. Increase the grill's temperature to 300°F.
7. Fold in three sides of the foil around the ribs and add the cola. Fold in the last side, completely enclosing the ribs and liquid. Return the ribs to the grill and cook for 30 to 45 minutes.
8. Remove the ribs from the grill and unwrap them from the foil.
9. In a small bowl, stir together the barbecue sauce and remaining 6 tablespoons of maple syrup. Use this to baste the ribs. Return the ribs to the grill, without the foil, and cook for 15 minutes to caramelize the sauce.
10. Cut into individual ribs and serve immediately.

Citrus Pork Chops

Servings: 4
Cooking Time: 30 Minutes
Ingredients:
- 2 oranges, sliced into wedges
- 2 lemons, sliced into wedges
- 6 sprigs rosemary, chopped
- 2 sticks butter, softened
- 1 clove garlic, minced
- 4 tablespoons fresh thyme leaves, chopped
- 1 teaspoon black pepper
- 5 pork chops

Directions:
1. Set the wood pellet grill to smoke.
2. Wait for it to establish fire for 5 minutes.
3. Set temperature to high.
4. Squeeze lemons and oranges into a bowl.
5. Stir in the rest of the ingredients except the pork chops.
6. Marinate the pork chops in the mixture for 3 hours.
7. Grill for 10 minutes per side.
8. Tips: Use bone-in pork chops for this recipe.

Crown Rack Of Lamb

Servings: 6
Cooking Time: 30 Minutes
Ingredients:
- 2 racks of lamb. Frenched
- 1 tbsp garlic, crushed
- 1 tbsp rosemary
- 1/2 cup olive oil
- Kitchen twine

Directions:
1. Preheat your to 450F.
2. Rinse the lab with clean cold water then pat it dry with a paper towel.
3. Lay the lamb flat on a chopping board and score a ¼ inch down between the bones. Repeat the process between the bones on each lamb rack. Set aside.
4. In a small mixing bowl, combine garlic, rosemary, and oil. Brush the lamb of rack generously with the mixture.
5. Bend the lamb rack into a semicircle then place the racks together such that the bones will be up and will form a crown shape.
6. Wrap around 4 times starting from the base moving upward. Tie tightly to keep the racks together.
7. Place the lambs on a baking sheet and set in the Traeger. Cook on high heat for 10 minutes. Reduce the temperature to 300F and cook for 20 more minutes or until the internal temperature reaches 130F.
8. Remove the lamb rack from the and let rest while wrapped in a foil for 15 minutes.
9. Serve when hot.
Nutrition Info: Calories 390, Total fat 35g, Saturated fat 15g, Total carbs 0g, Net carbs 0g Protein 17g, Sugars 0g, Fiber 0g, Sodium 65mg

Shredded Pork Tacos

Servings: 8
Cooking Time: 7 Hours
Ingredients:
- 5 lb pork shoulder, bone-in
- Dry Rub
- 3 tbsp. brown sugar
- 1 tbsp. salt
- 1 tbsp. garlic powder
- 1 tbsp. paprika
- 1 tbsp. onion powder
- 1/4 tbsp. cumin
- 1 tbsp. cayenne pepper

Directions:
1. Combine the dry rub ingredients in a mixing bowl then rub the pork roast.
2. Place the pork on the at 250F at indirect heat for 7 hours or until the internal temperature reaches 145F.
3. Remove the pork from the and let rest for 10 minutes before shredding.
4. Serve with tacos and enjoy
Nutrition Info: Calories 566, Total fat 41g, Saturated fat 0g, Total carbs 4g, Net carbs 4g Protein 44g, Sugars 3g, Fiber 0g, Sodium 659mg

Blackened Pork Chops

Servings: 6
Cooking Time: 20 Minutes
Ingredients:
- 6 pork chops
- 1/4 cup blackening seasoning
- Salt and pepper

Directions:
1. Preheat your to 375F.
2. Generously season the pork chops with the blackening seasoning, salt, and pepper.
3. Place the chops on the grill and cook for 8 minutes on one side then flip.
4. Cook until the internal temperature reaches 1420F.
5. Let the pork chops rest for 10 minutes before slicing and serving.
Nutrition Info: Calories 333, Total fat 18g, Saturated fat 6g, Total carbs 1g, Net carbs 0g Protein 40g, Sugars 0g, Fiber 1g, Sodium 3175mg

Buttered Tenderloin

Servings: 8
Cooking Time: 45 Minutes
Ingredients:
- 1 (4-lb.) beef tenderloin, trimmed
- Smoked salt and cracked black pepper, to taste
- 3 tbsp. butter, melted

Directions:
1. Set the temperature of Grill to 300 degrees F and preheat with closed lid for 15 minutes.
2. Season the tenderloin with salt and black pepper generously and then rub with butter.
3. Place the tenderloin onto the grill and cook for about 45 minutes.
4. Remove the tenderloin from grill and place onto a cutting board for about 10-15 minutes before serving.
5. With a sharp knife, cut the tenderloin into desired-sized slices and serve.
Nutrition Info: Calories per serving: 505; Carbohydrates: 0g; Protein: 65.7g; Fat: 25.1g; Sugar: 0g; Sodium: 184mg; Fiber: 0g

Buttermilk Pork Loin Roast

Servings: 4-6
Cooking Time: 3-3.5 Hours
Ingredients:
- 1 (3-3½lb) pork loin roast
- 1-quart buttermilk brine

Directions:
1. Cut out all fat and silver skin of pork roast.
2. Place the roast and buttermilk brine in a 1-gallon sealable plastic bag or brine container.
3. Refrigerate overnight, rotating roast every few hours if possible.
4. Use of wood pellet smokers and grills
5. Remove the salted pork roast from the salt water and dry it lightly with a paper towel.
6. In the part where the roast is thickest, incorporate the meat probe
7. Set the wood pellet smoker grill for indirect cooking and preheat to 225 ° F using apple or cherry pellets.
8. Suck roast for 3 to 3 1/2 hours until internal temperature reaches 145 ° F.
9. Place the roast under a loose foil tent for 15 minutes and carve it towards the grain.
Nutrition Info: Calories: 126 Cal Fat: 3 g Carbohydrates: 2 g Protein: 21 g Fiber: 0 g

Braised Mediterranean Beef Brisket

Servings: 16
Cooking Time: 5 Hours
Ingredients:
- 3 tablespoons dried rosemary
- 2 tablespoons cumin seeds, ground
- 2 tablespoons dried coriander
- 1 tablespoon dried oregano
- 2 teaspoons ground cinnamon
- ½ teaspoon salt
- 8 pounds beef brisket, sliced into chunks
- 1 cup beef stock

Directions:
1. Mix the rosemary, cumin, coriander, oregano, cinnamon, and salt in a bowl.
2. Massage the spice mix into the beef brisket and allow to rest in the fridge for 12 hours.
3. When ready to cook, fire the Grill to 180F. Use desired wood pellets when cooking. Close the lid and preheat for 15 minutes.
4. Place the brisket fat side down on the grill grate and cook for 4 hours.
5. After 4 hours, turn up the heat to 250F.
6. Continue cooking the beef brisket until the internal temperature reaches 160F. Remove and place on a foil. Crimp the edges of the foil to create a sleeve. Pour in the beef stock.
7. Return the brisket in the foil sleeve and continue cooking for another hour.
Nutrition Info: Calories per serving: 453 ; Protein: 33.5g; Carbs: 1g; Fat: 34g Sugar: 0.1g

Smoked Baby Back Ribs

Servings: 10
Cooking Time: 2 Hours
Ingredients:
- 3 racks baby back ribs
- Salt and pepper to taste

Directions:
1. Clean the ribs by removing the extra membrane that covers it. Pat dry the ribs with a clean paper towel. Season the baby back ribs with salt and pepper to taste. Allow to rest in the fridge for at least 4 hours before cooking.
2. Once ready to cook, fire the Grill to 225F. Use hickory wood pellets when cooking the ribs. Close the lid and preheat for 15 minutes.
3. Place the ribs on the grill grate and cook for two hours. Carefully flipping the ribs halfway through the cooking time for even cooking.
Nutrition Info: Calories per serving: 1037; Protein: 92.5g; Carbs: 1.4g; Fat: 73.7g Sugar: 0.2g

Smoked Texas Bbq Brisket

Servings: 4
Cooking Time: 5 Hours
Ingredients:
- 6 pounds whole packer brisket
- Commercial BBQ rub of your choice

Directions:
1. Trim the brisket from any membrane and loose fat. Trim the fat side to ¼ inch thick.
2. Season all sides of the brisket with the BBQ rub and allow to rest for 30 minutes inside the fridge.
3. When ready to cook, fire the Grill to 275F. Use mesquite wood pellets when cooking. Close the lid and preheat for 15 minutes.
4. Place the brisket fat side up on the grill grate and cook for 5 hours or until the internal temperature reaches 165F.
5. Once cooked, remove the brisket from the grill and allow to rest before slicing.
Nutrition Info: Calories per serving: 703; Protein: 93.9g; Carbs: 0 g; Fat: 33.4g Sugar: 0g

Wood Pellet Grilled Shredded Pork Tacos

Servings: 8
Cooking Time: 7 Hours
Ingredients:
- 5 lb pork shoulder, bone-in
- Dry Rub
- 3 tbsp brown sugar
- 1 tbsp salt
- 1 tbsp garlic powder
- 1 tbsp paprika
- 1 tbsp onion powder
- 1/4 tbsp cumin
- 1 tbsp cayenne pepper

Directions:
1. Mix all the dry rub ingredients and rub on the pork shoulder.
2. Preheat the grill to 275°F and cook the pork directly for 6 hours or until the internal temperature has reached 145°F.
3. If you want to fall off the bone tender pork, then cook until the internal temperature is 190°F.
4. Let rest for 10 minutes before serving. Enjoy

Nutrition Info: Calories 566, Total fat 41g, Saturated fat 15g, Total Carbs 4g, Net Carbs 4g, Protein 44g, Sugar 3g, Fiber 0g, Sodium: 659mg

Cocoa Crusted Pork Tenderloin

Servings: 5
Cooking Time: 25 Minutes
Ingredients:
- 1 pork tenderloin
- 1/2 tbsp fennel, ground
- 2 tbsp cocoa powder, unsweetened
- 1 tbsp smoked paprika
- 1/2 tbsp kosher salt
- 1/2 tbsp black pepper
- 1 tbsp extra virgin olive oil
- 3 green onion

Directions:
1. Remove the silver skin and the connective tissues from the pork loin.
2. Combine the rest of the ingredients in a mixing bowl, then rub the mixture on the pork. Refrigerate for 30 minutes.
3. Preheat the wood pellet grill for 15 minutes with the lid closed.
4. Sear all sides of the loin at the front of the grill then reduce the temperature to 350°F and move the pork to the centre grill.
5. Cook for 15 more minutes or until the internal temperature is 145°F.
6. Remove from grill and let rest for 10 minutes before slicing. Enjoy

Nutrition Info: Calories 264, Total fat 13.1g, Saturated fat 6g, Total Carbs 4.6g, Net Carbs 1.2g, Protein 33g, Sugar 0g, Fiber 3.4g, Sodium: 66mg

Best Pork Butt Roast

Servings: 14
Cooking Time: 14 Hours
Ingredients:
- ¼ C. brown sugar
- 2 tbsp. New Mexico chile powder
- 2 tbsp. garlic powder
- Salt, to taste
- 1 (7-lb.) fresh pork butt roast

Directions:
1. Set the temperature of Grill to 200-225 degrees F and preheat with closed lid for 15 minutes.
2. In a bowl, place all ingredients except for pork roast and mix well.
3. Rub the pork roast with spice mixture generously.
4. Arrange a roasting rack in a drip pan.
5. Place the pork roast onto the rack in drip pan.
6. Place the drip pan onto the grill and cook for about 8-14 hours or until desired doneness.
7. Remove the roast from grill and place onto a cutting board for about 10-15 minutes before slicing.
8. With a sharp knife, cut the roast into desired-sized slices and serve.

Nutrition Info: Calories per serving: 439; Carbohydrates: 4g; Protein: 40.g; Fat: 28.3g; Sugar: 2.9g; Sodium: 164mg; Fiber: 0.5g

Summertime Pork Chops

Servings: 4
Cooking Time: 1 Hour 35 Minutes
Ingredients:
- For Brine:
- 8 C. apple juice
- 1 C. light brown sugar
- ½ C. kosher salt
- ½ C. BBQ rub
- For Pork Chops:
- 4 thick-cut pork loin chops
- 2 tbsp. BBQ rub
- 1 tbsp. Montreal steak seasoning

Directions:
1. For brine: in a large pan, add 4 C. of apple juice and cook until heated completely.
2. Add sugar, salt and dry rub and cook until dissolved, stirring continuously.
3. Remove the pan from heat and stir in remaining apple juice.

4. Set aside to cool completely.
5. In a larger zip lock, add brine mixture and chops.
6. Seal the bag and refrigerate for about 2 hours.
7. Set the temperature of Grill to 250 degrees F and preheat with closed lid for 15 minutes.
8. Remove the chops from brine and set aside for about 10-15 minutes.
9. Now, season the chops with BBQ rub and steak seasoning evenly
10. Place the chops onto the grill and cook for about 1½ hours.
11. Remove the chops from grill and set aside for about 5 minutes before serving.

Nutrition Info: Calories per serving: 609; Carbohydrates: 92.6g; Protein: 29.5; Fat: 12.6; Sugar: 84.2g; Sodium: 299mg; Fiber: 1g

6. For sauce: in a bowl, add all ingredients and beat until well combined.
7. Remove the pan from grill and drain excess grease from meatloaf.
8. Place sauce over meatloaf evenly and place the pan onto the grill.
9. Cook for about 30 minutes.
10. Remove the meatloaf from grill and set aside for about 10 minutes before serving.
11. Carefully, invert the meatloaf onto a platter.
12. Cut the meatloaf into desired-sized slices and serve.

Nutrition Info: Calories per serving: 423; Carbohydrates: 15.7g; Protein: 54.9; Fat: 13; Sugar: 12.3g; Sodium: 299mg; Fiber: 1.5g

Comforting Beef Meatloaf

Servings: 8
Cooking Time: 2½ Hours
Ingredients:
- For Meatloaf:
- 3 lb. ground beef
- 3 eggs
- ½ C. panko breadcrumbs
- 1 (10-oz.) can diced tomatoes with green chile peppers
- 1 large white onion, chopped
- 2 hot banana peppers, chopped
- 2 tbsp. seasoned salt
- 2 tsp. liquid smoke flavoring
- 2 tsp. smoked paprika
- 1 tsp. onion salt
- 1 tsp. garlic salt
- Salt and freshly ground black pepper, to taste
- For Sauce:
- ½ C. ketchup
- ¼ C. tomato-based chile sauce
- ¼ C. white sugar
- 2 tsp. Worcestershire sauce
- 2 tsp. hot pepper sauce
- 1 tsp. red pepper flakes, crushed
- 1 tsp. red chili pepper
- Salt and freshly ground black pepper, to taste

Directions:
1. Set the temperature of Grill to 225 degrees F and preheat with closed lid for 15 minutes, using charcoal.
2. Grease a loaf pan.
3. For meatloaf: in a bowl, add all ingredients and with your hands, mix until well combined.
4. Place the mixture into prepared loaf pan evenly.
5. Place the pan onto the grill and cook for about 2 hours.

Smoked Lamb Meatballs

Servings: 5
Cooking Time: 1 Hour
Ingredients:
- 1 lb lamb shoulder, ground
- 3 garlic cloves, finely diced
- 3 tbsp shallot, diced
- 1 tbsp salt
- 1 egg
- 1/2 tbsp pepper
- 1/2 tbsp cumin
- 1/2 tbsp smoked paprika
- 1/4 tbsp red pepper flakes
- 1/4 tbsp cinnamon, ground
- 1/4 cup panko breadcrumbs

Directions:
1. Set the wood pellet smoker to 250 F using a fruitwood.
2. In a mixing bowl, combine all meatball ingredients until well mixed.
3. Form small-sized balls and place them on a baking sheet. Place the baking sheet in the smoker and smoke until the internal temperature reaches 160 F.
4. Remove from the smoker and serve. Enjoy.

Nutrition Info: Calories 73, Total fat 5.2g, Saturated fat 1.6g, Total Carbs 1.5g, Net Carbs 1.4g, Protein 4.9g, Sugar 0g, Fiber 0.1g, Sodium: 149mg, Potassium 72mg

Beef Shoulder Clod

Servings: 16-20
Cooking Time: 12-16 Hours
Ingredients:
- ½ cup sea salt
- ½ cup freshly ground black pepper

- 1 tablespoon red pepper flakes
- 1 tablespoon minced garlic
- 1 tablespoon cayenne pepper
- 1 tablespoon smoked paprika
- 1 (13- to 15-pound) beef shoulder clod

Directions:
1. Combine spices
2. Generously apply it to the beef shoulder.
3. Supply your smoker with wood pellets and follow the manufacturer's specific start-up procedure. Preheat, with the lid closed, to 250°F.
4. Put the meat on the grill grate, close the lid, and smoke for 12 to 16 hours, or until a meat thermometer inserted deeply into the beef reads 195°F. You may need to cover the clod with aluminum foil toward the end of smoking to prevent overbrowning.
5. Let the meat rest and serve

Nutrition Info: Calories: 290 Cal Fat: 22 g Carbohydrates: 0 g Protein: 20 g Fiber: 0 g

French Onion Burgers

Servings: 4
Cooking Time: 20-25 Minutes
Ingredients:
- 1-pound lean ground beef
- 1 tablespoon minced garlic
- 1 teaspoon Better Than Bouillon Beef Base
- 1 teaspoon dried chives
- 1 teaspoon freshly ground black pepper
- 8 slices Gruyère cheese, divided
- ½ cup soy sauce
- 1 tablespoon extra-virgin olive oil
- 1 teaspoon liquid smoke
- 3 medium onions, cut into thick slices (do not separate the rings)
- 1 loaf French bread, cut into 8 slices
- 4 slices provolone cheese

Directions:
1. In a large bowl, mix together the ground beef, minced garlic, beef base, chives, and pepper until well blended.
2. Divide the meat mixture and shape into 8 thin burger patties.
3. Top each of 4 patties with one slice of Gruyère, then top with the remaining 4 patties to create 4 stuffed burgers.
4. Supply your smoker with wood pellets and follow the manufacturer's specific start-up procedure. Preheat, with the lid closed, to 425°F.
5. Arrange the burgers directly on one side of the grill, close the lid, and smoke for 10 minutes. Flip and smoke with the lid closed for 10 to 15 minutes more, or until a meat thermometer inserted in the burgers

reads 160°F. Add another Gruyère slice to the burgers during the last 5 minutes of smoking to melt.
6. Meanwhile, in a small bowl, combine the soy sauce, olive oil, and liquid smoke.
7. Arrange the onion slices on the grill and baste on both sides with the soy sauce mixture. Smoke with the lid closed for 20 minutes, flipping halfway through.
8. Lightly toast the French bread slices on the grill. Layer each of 4 slices with a burger patty, a slice of provolone cheese, and some of the smoked onions. Top each with another slice of toasted French bread. Serve immediately.

Nutrition Info: Calories: 704 Cal Fat: 43 g Carbohydrates: 28 g Protein: 49 g Fiber: 2 g

Roasted Pork With Blackberry Sauce

Servings: 4
Cooking Time: 50 Minutes
Ingredients:
- 2 lb. pork tenderloin
- 2 tablespoons dried rosemary
- Salt and pepper to taste
- 2 tablespoons olive oil
- 12 blackberries, sliced
- 1 cup balsamic vinegar
- 4 tablespoons sugar

Directions:
1. Preheat the wood pellet grill to 350 degrees F for 15 minutes while the lid is closed.
2. Season the pork with the rosemary, salt and pepper.
3. In a pan over high heat, pour in the oil and sear pork for 2 minutes per side.
4. Transfer to the grill and cook for 20 minutes.
5. Take the pan off the grill.
6. Let rest for 10 minutes.
7. In a pan over medium heat, simmer the blackberries in vinegar and sugar for 30 minutes.
8. Pour sauce over the pork and serve.
9. Tips: You can also simmer the pork in the blackberry sauce for 10 minutes.

Smoked Apple Pork Tenderloin

Servings: 8
Cooking Time: 3 Hours
Ingredients:
- ½ cup apple juice
- 3 tablespoons honey
- 3 tablespoons Pork and Poultry Rub
- ¼ cup brown sugar
- 2 tablespoons thyme leaves
- ½ tablespoons black pepper

93

- 2 pork tenderloin roasts, skin removed

Directions:
1. In a bowl, mix together the apple juice, honey, pork and poultry rub, brown sugar, thyme, and black pepper. Whisk to mix everything.
2. Add the pork loins into the marinade and allow to soak for 3 hours in the fridge.
3. Once ready to cook, fire the Grill to 225F. Use hickory wood pellets when cooking the ribs. Close the lid and preheat for 15 minutes.
4. Place the marinated pork loin on the grill grate and cook until the temperature registers to 145F. Cook for 2 to 3 hours on low heat.
5. Meanwhile, place the marinade in a saucepan. Place the saucepan in the grill and allow to simmer until the sauce has reduced.
6. Before taking the meat out, baste the pork with the reduced marinade.
7. Allow to rest for 10 minutes before slicing.

Nutrition Info: Calories per serving: 203 ; Protein: 26.4g; Carbs: 15.4g; Fat: 3.6g Sugar: 14.6g

Supper Beef Roast

Servings: 7
Cooking Time: 3 Hours
Ingredients:
- 3-1/2 beef top round
- 3 tbsp vegetable oil
- Prime rib rub
- 2 cups beef broth
- 1 russet potato, peeled and sliced
- 2 carrots, peeled and sliced
- 2 celery stalks, chopped
- 1 onion, sliced
- 2 thyme sprigs

Directions:
1. Rub the roast with vegetable oil and place it on the roasting fat side up. Season with prime rib rub then pour the beef broth.
2. Set the temperature to 500°F and preheat the wood pellet grill for 15 minutes with the lid closed.
3. Cook for 30 minutes or until the roast is well seared.
4. Reduce temperature to 225°F. Add the veggies and thyme and cover with foil. Cook for 3 more hours o until the internal temperature reaches 135°F.
5. Remove from the grill and let rest for 10 minutes. Slice against the grain and serve with vegetables and the pan dippings.
6. Enjoy.

Nutrition Info: Calories 697, Total fat 10g, Saturated fat 4.7g, Total Carbs 127g, Net Carbs 3106g, Protein 34g, Sugar 14g, Fiber 22g, Sodium: 3466mg, Potassium 2329mg

Lamb Skewers

Servings: 6
Cooking Time: 8-12 Minutes
Ingredients:
- One lemon, juiced
- Two crushed garlic cloves
- Two chopped red onions
- One t. chopped thyme
- Pepper
- Salt
- One t. oregano
- 1/3 c. oil
- ½ t. cumin
- Two pounds cubed lamb leg

Directions:
1. Refrigerate the chunked lamb.
2. The remaining ingredients should be mixed together. Add in the meat. Refrigerate overnight.
3. Pat the meat dry and thread onto some metal or wooden skewers. Wooden skewers should be soaked in water.
4. Add wood pellets to your smoker and follow your cooker's startup procedure. Preheat your smoker, with your lid closed, until it reaches 450.
5. Grill, covered, for 4-6 minutes on each side.
6. Serve.

Nutrition Info: Calories: 201 Cal Fat: 9 g Carbohydrates: 3 g Protein: 24 g Fiber: 1 g

Smoked, Candied, And Spicy Bacon

Servings: 10
Cooking Time: 40 Minutes
Ingredients:
- Center-cut bacon - 1 lb.
- Brown sugar - ½ cup
- Maple syrup - ½ cup
- Hot sauce - 1 tbsp
- Pepper - ½ tbsp

Directions:
1. Mix the maple syrup, brown sugar, hot sauce, and pepper in a bowl.
2. Preheat your wood pellet grill to 300 degrees.
3. Line a baking sheet and place the bacon slices on it.
4. Generously spread the brown sugar mix on both sides of the bacon slices.
5. Place the pan on the wood pellet grill for 20 minutes. Flip the bacon pieces.
6. Leave them for another 15 minutes until the bacon looks cooked, and the sugar is melted.

7. Remove from the grill and let it stay for 10-15 minutes.
8. Voila! Your bacon candy is ready!
Nutrition Info: Carbohydrates: 37 g Protein: 9 g Sodium: 565 mg Cholesterol: 49 mg

Stunning Prime Rib Roast

Servings: 10
Cooking Time: 3 Hours 50 Minutes
Ingredients:
- 1 (5-lb.) prime rib roast
- Salt, to taste
- 5 tbsp. olive oil
- 4 tsp. dried rosemary, crushed
- 2 tsp. garlic powder
- 1 tsp. onion powder
- 1 tsp. paprika
- ½ tsp. cayenne pepper
- Freshly ground black pepper, to taste

Directions:
1. Season the roast with salt generously.
2. With a plastic wrap, cover the roast and refrigerate for about 24 hours.
3. In a bowl, mix together remaining ingredients and set aside for about 1 hour.
4. Rub the roast with oil mixture from both sides evenly.
5. Arrange the roast in a large baking sheet and refrigerate for about 6-12 hours.
6. Set the temperature of Grill to 225-230 degrees F and preheat with closed lid for 15 minutes. , using pecan wood chips.
7. Place the roast onto the grill and cook for about 3-3½ hours.
8. Meanwhile, preheat the oven to 500 degrees F.
9. Remove the roast from grill and place onto a large baking sheet.
10. Place the baking sheet in oven and roast for about 15-20 minutes.
11. Remove the roast from oven and place onto a cutting board for about 10-15 minutes before serving.
12. With a sharp knife, cut the roast into desired-sized slices and serve.
Nutrition Info: Calories per serving: 605; Carbohydrates: 3.8g; Protein: 38g; Fat: 47.6g; Sugar: 0.3g; Sodium: 1285mg; Fiber: 0.3g Stunning Prime Rib Roast

Perfect Beef Tenderloin

Servings: 12
Cooking Time: 1 Hour 19 Minutes
Ingredients:
- 1 (5-lb.) beef tenderloin, trimmed

- Kosher salt, to taste
- ¼ C. olive oil
- Freshly ground black pepper, to taste

Directions:
1. With kitchen strings, tie the tenderloin at 7-8 places.
2. Season tenderloin with kosher salt generously.
3. With a plastic wrap, cover the tenderloin and set aside at room temperature for about 1 hour.
4. Set the temperature of Grill to 225-250 degrees F and preheat with closed lid for 15 minutes.
5. Now, coat tenderloin with oil evenly and season with black pepper.
6. Arrange tenderloin onto the grill and cook for about 55-65 minutes.
7. Now, place cooking grate directly over hot coals and sear tenderloin for about 2 minutes per side.
8. Remove the tenderloin from grill and place onto a cutting board for about 10-15 minutes before serving.
9. With a sharp knife, cut the tenderloin into desired-sized slices and serve.
Nutrition Info: Calories per serving: 425; Carbohydrates: 0g; Protein: 54.7g; Fat: 21.5g; Sugar: 0g; Sodium: 123mg; Fiber: 0g

Bacon Stuffed Smoked Pork Loin

Servings: 4 To 6
Cooking Time: 1 Hour
Ingredients:
- 3 Pound Pork Loin, Butterflied
- As Needed Pork Rub
- 1/4 Cup Walnuts, Chopped
- 1/3 Cup Craisins
- 1 Tablespoon Oregano, fresh
- 1 Tablespoon fresh thyme
- 6 Pieces Asparagus, fresh
- 6 Slices Bacon, sliced
- 1/3 Cup Parmesan cheese, grated
- As Needed Bacon Grease

Directions:
1. Lay down 2 large pieces of butcher's twine on your work surface. Place butterflied pork loin perpendicular to twine.
2. Season the inside of the pork loin with the pork rub.
3. On one end of the loin, layer in a line all of the ingredients, beginning with the chopped walnuts, craisins, oregano, thyme, and asparagus.
4. Add bacon and top with the parmesan cheese.
5. Starting at the end with all of the fillings, carefully roll up the pork loin and secure on both ends with butcher's twine.

6. Roll the pork loin in the reserved bacon grease and season the outside with more Pork Rub.

7. When ready to cook, set temperature to 180°F and preheat, lid closed for 15 minutes. Place stuffed pork loin directly on the grill grate and smoke for 1 hour.

8. Remove the pork loin; increase the temperature to 350°F and allow to preheat.

9. Place the loin back on the and grill for approximately 30 to 45 minutes or until the temperature reads 135°F on an instant-read thermometer.

10. Move the pork loin to a plate and tent it with aluminum foil. Let it rest for 15 minutes before slicing and serving. Enjoy!

Slow Roasted Shawarma

Servings: 6-8
Cooking Time: 4 Hours 55 Minutes
Ingredients:
- Top sirloin - 5.5 lbs
- Lamb fat - 4.5 lbs
- Boneless, skinless chicken thighs- 5.5 lbs
- Pita bread
- rub - 4 tbsp
- Double skewer - 1
- Large yellow onions - 2
- Variety of topping options such as tomatoes, cucumbers, pickles, tahini, Israeli salad, fries, etc.
- Cast iron griddle

Directions:
1. Assemble the stack of shawarma the night before you wish to cook it.

2. Slice all the meat and fat into ½-inch slices. Place them into 3 bowls. If you partially freeze them, it will be much easier to slice them.

3. Season the bowl with the rub, massaging it thoroughly into the meat.

4. Place half a yellow onion on the bottom of the skewers to ensure a firm base. Add 2 layers at a time from each bowl. Try to make the entire stack symmetrical. Place the other 2 onions on top. Wrap them in plastic wrap and refrigerate overnight.

5. When the meat is ready to cook, preheat the pellet grill for about 15 minutes with the lid closed at a temperature of 275 degrees Fahrenheit.

6. Lay the shawarma directly on the grill grate and cook it for at least 3-4 hours. Rotate the skewers at least once.

7. Remove them from the grill and increase its temperature to 445 degrees Fahrenheit. When the grill is preheating, place a cast iron griddle directly on the grill grate and brush it with some olive oil.

8. Once the griddle is hot enough, place the shawarma directly on the cast iron. Sear it on each side for 5-10 minutes. Remove it from the grill and slice off the edges. Repeat the process with the remaining shawarma.

9. Serve in pita bread and favorite toppings, such as tomatoes, cucumbers, Israeli salad, fries, pickles, or tahini. Enjoy!

Nutrition Info: Carbohydrates: 4.6 g Protein: 30.3 g Fat: 26.3 g Sodium: 318.7 mg Cholesterol: 125.5 mg

Smoked Beef Roast

Servings: 6
Cooking Time: 6 Hours
Ingredients:
- 1-3/4 pounds beef sirloin tip roast
- 1/2 cup barbeque rub
- 2 bottles amber beer
- 1 bottle BBQ sauce

Directions:
1. Turn the onto the smoke setting.

2. Rub the beef with barbeque rub until well coated then place on the grill. Let smoke for 4 hours while flipping every 1 hour.

3. Transfer the beef to a pan and add the beer. The beef should be 1/2 way covered.

4. Braise the beef until fork tender. It will take 3 hours on the stovetop and 60 minutes on the instant pot.

5. Remove the beef from the ban and reserve 1 cup of the cooking liquid.

6. Use 2 forks to shred the beef into small pieces then return to the pan with the reserved braising liquid. Add BBQ sauce and stir well then keep warm until serving. You can also reheat if it gets cold.

Nutrition Info: Calories: 829 Cal Fat: 18 g Carbohydrates: 4 g Protein: 86 g Fiber: 0 g

FISH AND SEAFOOD RECIPES

Wine Infused Salmon

Servings: 4
Cooking Time: 5 Hours
Ingredients:
- 2 C. low-sodium soy sauce
- 1 C. dry white wine
- 1 C. water
- ½ tsp. Tabasco sauce
- 1/3 C. sugar
- ¼ C. salt
- ½ tsp. garlic powder
- ½ tsp. onion powder
- Freshly ground black pepper, to taste
- 4 (6-oz.) salmon fillets

Directions:
1. In a large bowl, add all ingredients except salmon and stir until sugar is dissolved.
2. Add salmon fillets and coat with brine well.
3. Refrigerate, covered overnight.
4. Remove salmon from bowl and rinse under cold running water.
5. With paper towels, pat dry the salmon fillets.
6. Arrange a wire rack in a sheet pan.
7. Place the salmon fillets onto wire rack, skin side down and set aside to cool for about 1 hour.
8. Set the temperature of Grill to 165 degrees F and preheat with closed lid for 15 minutes, using charcoal.
9. Place the salmon fillets onto the grill, skin side down and cook for about 3-5 hours or until desired doneness.
10. Remove the salmon fillets from grill and serve hot.

Nutrition Info: Calories per serving: 377; Carbohydrates: 26.3g; Protein: 41.1g; Fat: 10.5g; Sugar: 25.1g; Sodium: 14000mg; Fiber: 0g

Dijon-smoked Halibut

Servings: 6
Cooking Time: 2 Hours
Ingredients:
- 4 (6-ounce) halibut steaks
- ¼ cup extra-virgin olive oil
- 2 teaspoons kosher salt
- 1 teaspoon freshly ground black pepper
- ½ cup mayonnaise
- ½ cup sweet pickle relish
- ¼ cup finely chopped sweet onion
- ¼ cup chopped roasted red pepper
- ¼ cup finely chopped tomato
- ¼ cup finely chopped cucumber
- 2 tablespoons Dijon mustard
- 1 teaspoon minced garlic

Directions:
1. Rub the halibut steaks with the olive oil and season on both sides with the salt and pepper. Transfer to a plate, cover with plastic wrap, and refrigerate for 4 hours.
2. Supply your smoker with wood pellets and follow the manufacturer's specific start-up procedure. Preheat, with the lid closed, to 200°F.
3. Remove the halibut from the refrigerator and rub with the mayonnaise.
4. Put the fish directly on the grill grate, close the lid, and smoke for 2 hours, or until opaque and an instant-read thermometer inserted in the fish reads 140°F.
5. While the fish is smoking, combine the pickle relish, onion, roasted red pepper, tomato, cucumber, Dijon mustard, and garlic in a medium bowl. Refrigerate the mustard relish until ready to serve.
6. Serve the halibut steaks hot with the mustard relish.

Grilled Shrimp Scampi

Servings: 4
Cooking Time: 10 Minutes
Ingredients:
- 1 lb raw shrimp, tail on
- 1/2 cup salted butter, melted
- 1/4 cup white wine, dry
- 1/2 tbsp fresh garlic, chopped
- 1 tbsp lemon juice
- 1/2 tbsp garlic powder
- 1/2 tbsp salt

Directions:
1. Preheat your wood pellet grill to 400°F with a cast iron inside.
2. In a mixing bowl, mix butter, wine, garlic, and juice then pour in the cast iron. Let the mixture mix for 4 minutes.
3. Sprinkle garlic and salt on the shrimp then place it on the cast iron. Grill for 10 minutes with the lid closed.
4. Remove the shrimp from the grill and serve when hot. Enjoy.

Nutrition Info: Calories 298, Total fat 24g, Saturated fat 15g, Total Carbs 2g, Net Carbs 2g, Protein 16g, Sugar 0g, Fiber 0g, Sodium: 1091mg, Potassium 389mg

Sriracha Salmon

Servings: 4
Cooking Time: 25 Minutes
Ingredients:
- 3-pound salmon, skin on
- For the Marinade:
- 1 teaspoon lime zest
- 1 tablespoon minced garlic
- 1 tablespoon grated ginger
- Sea salt as needed
- Ground black pepper as needed
- 1/4 cup maple syrup
- 2 tablespoons soy sauce
- 2 tablespoons Sriracha sauce
- 1 tablespoon toasted sesame oil
- 1 tablespoon rice vinegar
- 1 teaspoon toasted sesame seeds

Directions:
1. Prepare the marinade and for this, take a small bowl, place all of its ingredients in it, stir until well combined, and then pour the mixture into a large plastic bag.
2. Add salmon in the bag, seal it, turn it upside down to coat salmon with the marinade and let it marinate for a minimum of 2 hours in the refrigerator.
3. When ready to cook, switch on the grill, fill the grill hopper with flavored wood pellets, power the grill on by using the control panel, select 'smoke' on the temperature dial, or set the temperature to 450 degrees F and let it preheat for a minimum of 5 minutes.
4. Meanwhile, take a large baking sheet, line it with parchment paper, place salmon on it skin-side down and then brush with the marinade.
5. When the grill has preheated, open the lid, place baking sheet containing salmon on the grill grate, shut the grill and smoke for 25 minutes until thoroughly cooked.
6. When done, transfer salmon to a dish and then serve.

Nutrition Info: Calories: 360 Cal ;Fat: 21 g ;Carbs: 28 g ;Protein: 16 g ;Fiber: 1.5 g

Rockfish

Servings: 6
Cooking Time: 20 Minutes
Ingredients:
- 6 rockfish fillets
- 1 lemon, sliced
- 3/4 tbsp salt
- 2 tbsp fresh dill, chopped
- 1/2 tbsp garlic powder
- 1/2 tbsp onion powder

- 6 tbsp butter

Directions:
1. Preheat your to 400F.
2. Season the fish with salt, dill, garlic and onion powder on both sides then place it in a baking dish.
3. Place a pat of butter and a lemon slice on each fillet. Place the baking dish in the and close the lid.
4. Cook for 20 minutes or until the fish is no longer translucent and is flaky.
5. Remove from and let rest for 5 minutes before serving.

Nutrition Info: Calories 270, Total fat 17g, Saturated fat 9g, Total carbs 2g, Net carbs 2g Protein 28g, Sugars 0g, Fiber 0g, Sodium 381mg

Crazy Delicious Lobster Tails

Servings: 4
Cooking Time: 25 Minutes
Ingredients:
- ½ C. butter, melted
- 2 garlic cloves, minced
- 2 tsp. fresh lemon juice
- Salt and freshly ground black pepper, to taste
- 4 (8-oz.) lobster tails

Directions:
1. Set the temperature of Grill to 450 degrees F and preheat with closed lid for 15 minutes.
2. In a metal pan, add all ingredients except for lobster tails and mix well.
3. Place the pan onto the grill and cook for about 10 minutes.
4. Meanwhile, cut down the top of the shell and expose lobster meat.
5. Remove pan of butter mixture from grill.
6. Coat the lobster meat with butter mixture.
7. Place the lobster tails onto the grill and cook for about 15 minutes, coating with butter mixture once halfway through.
8. Remove from grill and serve hot.

Nutrition Info: Calories per serving: 409; Carbohydrates: 0.6g; Protein: 43.5g; Fat: 24.9g; Sugar: 0.1g; Sodium: 1305mg; Fiber: 0g

Grilled Shrimp

Servings: 4
Cooking Time: 15 Minutes
Ingredients:
- Jumbo shrimp peeled and cleaned - 1 lb.
- Oil - 2 tbsp
- Salt - ½ tbsp
- Skewers - 4-5
- Pepper - ⅛ tbsp
- Garlic salt - ½ tbsp

Directions:
1. Preheat the wood pellet grill to 375 degrees.
2. Mix all the ingredients in a small bowl.
3. After washing and drying the shrimp, mix it well with the oil and seasonings.
4. Add skewers to the shrimp and set the bowl of shrimp aside.
5. Open the skewers and flip them.
6. Cook for 4 more minutes. Remove when the shrimp is opaque and pink.

Nutrition Info: Carbohydrates: 1.3 g Protein: 19 g Fat: 1.4 g Sodium: 805 mg Cholesterol: 179 mg

Oysters In The Shell

Servings: 4
Cooking Time: 20 Minutes
Ingredients:
- 8 medium oysters, unopened, in the shell, rinsed and scrubbed
- 1 batch Lemon Butter Mop for Seafood

Directions:
1. Supply your smoker with wood pellets and follow the manufacturer's specific start-up procedure. Preheat the grill, with the lid closed, to 375°F.
2. Place the unopened oysters directly on the grill grate and grill for about 20 minutes, or until the oysters are done and their shells open.
3. Discard any oysters that do not open. Shuck the remaining oysters, transfer them to a bowl, and add the mop. Serve immediately.

Charleston Crab Cakes With Remoulade

Servings: 4
Cooking Time: 45 Minutes
Ingredients:
- 1¼ cups mayonnaise
- ¼ cup yellow mustard
- 2 tablespoons sweet pickle relish, with its juices
- 1 tablespoon smoked paprika
- 2 teaspoons Cajun seasoning
- 2 teaspoons prepared horseradish
- 1 teaspoon hot sauce
- 1 garlic clove, finely minced
- 2 pounds fresh lump crabmeat, picked clean
- 20 butter crackers (such as Ritz brand), crushed
- 2 tablespoons Dijon mustard
- 1 cup mayonnaise
- 2 tablespoons freshly squeezed lemon juice
- 1 tablespoon salted butter, melted
- 1 tablespoon Worcestershire sauce
- 1 tablespoon Old Bay seasoning
- 2 teaspoons chopped fresh parsley
- 1 teaspoon ground mustard
- 2 eggs, beaten
- ¼ cup extra-virgin olive oil, divided

Directions:
1. For the remoulade:
2. In a small bowl, combine the mayonnaise, mustard, pickle relish, paprika, Cajun seasoning, horseradish, hot sauce, and garlic.
3. Refrigerate until ready to serve.
4. For the crab cakes:
5. Supply your smoker with wood pellets and follow the manufacturer's specific start-up procedure. Preheat, with the lid closed, to 375°F.
6. Spread the crabmeat on a foil-lined baking sheet and place over indirect heat on the grill, with the lid closed, for 30 minutes.
7. Remove from the heat and let cool for 15 minutes.
8. While the crab cools, combine the crushed crackers, Dijon mustard, mayonnaise, lemon juice, melted butter, Worcestershire sauce, Old Bay, parsley, ground mustard, and eggs until well incorporated.
9. Fold in the smoked crabmeat, then shape the mixture into 8 (1-inch-thick) crab cakes.
10. In a large skillet or cast-iron pan on the grill, heat 2 tablespoons of olive oil. Add half of the crab cakes, close the lid, and smoke for 4 to 5 minutes on each side, or until crispy and golden brown.
11. Remove the crab cakes from the pan and transfer to a wire rack to drain. Pat them to remove any excess oil.
12. Repeat steps 6 and 7 with the remaining oil and crab cakes.
13. Serve the crab cakes with the remoulade.

Wood Pellet Garlic Dill Smoked Salmon

Servings: 12
Cooking Time: 4 Hours
Ingredients:
- 2 salmon fillets
- Brine
- 4 cups water
- 1 cup brown sugar
- 1/3 cup kosher salt
- Seasoning
- 3 tbsp minced garlic
- 1 tbsp fresh dill, chopped

Directions:
1. In a zip lock bag, combine the brine ingredients until all sugar has dissolved. Place the salmon in the bag and refrigerate overnight.
2. Remove the salmon from the brine, rinse with water and pat dry with a paper towel. Let it rest for 2-4 hours at room temperature.

3. Season the salmon with garlic and dill generously.
4. Fire up the wood pellet grill to smoke and place the salmon on a cooling rack that is coated with cooking spray.
5. Place the rack in the smoker and close the lid.
6. Smoke the salmon for 4 hours until the smoke is between 130-180°F.
7. Remove the salmon from the grill and serve with crackers. Enjoy
Nutrition Info: Calories 139, Total fat 5g, Saturated fat 1g, Total Carbs 16g, Net Carbs 16g, Protein 9g, Sugar 0g, Fiber 0g, Sodium: 3143mg

Lobster Tail

Servings: 2
Cooking Time: 25 Minutes
Ingredients:
- 2 lobster tails
- Salt
- Freshly ground black pepper
- 1 batch Lemon Butter Mop for Seafood

Directions:
1. Supply your smoker with wood pellets and follow the manufacturer's specific start-up procedure. Preheat the grill, with the lid closed, to 375°F.
2. Using kitchen shears, slit the top of the lobster shells, through the center, nearly to the tail. Once cut, expose as much meat as you can through the cut shell.
3. Season the lobster tails all over with salt and pepper.
4. Place the tails directly on the grill grate and grill until their internal temperature reaches 145°F. Remove the lobster from the grill and serve with the mop on the side for dipping.

Fish Fillets With Pesto

Servings: 6
Cooking Time: 15 Minutes
Ingredients:
- 2 cups fresh basil
- 1 cup parsley, chopped
- 1/2 cup walnuts
- 1/2 cup olive oil
- 1 cup Parmesan cheese, grated
- Salt and pepper to taste
- 4 white fish fillets

Directions:
1. Preheat the wood pellet grill to high for 15 minutes while the lid is closed.
2. Add all the ingredients except fish to a food processor.
3. Pulse until smooth. Set aside.

4. Season fish with salt and pepper.
5. Grill for 6 to 7 minutes per side.
6. Serve with the pesto sauce.
7. Tips: You can also spread a little bit of the pesto on the fish before grilling.

Buttered Crab Legs

Servings: 4
Cooking Time: 10 Minutes
Ingredients:
- 12 tablespoons butter
- 1 tablespoon parsley, chopped
- 1 tablespoon tarragon, chopped
- 1 tablespoon chives, chopped
- 1 tablespoon lemon juice
- 4 lb. king crab legs, split in the center

Directions:
1. Set the wood pellet grill to 375 degrees F.
2. Preheat it for 15 minutes while lid is closed.
3. In a pan over medium heat, simmer the butter, herbs and lemon juice for 2 minutes.
4. Place the crab legs on the grill.
5. Pour half of the sauce on top.
6. Grill for 10 minutes.
7. Serve with the reserved butter sauce.
8. Tips: You can also use shrimp for this recipe.

Halibut With Garlic Pesto

Servings: 4
Cooking Time: 10 Minutes
Ingredients:
- 4 halibut fillets
- 1 cup olive oil
- Salt and pepper to taste
- 1/4 cup garlic, chopped
- 1/4 cup pine nuts

Directions:
1. Set the wood pellet grill to smoke.
2. Establish fire for 5 minutes.
3. Set temperature to high.
4. Place a cast iron on a grill.
5. Season fish with salt and pepper.
6. Add fish to the pan.
7. Drizzle with a little oil.
8. Sear for 4 minutes per side.
9. Prepare the garlic pesto by pulsing the remaining ingredients in the food processor until smooth.
10. Serve fish with garlic pesto.
11. Tips: You can also use other white fish fillets for this recipe.

Salmon With Togarashi

Servings: 3
Cooking Time: 20 Minutes
Ingredients:
- 1 salmon fillet
- 1/4 cup olive oil
- 1/2 tbsp kosher salt
- 1 tbsp Togarashi seasoning

Directions:
1. Preheat your to 400F.
2. Place the salmon on a sheet lined with non-stick foil with the skin side down.
3. Rub the oil into the meat then sprinkle salt and Togarashi.
4. Place the salmon on the grill and cook for 20 minutes or until the internal temperature reaches 145F with the lid closed.
5. Remove from the and serve when hot.

Nutrition Info: Calories 119, Total fat 10g, Saturated fat 2g, Total carbs 0g, Net carbs 0g Protein 0g, Sugars 0g, Fiber 0g, Sodium 720mg

Cod With Lemon Herb Butter

Servings: 4
Cooking Time: 15 Minutes
Ingredients:
- 4 tablespoons butter
- 1 clove garlic, minced
- 1 tablespoon tarragon, chopped
- 1 tablespoon lemon juice
- 1 teaspoon lemon zest
- Salt and pepper to taste
- 1 lb. cod fillet

Directions:
1. Preheat the wood pellet grill to high for 15 minutes while the lid is closed.
2. In a bowl, mix the butter, garlic, tarragon, lemon juice and lemon zest, salt and pepper.
3. Place the fish in a baking pan.
4. Spread the butter mixture on top.
5. Bake the fish for 15 minutes.
6. Tips: You can also use other white fish fillet for this recipe.

Blackened Salmon

Servings: 4
Cooking Time: 30 Minutes
Ingredients:
- 2 lb. salmon, fillet, scaled and deboned
- 2 tablespoons olive oil
- 4 tablespoons sweet dry rub
- 1 tablespoon cayenne pepper

- 2 cloves garlic, minced

Directions:
1. Turn on your wood pellet grill.
2. Set it to 350 degrees F.
3. Brush the salmon with the olive oil.
4. Sprinkle it with the dry rub, cayenne pepper, and garlic.
5. Grill for 5 minutes per side.

Nutrition Info: Calories: 460Fat: 23 gCholesterol: 140 mgCarbohydrates: 7 g Fiber: 5 g Sugars: 2 g Protein: 50 g

Blackened Catfish

Servings: 4
Cooking Time: 40 Minutes
Ingredients:
- Spice blend
- 1teaspoon granulated garlic
- 1/4 teaspoon cayenne pepper
- 1/2 cup Cajun seasoning
- 1teaspoon ground thyme
- 1teaspoon ground oregano
- 1teaspoon onion powder
- 1tablespoon smoked paprika
- 1teaspoon pepper
- Fish
- 4 catfish fillets
- Salt to taste
- 1/2 cup butter

Directions:
1. In a bowl, combine all the ingredients for the spice blend.
2. Sprinkle both sides of the fish with the salt and spice blend.
3. Set your wood pellet grill to 450 degrees F.
4. Heat your cast iron pan and add the butter. Add the fillets to the pan.
5. Cook for 5 minutes per side.
6. Serving Suggestion: Garnish with lemon wedges.
7. Tip: Smoke the catfish for 20 minutes before seasoning.

Nutrition Info: Calories: 181.5 Fat: 10.5 g Cholesterol: 65.8 mg Carbohydrates: 2.9 g Fiber: 1.8 g Sugars: 0.4 g Protein: 19.2 g

Wood-fired Halibut

Servings: 4
Cooking Time: 20 Minutes
Ingredients:
- 1 pound halibut fillet
- 1 batch Dill Seafood Rub

Directions:

1. Supply your smoker with wood pellets and follow the manufacturer's specific start-up procedure. Preheat the grill, with the lid closed, to 325°F.
2. Sprinkle the halibut fillet on all sides with the rub. Using your hands, work the rub into the meat.
3. Place the halibut directly on the grill grate and grill until its internal temperature reaches 145°F. Remove the halibut from the grill and serve immediately.

Grilled Teriyaki Salmon

Servings: 4
Cooking Time: 30 Minutes
Ingredients:
- 1 salmon fillet
- 1/8 cup olive oil
- 1/2 tbsp salt
- 1/4 tbsp pepper
- 1/4 tbsp garlic salt
- 1/4 cup butter, sliced
- 1/4 teriyaki sauce
- 1 tbsp sesame seeds

Directions:
1. Preheat the grill to 400°F.
2. Place the salmon fillet on a non-stick foil sheet. Drizzle the salmon with oil, seasonings, and butter on top.
3. Pace the foil tray on the grill and close the lid. Cook for 8 minutes then open the lid.
4. Brush the salmon with teriyaki sauce and repeat after every 5 minutes until all sauce is finished. The internal temperature should be 145°F.
5. Remove the salmon from the grill and sprinkle with sesame seeds.
6. Serve and enjoy with your favorite side dish.
Nutrition Info: Calories 296, Total fat 25g, Saturated fat 10g, Total Carbs 3g, Net Carbs 3g, Protein 14g, Sugar 3g, Fiber 0g, Sodium: 1179mg, Potassium 459mg

Lobster Tails

Servings: 4
Cooking Time: 35 Minutes
Ingredients:
- 2 lobster tails, each about 10 ounces
- For the Sauce:
- 2 tablespoons chopped parsley
- 1/4 teaspoon garlic salt
- 1 teaspoon paprika
- 1/4 teaspoon ground black pepper
- 1/4 teaspoon old bay seasoning
- 8 tablespoons butter, unsalted

- 2 tablespoons lemon juice

Directions:
1. Switch on the grill, fill the grill hopper with flavored wood pellets, power the grill on by using the control panel, select 'smoke' on the temperature dial, or set the temperature to 450 degrees F and let it preheat for a minimum of 15 minutes.
2. Meanwhile, prepare the sauce and for this, take a small saucepan, place it over medium-low heat, add butter in it and when it melts, add remaining ingredients for the sauce and stir until combined, set aside until required.
3. Prepare the lobster and for this, cut the shell from the middle to the tail by using kitchen shears and then take the meat from the shell, keeping it attached at the base of the crab tail.
4. Then butterfly the crab meat by making a slit down the middle, then place lobster tails on a baking sheet and pour 1 tablespoon of sauce over each lobster tail, reserve the remaining sauce.
5. When the grill has preheated, open the lid, place crab tails on the grill grate, shut the grill and smoke for 30 minutes until opaque.
6. When done, transfer lobster tails to a dish and then serve with the remaining sauce.
Nutrition Info: Calories: 290 Cal ;Fat: 22 g ;Carbs: 1 g ;Protein: 20 g ;Fiber: 0.3 g

Wood Pellet Grilled Scallops

Servings: 4
Cooking Time: 15 Minutes
Ingredients:
- 2 lb sea scallops, dried with a paper towel
- 1/2 tbsp garlic salt
- 2 tbsp kosher salt
- 4 tbsp salted butter
- Squeeze lemon juice

Directions:
1. Preheat the wood pellet grill to 400°F with the cast pan inside.
2. Sprinkle with both salts, pepper on both sides of the scallops.
3. Place the butter on the cast iron then add the scallops. Close the lid and cook for 8 minutes.
4. Flip the scallops and close the lid once more. Cook for 8 more minutes.
5. Remove the scallops from the grill and give a lemon squeeze. Serve immediately and enjoy.
Nutrition Info: Calories 177, Total fat 7g, Saturated fat 4g, Total Carbs 6g, Net Carbs 6g, Protein 23g, Sugar 0g, Fiber 0g, Sodium: 1430mg, Potassium 359mg

Grilled Lingcod

Servings: 6
Cooking Time: 15 Minutes
Ingredients:
- 2 lb lingcod fillets
- 1/2 tbsp salt
- 1/2 tbsp white pepper
- 1/4 tbsp cayenne
- Lemon wedges

Directions:
1. Preheat the wood pellet grill to 375°F.
2. Place the lingcod on a parchment paper and season it with salt, white pepper, cayenne pepper then top with the lemon.
3. Place the fish on the grill and cook for 15 minutes or until the internal temperature reaches 145°F.
4. Serve and enjoy.

Nutrition Info: Calories 245, Total fat 2g, Saturated fat 0g, Total Carbs 2g, Net Carbs 1g, Protein 52g, Sugar 1g, Fiber 1g, Sodium: 442mg, Potassium 649mg

Pacific Northwest Salmon

Servings: 4
Cooking Time: 1 Hour, 15 Minutes
Ingredients:
- 1 (2-pound) half salmon fillet
- 1 batch Dill Seafood Rub
- 2 tablespoons butter, cut into 3 or 4 slices

Directions:
1. Supply your smoker with wood pellets and follow the manufacturer's specific start-up procedure. Preheat the grill, with the lid closed, to 180°F.
2. Season the salmon all over with the rub. Using your hands, work the rub into the flesh.
3. Place the salmon directly on the grill grate, skin-side down, and smoke for 1 hour.
4. Place the butter slices on the salmon, equally spaced. Increase the grill's temperature to 300°F and continue to cook until the salmon's internal temperature reaches 145°F. Remove the salmon from the grill and serve immediately.

Togarashi Smoked Salmon

Servings: 10
Cooking Time: 20 Hours 15 Minutes
Ingredients:
- Salmon filet - 2 large
- Togarashi for seasoning
- For Brine:
- Brown sugar - 1 cup

- Water - 4 cups
- Kosher salt - ⅓ cup

Directions:
1. Remove all the thorns from the fish filet.
2. Mix all the brine ingredients until the brown sugar is dissolved completely.
3. Put the mix in a big bowl and add the filet to it.
4. Leave the bowl to refrigerate for 16 hours.
5. After 16 hours, remove the salmon from this mix. Wash and dry it.
6. Place the salmon in the refrigerator for another 2-4 hours. (This step is important. DO NOT SKIP IT.)
7. Season your salmon filet with Togarashi.
8. Start the wood pellet grill with the 'smoke' option and place the salmon on it.
9. Smoke for 4 hours.
10. Make sure the temperature does not go above 180 degrees or below 130 degrees.
11. Remove from the grill and serve it warm with a side dish of your choice.

Nutrition Info: Carbohydrates: 19 g Protein: 10 g Fat: 6 g Sodium: 3772 mg Cholesterol: 29 mg

Mango Shrimp

Servings: 4
Cooking Time: 15 Minutes
Ingredients:
- 1lb. shrimp, peeled and deveined but tail intact
- 2 tablespoons olive oil
- Mango seasoning

Directions:
1. Turn on your wood pellet grill.
2. Preheat it to 425 degrees F.
3. Coat the shrimp with the oil and season with the mango seasoning.
4. Thread the shrimp into skewers.
5. Grill for 3 minutes per side.
6. Serving Suggestion: Garnish with chopped parsley.

Nutrition Info: Calories: 223.1 Fat: 4.3 g Cholesterol: 129.2 mg Carbohydrates: 29.2 g Fiber: 4.4 g Sugars: 15. 6g Protein: 19.5 g

Spot Prawn Skewers

Servings: 6
Cooking Time: 10 Minutes
Ingredients:
- 2 lb spot prawns
- 2 tbsp oil
- Salt and pepper to taste

Directions:
1. Preheat your to 400F.

2. Skewer your prawns with soaked skewers then generously sprinkle with oil, salt, and pepper.
3. Place the skewers on the grill and cook with the lid closed for 5 minutes on each side.
4. Remove the skewers and serve when hot.
Nutrition Info: Calories 221, Total fat 7g, Saturated fat 1g, Total carbs 2g, Net carbs 2g Protein 34g, Sugars 0g, Fiber 0g, Sodium 1481mg

Jerk Shrimp

Servings: 12
Cooking Time: 6 Minutes
Ingredients:
- 2 pounds shrimp, peeled, deveined
- 3 tablespoons olive oil
- For the Spice Mix:
- 1 teaspoon garlic powder
- 1 teaspoon of sea salt
- 1/4 teaspoon ground cayenne
- 1 tablespoon brown sugar
- 1/8 teaspoon smoked paprika
- 1 tablespoon smoked paprika
- 1/4 teaspoon ground thyme
- 1 lime, zested

Directions:
1. Switch on the grill, fill the grill hopper with flavored wood pellets, power the grill on by using the control panel, select 'smoke' on the temperature dial, or set the temperature to 450 degrees F and let it preheat for a minimum of 5 minutes.
2. Meanwhile, prepare the spice mix and for this, take a small bowl, place all of its ingredients in it and stir until mixed.
3. Take a large bowl, place shrimps in it, sprinkle with prepared spice mix, drizzle with oil and toss until well coated.
4. When the grill has preheated, open the lid, place shrimps on the grill grate, shut the grill and smoke for 3 minutes per side until firm and thoroughly cooked.
5. When done, transfer shrimps to a dish and then serve.
Nutrition Info: Calories: 131 Cal ;Fat: 4.3 g ;Carbs: 0 g ;Protein: 22 g ;Fiber: 0 g

Grilled Lobster Tail

Servings: 4
Cooking Time: 15 Minutes
Ingredients:
- 2 (8 ounces each) lobster tails
- 1/4 tsp old bay seasoning
- ½ tsp oregano

- 1 tsp paprika
- Juice from one lemon
- 1/4 tsp Himalayan salt
- 1/4 tsp freshly ground black pepper
- 1/4 tsp onion powder
- 2 tbsp freshly chopped parsley
- ¼ cup melted butter

Directions:
1. Slice the tail in the middle with a kitchen shear. Pull the shell apart slightly and run your hand through the meat to separate the meat partially
2. Combine the seasonings
3. Drizzle lobster tail with lemon juice and season generously with the seasoning mixture.
4. Preheat your wood pellet smoker to 450°F, using apple wood pellets.
5. Place the lobster tail directly on the grill grate, meat side down. Cook for about 15 minutes.
6. The tails must be pulled off and it must cool down for a few minutes
7. Drizzle melted butter over the tails.
8. Serve and garnish with fresh chopped parsley.
Nutrition Info: Calories: 146 Cal Fat: 11.7 g Carbohydrates: 2.1 g Protein: 9.3 g Fiber: 0.8 g

Lobster Tail

Servings: 2
Cooking Time: 15 Minutes
Ingredients:
- 10 oz lobster tail
- 1/4 tbsp old bay seasoning
- 1/4 tbsp Himalayan salt
- 2 tbsp butter, melted
- 1 tbsp fresh parsley, chopped

Directions:
1. Preheat your to 450F.
2. Slice the tail down the middle then season it with bay seasoning and salt.
3. Place the tails directly on the grill with the meat side down. Grill for 15 minutes or until the internal temperature reaches 140F.
4. Remove from the and drizzle with butter.
5. Serve when hot garnished with parsley.
Nutrition Info: Calories 305, Total fat 14g, Saturated fat 8g, Total carbs 5g, Net carbs 5g Protein 38g, Sugars 0g, Fiber 0g, Sodium 684mg

Wood Pellet Salt And Pepper Spot Prawn Skewers

Servings: 6
Cooking Time: 10 Minutes
Ingredients:

- 2 lb spot prawns, clean
- 2 tbsp oil
- Salt and pepper to taste

Directions:
1. Preheat your grill to 400°F.
2. Meanwhile, soak the skewers then skewer with the prawns.
3. Brush with oil then season with salt and pepper to taste.
4. Place the skewers in the grill, close the lid, and cook for 5 minutes on each side.
5. Remove from the grill and serve. Enjoy.

Nutrition Info: Calories 221, Total fat 7g, Saturated fat 1g, Total Carbs 2g, Net Carbs 2g, Protein 34g, Sugar 0g, Fiber 0g, Sodium: 1481mg, Potassium 239mg

Grilled King Crab Legs

Servings: 4
Cooking Time: 25 Minutes
Ingredients:
- 4 pounds king crab legs (split)
- 4 tbsp lemon juice
- 2 tbsp garlic powder
- 1 cup butter (melted)
- 2 tsp brown sugar
- 2 tsp paprika
- Black pepper (depends to your liking)

Directions:
1. In a mixing bowl, combine the lemon juice, butter, sugar, garlic, paprika and pepper.
2. Arrange the split crab on a baking sheet, split side up. Drizzle ¾ of the butter mixture over the crab legs. Configure your pellet grill for indirect cooking and preheat it to 225°F, using mesquite wood pellets.
3. Arrange the crab legs onto the grill grate, shell side down. Cover the grill and cook 25 minutes.
4. Remove the crab legs from the grill. Serve and top with the remaining butter mixture.

Nutrition Info: Calories: 480 Cal Fat: 53.2 g Carbohydrates: 6.1 g Protein: 88.6 g Fiber: 1.2 g

Smoked Scallops

Servings: 6
Cooking Time: 15 Minutes
Ingredients:
- 2 pounds sea scallops
- 4 tbsp salted butter
- 2 tbsp lemon juice
- ½ tsp ground black pepper
- 1 garlic clove (minced)
- 1 kosher tsp salt

- 1 tsp freshly chopped tarragon

Directions:
1. Let the scallops dry using paper towels and drizzle all sides with salt and pepper to season
2. Place you're a cast iron pan in your grill and preheat the grill to 400°F with lid closed for 15 minutes.
3. Combine the butter and garlic in hot cast iron pan. Add the scallops and stir. Close grill lid and cook for 8 minutes. Flip the scallops and cook for an additional 7 minutes.
4. Remove the scallop from heat and let it rest for a few minutes.
5. Stir in the chopped tarragon. Serve and top with lemon juice.

Nutrition Info: Calories: 204 Cal Fat: 8.9 g Carbohydrates: 4 g Protein: 25.6 g Fiber: 0.1 g

Yummy Buttery Clams

Servings: 6
Cooking Time: 8 Minutes
Ingredients:
- 24 littleneck clams
- ½ C. cold butter, chopped
- 2 tbsp. fresh parsley, minced
- 3 garlic cloves, minced
- 1 tsp. fresh lemon juice

Directions:
1. Set the temperature of Grill to 450 degrees F and preheat with closed lid for 15 minutes.
2. Scrub the clams under cold running water.
3. In a large casserole dish, mix together remaining ingredients.
4. Place the casserole dish onto the grill.
5. Now, arrange the clams directly onto the grill and cook for about 5-8 minutes or until they are opened. (Discard any that fail to open).
6. With tongs, carefully transfer the opened clams into the casserole dish and remove from grill.
7. Serve immediately.

Nutrition Info: Calories per serving: 306; Carbohydrates: 6.4g; Protein: 29.3g; Fat: 7.6g; Sugar: 0.1g; Sodium: 237mg; Fiber: 0.1g

Wood Pellet Grilled Lobster Tail

Servings: 2
Cooking Time: 15 Minutes
Ingredients:
- 10 oz lobster tail
- 1/4 tbsp old bay seasoning
- 1/4 tbsp Himalayan sea salt
- 2 tbsp butter, melted
- 1 tbsp fresh parsley, chopped

Directions:
1. Preheat the wood pellet to 450°F.
2. Slice the tails down the middle using a knife.
3. Season with seasoning and salt then place the tails on the grill grate.
4. Grill for 15 minutes or until the internal temperature reaches 140°F..
5. Remove the tails and drizzle with butter and garnish with parsley.
6. Serve and enjoy.

Nutrition Info: Calories 305, Total fat 14g, Saturated fat 8g, Total Carbs 5g, Net Carbs 5g, Protein 18g, Sugar 0g, Fiber 0g, Sodium: 685mg, Potassium 159mg

Super-tasty Trout

Servings: 8
Cooking Time: 5 Hours
Ingredients:
- 1 (7-lb.) whole lake trout, butterflied
- ½ C. kosher salt
- ½ C.fresh rosemary, chopped
- 2 tsp. lemon zest, grated finely

Directions:
1. Rub the trout with salt generously and then, sprinkle with rosemary and lemon zest.
2. Arrange the trout in a large baking dish and refrigerate for about 7-8 hours.
3. Remove the trout from baking dish and rinse under cold running water to remove the salt.
4. With paper towels, pat dry the trout completely.
5. Arrange a wire rack in a sheet pan.
6. Place the trout onto the wire rack, skin side down and refrigerate for about 24 hours.
7. Set the temperature of Grill to 180 degrees F and preheat with closed lid for 15 minutes, using charcoal.
8. Place the trout onto the grill and cook for about 2-4 hours or until desired doneness.
9. Remove the trout from grill and place onto a cutting board for about 5 minutes before serving.

Nutrition Info: Calories per serving: 633; Carbohydrates: 2.4g; Protein: 85.2g; Fat: 31.8g; Sugar: 0g; Sodium: 5000mg; Fiber: 1.6g

Citrus Salmon

Servings: 6
Cooking Time: 30 Minutes
Ingredients:
- 2 (1-lb.) salmon fillets
- Salt and freshly ground black pepper, to taste
- 1 tbsp. seafood seasoning
- 2 lemons, sliced

- 2 limes, sliced

Directions:
1. Set the temperature of Grill to 225 degrees F and preheat with closed lid for 15 minutes.
2. Season the salmon fillets with salt, black pepper and seafood seasoning evenly.
3. Place the salmon fillets onto the grill and top each with lemon and lime slices evenly.
4. Cook for about 30 minutes.
5. Remove the salmon fillets from grill and serve hot.

Nutrition Info: Calories per serving: 327; Carbohydrates: 1g; Protein: 36.1g; Fat: 19.8g; Sugar: 0.2g; Sodium: 237mg; Fiber: 0.3g

Peppercorn Tuna Steaks

Servings: 3
Cooking Time: 10 Minutes
Ingredients:
- ¼ cup of salt
- 2 pounds yellowfin tuna
- ¼ cup Dijon mustard
- Freshly ground black pepper
- 2 tablespoons peppercorn

Directions:
1. Take a large-sized container and dissolve salt in warm water (enough water to cover fish)
2. Transfer tuna to the brine and cover, refrigerate for 8 hours
3. Preheat your smoker to 250 degrees Fahrenheit with your preferred wood
4. Remove tuna from bring and pat it dry
5. Transfer to grill pan and spread Dijon mustard all over
6. Season with pepper and sprinkle peppercorn on top
7. Transfer tuna to smoker and smoker for 1 hour
8. Enjoy!

Nutrition Info: Calories: 707 Fats: 57g Carbs: 10g Fiber: 2g

Smoked Shrimp

Servings: 6
Cooking Time: 10 Minutes
Ingredients:
- 1 lb tail-on shrimp, uncooked
- 1/2 tbsp onion powder
- 1/2 tbsp garlic powder
- 1/2 tbsp salt
- 4 tbsp teriyaki sauce
- 2 tbsp green onion, minced
- 4 tbsp sriracha mayo

Directions:

1. Peel the shrimp shells leaving the tail on then wash well and rise.
2. Drain well and pat dry with a paper towel.
3. Preheat your to 450F.
4. Season the shrimp with onion powder, garlic powder, and salt. Place the shrimp in the and cook for 6 minutes on each side.
5. Remove the shrimp from the and toss with teriyaki sauce then garnish with onions and mayo.
Nutrition Info: Calories 87, Total fat 0g, Saturated fat 0g, Total carbs 2g, Net carbs 2g Protein 16g, Sugars 0g, Fiber 0g, Sodium 1241mg

Grilled Blackened Salmon

Servings: 4
Cooking Time: 30 Minutes
Ingredients:
- 4 salmon fillet
- Blackened dry rub
- Italian seasoning powder

Directions:
1. Season salmon fillets with dry rub and seasoning powder.
2. Grill in the wood pellet grill at 325 degrees F for 10 to 15 minutes per side.
3. Tips: You can also drizzle salmon with lemon juice

Wood Pellet Grilled Salmon Sandwich

Servings: 4
Cooking Time: 15 Minutes
Ingredients:
- Salmon Sandwiches
- 4 salmon fillets
- 1 tbsp olive oil
- Fin and feather rub
- 1 tbsp salt
- 4 toasted bun
- Butter lettuce
- Dill Aioli
- 1/2 cup mayonnaise
- 1/2 tbsp lemon zest
- 2 tbsp lemon juice
- 1/4 tbsp salt
- 1/2 tbsp fresh dill, minced

Directions:
1. Mix all the dill aioli ingredients and place them in the fridge.
2. Preheat the wood pellet grill to 450°F.
3. Brush the salmon fillets with oil, rub, and salt. Place the fillets on the grill and cook until the internal temperature reaches 135°F.

4. Remove the fillets from the grill and let rest for 5 minutes.
5. Spread the aioli on the buns then top with salmon, lettuce, and the top bun.
6. Serve when hot.
Nutrition Info: Calories 852, Total fat 54g, Saturated fat 10g, Total Carbs 30g, Net Carbs 28g, Protein 57g, Sugar 5g, Fiber 2g, Sodium: 1268mg, Potassium 379mg

Grilled Salmon

Servings: 4
Cooking Time: 25 Minutes
Ingredients:
- 1 (2-pound) half salmon fillet
- 3 tablespoons mayonnaise
- 1 batch Dill Seafood Rub

Directions:
1. Supply your smoker with wood pellets and follow the manufacturer's specific start-up procedure. Preheat the grill, with the lid closed, to 325°F.
2. Using your hands, rub the salmon fillet all over with the mayonnaise and sprinkle it with the rub.
3. Place the salmon directly on the grill grate, skin-side down, and grill until its internal temperature reaches 145°F. Remove the salmon from the grill and serve immediately.

Omega-3 Rich Salmon

Servings: 6
Cooking Time: 20 Minutes
Ingredients:
- 6 (6-oz.) skinless salmon fillets
- 1/3 C. olive oil
- ¼ C. spice rub
- ¼ C. honey
- 2 tbsp. Sriracha
- 2 tbsp. fresh lime juice

Directions:
1. Set the temperature of Grill to 300 degrees F and preheat with closed lid for 15 minutes.
2. Coat salmon fillets with olive oil and season with rub evenly.
3. In a small bowl, mix together remaining ingredients.
4. Arrange salmon fillets onto the grill, flat-side up and cook for about 7-10 minutes per side, coating with honey mixture once halfway through.
5. Serve hot alongside remaining honey mixture.
Nutrition Info: Calories per serving: 384; Carbohydrates: 15.7g; Protein: 33g; Fat: 21.7g; Sugar: 11.6g; Sodium: 621mg; Fiber: 0g

Juicy Smoked Salmon

Servings: 5
Cooking Time: 50 Minutes
Ingredients:
- ½ cup of sugar
- 2 tablespoon salt
- 2 tablespoons crushed red pepper flakes
- ½ cup fresh mint leaves, chopped
- ¼ cup brandy
- 1(4 pounds) salmon, bones removed
- 2cups alder wood pellets, soaked in water

Directions:
1. Take a medium-sized bowl and add brown sugar, crushed red pepper flakes, mint leaves, salt, and brandy until a paste forms
2. Rub the paste all over your salmon and wrap the salmon with a plastic wrap
3. Allow them to chill overnight
4. Preheat your smoker to 220 degrees Fahrenheit and add wood Pellets
5. Transfer the salmon to the smoker rack and cook smoke for 45 minutes
6. Once the salmon has turned red-brown and the flesh flakes off easily, take it out and serve!

Nutrition Info: Calories: 370 Fats: 28g Carbs: 1g Fiber: 0g

Enticing Mahi-mahi

Servings: 4
Cooking Time: 10 Minutes
Ingredients:
- 4 (6-oz.) mahi-mahi fillets
- 2 tbsp. olive oil
- Salt and freshly ground black pepper, to taste

Directions:
1. Set the temperature of Grill to 350 degrees F and preheat with closed lid for 15 minutes.
2. Coat fish fillets with olive oil and season with salt and black pepper evenly.
3. Place the fish fillets onto the grill and cook for about 5 minutes per side.
4. Remove the fish fillets from grill and serve hot.

Nutrition Info: Calories per serving: 195; Carbohydrates: 0g; Protein: 31.6g; Fat: 7g; Sugar: 0g; Sodium: 182mg; Fiber: 0g

Lemon Garlic Scallops

Servings: 6
Cooking Time: 5 Minutes
Ingredients:
- 1 dozen scallops
- 2 tablespoons chopped parsley
- Salt as needed
- 1 tablespoon olive oil
- 1 tablespoon butter, unsalted
- 1 teaspoon lemon zest
- For the Garlic Butter:
- ½ teaspoon minced garlic
- 1 lemon, juiced
- 4 tablespoons butter, unsalted, melted

Directions:
1. Switch on the grill, fill the grill hopper with alder flavored wood pellets, power the grill on by using the control panel, select 'smoke' on the temperature dial, or set the temperature to 400 degrees F and let it preheat for a minimum of 15 minutes.
2. Meanwhile, remove frill from scallops, pat dry with paper towels and then season with salt and black pepper.
3. When the grill has preheated, open the lid, place a skillet on the grill grate, add butter and oil, and when the butter melts, place seasoned scallops on it and then cook for 2 minutes until seared.
4. Meanwhile, prepare the garlic butter and for this, take a small bowl, place all of its ingredients in it and then whisk until combined.
5. Flip the scallops, top with some of the prepared garlic butter, and cook for another minute.
6. When done, transfer scallops to a dish, top with remaining garlic butter, sprinkle with parsley and lemon zest, and then serve.

Nutrition Info: Calories: 184 Cal ;Fat: 10 g ;Carbs: 1 g ;Protein: 22 g ;Fiber: 0.2 g

Wood Pellet Togarashi Grilled Salmon

Servings: 6
Cooking Time: 20 Minutes
Ingredients:
- 1 salmon fillet
- 1/4 cup olive oil
- 1/2 tbsp kosher salt
- 1 tbsp Togarashi seasoning

Directions:
1. Preheat the wood pellet grill to 400°F.
2. Place the salmon fillet on a non-stick foil sheet with the skin side up.
3. Rub the olive oil on the salmon and sprinkle with salt and togarashi seasoning.
4. Place the salmon on the preheated grill and close the lid. Cook for 20 minutes or until the internal temperature reaches 145°F.
5. Remove from the grill and serve when hot. Enjoy.

Nutrition Info: Calories 119, Total fat 10g, Saturated fat 2g, Total Carbs 0g, Net Carbs 0g, Protein 6g, Sugar 0g, Fiber 0g, Sodium: 720mg

Spicy Shrimps Skewers

Servings: 4
Cooking Time: 6 Minutes
Ingredients:
- 2 pounds shrimp, peeled, and deveined
- For the Marinade:
- 6 ounces Thai chilies
- 6 cloves of garlic, peeled
- 1 ½ teaspoon sugar
- 2 tablespoons Napa Valley rub
- 1 ½ tablespoon white vinegar
- 3 tablespoons olive oil

Directions:
1. Prepare the marinade and for this, place all of its ingredients in a food processor and then pulse for 1 minute until smooth.
2. Take a large bowl, place shrimps on it, add prepared marinade, toss until well coated, and let marinate for a minimum of 30 minutes in the refrigerator.
3. When ready to cook, switch on the grill, fill the grill hopper with apple-flavored wood pellets, power the grill on by using the control panel, select 'smoke' on the temperature dial, or set the temperature to 450 degrees F and let it preheat for a minimum of 5 minutes.
4. Meanwhile, remove shrimps from the marinade and then thread onto skewers.
5. When the grill has preheated, open the lid, place shrimps' skewers on the grill grate, shut the grill and smoke for 3 minutes per side until firm.
6. When done, transfer shrimps' skewers to a dish and then serve.

Nutrition Info: Calories: 187.2 Cal ;Fat: 2.7 g ;Carbs: 2.7 g ;Protein: 23.2 g ;Fiber: 0.2 g

Halibut

Servings: 4
Cooking Time: 3o Minutes
Ingredients:
- 1-pound fresh halibut filet (cut into 4 equal sizes)
- 1 tbsp fresh lemon juice
- 2 garlic cloves (minced)
- 2 tsp soy sauce
- ½ tsp ground black pepper
- ½ tsp onion powder
- 2 tbsp honey
- ½ tsp oregano

- 1 tsp dried basil
- 2 tbsp butter (melted)
- Maple syrup for serving

Directions:
1. Combine the lemon juice, honey, soy sauce, onion powder, oregano, dried basil, pepper and garlic.
2. Brush the halibut filets generously with the filet the mixture. Wrap the filets with aluminum foil and refrigerate for 4 hours.
3. Remove the filets from the refrigerator and let them sit for about 2 hours, or until they are at room temperature.
4. Activate your wood pellet grill on smoke, leaving the lid opened for 5 minutes or until fire starts.
5. The lid must not be opened for it to be preheated and reach 275°F 15 minutes, using fruit wood pellets.
6. Place the halibut filets directly on the grill grate and smoke for 30 minutes
7. Remove the filets from the grill and let them rest for 10 minutes.
8. Serve and top with maple syrup to taste

Nutrition Info: Calories: 180 Cal Fat: 6.3 g Carbohydrates: 10 g Protein: 20.6 g Fiber: 0.3 g

Grilled Shrimp Kabobs

Servings: 4
Cooking Time: 10 Minutes
Ingredients:
- 1 lb. colossal shrimp, peeled and deveined
- 2 tbsp. oil
- 1/2 tbsp. garlic salt
- 1/2 tbsp. salt
- 1/8 tbsp. pepper
- 6 skewers

Directions:
1. Preheat your to 375F.
2. Pat the shrimp dry with a paper towel.
3. In a mixing bowl, mix oil, garlic salt, salt, and pepper
4. Toss the shrimp in the mixture until well coated.
5. Skewer the shrimps and cook in the with the lid closed for 4 minutes.
6. Open the lid, flip the skewers and cook for another 4 minutes or until the shrimp is pink and the flesh is opaque.
7. Serve.

Nutrition Info: Calories 325, Total fat 0g, Saturated fat 0g, Total carbs 0g, Net carbs 0g Protein 20g, Sugars 0g, Fiber 0g, Sodium 120mg

Cajun Seasoned Shrimp

Servings: 4

Cooking Time: 16-20 Minutes

Ingredients:

- 20 pieces of jumbo Shrimp
- 1/2 teaspoon of Cajun seasoning
- 1tablespoon of Canola oil
- 1teaspoon of magic shrimp seasoning

Directions:

1. Take a large bowl and add canola oil, shrimp, and seasonings.
2. Mix well for fine coating.
3. Now put the shrimp on skewers.
4. Put the grill grate inside the grill and set a timer to 8 minutes at high for preheating.
5. Once the grill is preheated, open the unit and place the shrimp skewers inside.
6. Cook the shrimp for 2 minutes.
7. Open the unit to flip the shrimp and cook for another 2 minutes at medium.
8. Own done, serve.

Nutrition Info: Calories: 382 Total Fat: 7.4g Saturated Fat: 0g Cholesterol: 350mg Sodium: 2208mg Total Carbohydrate: 23.9g Dietary Fiber 2.6g Total Sugars: 2.6g Protein: 50.2g

Citrus-smoked Trout

Servings: 6
Cooking Time: 1 To 2 Hours

Ingredients:

- 6 to 8 skin-on rainbow trout, cleaned and scaled
- 1 gallon orange juice
- ½ cup packed light brown sugar
- ¼ cup salt
- 1 tablespoon freshly ground black pepper
- Nonstick spray, oil, or butter, for greasing
- 1 tablespoon chopped fresh parsley
- 1 lemon, sliced

Directions:

1. Fillet the fish and pat dry with paper towels.
2. Pour the orange juice into a large container with a lid and stir in the brown sugar, salt, and pepper.
3. Place the trout in the brine, cover, and refrigerate for 1 hour.
4. Cover the grill grate with heavy-duty aluminum foil. Poke holes in the foil and spray with cooking spray (see Tip).
5. Supply your smoker with wood pellets and follow the manufacturer's specific start-up procedure. Preheat, with the lid closed, to 225°F.
6. Remove the trout from the brine and pat dry. Arrange the fish on the foil-covered grill grate, close the lid, and smoke for 1 hour 30 minutes to 2 hours, or until flaky.
7. Remove the fish from the heat. Serve garnished with the fresh parsley and lemon slices.

Bacon-wrapped Scallops

Servings: 4
Cooking Time: 30 Minutes

Ingredients:

- 12 scallops
- 12 bacon slices
- 3 tablespoons lemon juice
- Pepper to taste

Directions:

1. Turn on your wood pellet grill.
2. Set it to smoke.
3. Let it burn for 5 minutes while the lid is open.
4. Set it to 400 degrees F.
5. Wrap the scallops with bacon.
6. Secure with a toothpick.
7. Drizzle with the lemon juice and season with pepper.
8. Add the scallops to a baking tray.
9. Place the tray on the grill.
10. Grill for 20 minutes.
11. Serving Suggestion: Serve with sweet chili sauce.

Nutrition Info: Calories: 180.3 Fat: 8 g Cholesterol: 590.2 mg Carbohydrates: 3 g Fiber: 0 g Sugars: 0 g Protein: 22 g

Smoked Shrimp

Servings: 4
Cooking Time: 10 Minutes

Ingredients:

- 4 tablespoons olive oil
- 1 tablespoon Cajun seasoning
- 2 cloves garlic, minced
- 1 tablespoon lemon juice
- Salt to taste
- 2 lb. shrimp, peeled and deveined

Directions:

1. Combine all the ingredients in a sealable plastic bag.
2. Toss to coat evenly.
3. Marinate in the refrigerator for 4 hours.
4. Set the wood pellet grill to high.
5. Preheat it for 15 minutes while the lid is closed.
6. Thread shrimp onto skewers.
7. Grill for 4 minutes per side.
8. Tips: Soak skewers first in water if you are using wooden skewers.

Grilled Rainbow Trout

Servings: 6
Cooking Time: 2 Hours

Ingredients:
- 6 rainbow trout, cleaned, butterfly
- For the Brine:
- 1/4 cup salt
- 1 tablespoon ground black pepper
- 1/2 cup brown sugar
- 2 tablespoons soy sauce
- 16 cups water

Directions:
1. Prepare the brine and for this, take a large container, add all of its ingredients in it, stir until sugar has dissolved, then add trout and let soak for 1 hour in the refrigerator.
2. When ready to cook, switch on the grill, fill the grill hopper with oak flavored wood pellets, power the grill on by using the control panel, select 'smoke' on the temperature dial, or set the temperature to 225 degrees F and let it preheat for a minimum of 15 minutes.
3. Meanwhile, remove trout from the brine and pat dry with paper towels.
4. When the grill has preheated, open the lid, place trout on the grill grate, shut the grill and smoke for 2 hours until thoroughly cooked and tender.
5. When done, transfer trout to a dish and then serve.

Nutrition Info: Calories: 250 Cal ;Fat: 12 g ;Carbs: 1.4 g ;Protein: 33 g ;Fiber: 0.3 g

Hot-smoked Salmon

Servings: 4
Cooking Time: 4 To 6 Hours
Ingredients:
- 1 (2-pound) half salmon fillet
- 1 batch Dill Seafood Rub

Directions:
1. Supply your smoker with wood pellets and follow the manufacturer's specific start-up procedure. Preheat the grill, with the lid closed, to 180°F.
2. Season the salmon all over with the rub. Using your hands, work the rub into the flesh.
3. Place the salmon directly on the grill grate, skin-side down, and smoke until its internal temperature reaches 145°F. Remove the salmon from the grill and serve immediately.

Flavor-bursting Prawn Skewers

Servings: 5
Cooking Time: 8 Minutes
Ingredients:
- ¼ C. fresh parsley leaves, minced
- 1 tbsp. garlic, crushed
- 2½ tbsp. olive oil

- 2 tbsp. Thai chili sauce
- 1 tbsp. fresh lime juice
- 1½ pounds prawns, peeled and deveined

Directions:
1. In a large bowl, add all ingredients except for prawns and mix well.
2. In a resealable plastic bag, add marinade and prawns.
3. Seal the bag and shake to coat well
4. Refrigerate for about 20-30 minutes.
5. Set the temperature of Grill to 450 degrees F and preheat with closed lid for 15 minutes.
6. Remove the prawns from marinade and thread onto metal skewers.
7. Arrange the skewers onto the grill and cook for about 4 minutes per side.
8. Remove the skewers from grill and serve hot.

Nutrition Info: Calories per serving: 234; Carbohydrates: 4.9g; Protein: 31.2g; Fat: 9.3g; Sugar: 1.7g; Sodium: 562mg; Fiber: 0.1g

Spicy Shrimp

Servings: 4
Cooking Time: 10 Minutes
Ingredients:
- 3 tablespoons olive oil
- 6 cloves garlic
- 2 tablespoons chicken dry rub
- 6 oz. chili
- 1 1/2 tablespoons white vinegar
- 1 1/2 teaspoons sugar
- 2 lb. shrimp, peeled and deveined

Directions:
1. Add olive oil, garlic, dry rub, chili, vinegar and sugar in a food processor.
2. Blend until smooth.
3. Transfer mixture to a bowl.
4. Stir in shrimp.
5. Cover and refrigerate for 30 minutes.
6. Preheat the wood pellet grill to hit for 15 minutes while the lid is closed.
7. Thread shrimp onto skewers.
8. Grill for 3 minute per side.
9. Tips: You can also add vegetables to the skewers.

Grilled Lingcod

Servings: 6
Cooking Time: 15 Minutes
Ingredients:
- 2 lb lingcod fillets
- 1/2 tbsp salt
- 1/2 tbsp white pepper

- 1/4 tbsp cayenne pepper
- Lemon wedges

Directions:
1. Preheat your to 375F.
2. Place the lingcod on a parchment paper or on a grill mat
3. Season the fish with salt, pepper, and top with lemon wedges.
4. Cook the fish for 15 minutes or until the internal temperature reaches 145F.

Nutrition Info: Calories 245, Total fat 2g, Saturated fat 0g, Total carbs 2g, Net carbs 0g Protein 52g, Sugars 1g, Fiber 1g, Sodium 442mg

Chilean Sea Bass

Servings: 6
Cooking Time: 40 Minutes
Ingredients:
- 4 sea bass fillets, skinless, each about 6 ounces
- Chicken rub as needed
- 8 tablespoons butter, unsalted
- 2 tablespoons chopped thyme leaves
- Lemon slices for serving
- For the Marinade:
- 1 lemon, juiced
- 4 teaspoons minced garlic
- 1 tablespoon chopped thyme
- 1 teaspoon blackened rub
- 1 tablespoon chopped oregano
- 1/4 cup oil

Directions:
1. Prepare the marinade and for this, take a small bowl, place all of its ingredients in it, stir until well combined, and then pour the mixture into a large plastic bag.
2. Add fillets in the bag, seal it, turn it upside down to coat fillets with the marinade and let it marinate for a minimum of 30 minutes in the refrigerator.
3. When ready to cook, switch on the grill, fill the grill hopper with apple-flavored wood pellets, power the grill on by using the control panel, select 'smoke' on the temperature dial, or set the temperature to 325 degrees F and let it preheat for a minimum of 15 minutes.
4. Meanwhile, take a large baking pan and place butter on it.
5. When the grill has preheated, open the lid, place baking pan on the grill grate, and wait until butter melts.
6. Remove fillets from the marinade, pour marinade into the pan with melted butter, then season fillets with chicken rubs until coated on all sides, then place them into the pan, shut the grill and cook for 30 minutes until internal temperature

reaches 160 degrees F, frequently basting with the butter sauce.
7. When done, transfer fillets to a dish, sprinkle with thyme and then serve with lemon slices.

Nutrition Info: Calories: 232 Cal ;Fat: 12.2 g ;Carbs: 0.8 g ;Protein: 28.2 g ;Fiber: 0.1 g

Wood Pellet Smoked Salmon

Servings: 8
Cooking Time: 4 Hours
Ingredients:
- Brine
- 4 cups water
- 1 cup brown sugar
- 1/3 cup kosher salt
- Salmon
- Salmon fillet, skin in
- Maple syrup

Directions:
1. Combine all the brine ingredients until the sugar has fully dissolved.
2. Add the brine to a ziplock bag with the salmon and refrigerate for 12 hours.
3. Remove the salmon from the brine, wash it and rinse with water. Pat dry with paper towel then let sit at room temperature for 2 hours.
4. Startup your wood pellet to smoke and place the salmon on a baking rack sprayed with cooking spray.
5. After cooking for an hour, baste the salmon with maple syrup. Do not let the smoker get above 180°F for accurate results.
6. Smoke for 3-4 hours or until the salmon flakes easily.

Nutrition Info: Calories 101, Total fat 2g, Saturated fat 0g, Total carbs 16g, Net carbs 16g, Protein 4g, Sugar 16g, Fiber 0g, Sodium: 3131mg

Stuffed Shrimp Tilapia

Servings: 5
Cooking Time: 45 Minutes
Ingredients:
- 5 ounces fresh, farmed tilapia fillets
- 2 tablespoons extra virgin olive oil
- 1and ½ teaspoons smoked paprika
- 1and ½ teaspoons Old Bay seasoning
- Shrimp stuffing
- 1pound shrimp, cooked and deveined
- 1tablespoon salted butter
- 1cup red onion, diced
- 1cup Italian bread crumbs
- ½ cup mayonnaise
- 1large egg, beaten

- 2teaspoons fresh parsley, chopped
- 1and ½ teaspoons salt and pepper

Directions:
1. Take a food processor and add shrimp, chop them up
2. Take a skillet and place it over medium-high heat, add butter and allow it to melt
3. Sauté the onions for 3 minutes
4. Add chopped shrimp with cooled Sautéed onion alongside remaining ingredients listed under stuffing ingredients and transfer to a bowl
5. Cover the mixture and allow it to refrigerate for 60 minutes
6. Rub both sides of the fillet with olive oil
7. Spoon 1/3 cup of the stuffing to the fillet
8. Flatten out the stuffing onto the bottom half of the fillet and fold the Tilapia in half
9. Secure with 2 toothpicks
10. Dust each fillet with smoked paprika and Old Bay seasoning
11. Preheat your smoker to 400 degrees Fahrenheit
12. Add your preferred wood Pellets and transfer the fillets to a non-stick grill tray
13. Transfer to your smoker and smoker for 30-45 minutes until the internal temperature reaches 145 degrees Fahrenheit
14. Allow the fish to rest for 5 minutes and enjoy!

Nutrition Info: Calories: 620 Fats: 50g Carbs: 6g Fiber: 1g

Mussels With Pancetta Aïoli

Servings: 4
Cooking Time: 30 Minutes
Ingredients:
- ¾ cup mayonnaise (to make your own, see page 460)
- 1tablespoon minced garlic, or more to taste
- 1.4-ounce slice pancetta, chopped
- Salt and pepper
- 4 pounds mussels
- 8 thick slices Italian bread
- ¼ cup good-quality olive oil

Directions:
1. Whisk the mayonnaise and garlic together in a small bowl. Put the pancetta in a small cold skillet, turn the heat to low; cook, occasionally stir, until most of the fat is rendered and the meat turns golden and crisp about 5 minutes. Drain on a paper towel, then stir into the mayonnaise along with 1 teaspoon of the rendered fat from the pan. Taste and add more garlic and some salt if you like. Cover and refrigerate until you're ready to serve. (You can make the aïoli up to several days ahead; refrigerate in an airtight container.)

2. Start the coals or heat a gas grill for direct hot cooking. Make sure the grates are clean.
3. Rinse the mussels and pull off any beards. Discard any that are broken or don't close when tapped.
4. Brush both sides of the bread slices with the oil. Put the bread on the grill directly over the fire. Close the lid and toast, turning once, until it develops grill marks with some charring, 1 to 2 minutes per side. Remove from the grill and keep warm.
5. Scatter the mussels onto the grill directly over the fire, spreading them out, so they are in a single layer. Immediately close the lid and cook for 3 minutes. Transfer the open mussels to a large bowl with tongs. If any have not opened, leave them on the grill, close the lid, and cook for another minute or 2, checking frequently and removing open mussels until they are all off the grill.
6. Dollop the aïoli over the tops of the mussels and use a large spoon to turn them over to coat them. Serve the mussels drizzled with their juices, either over (or alongside) the bread.

Nutrition Info: Calories: 159 Fats: 6.1 g Cholesterol: 0 mg Carbohydrates: 14.95 g Fiber: 0 g Sugars: 0 g Proteins: 9.57 g

Grilled Herbed Tuna

Servings: 6
Cooking Time: 10 Minutes
Ingredients:
- 6 tuna steaks
- 1 tablespoon lemon zest
- 1 tablespoon fresh thyme, chopped
- 1 tablespoon fresh parsley, chopped
- Garlic salt to taste

Directions:
1. Sprinkle the tuna steaks with lemon zest, herbs and garlic salt.
2. Cover with foil.
3. Refrigerate for 4 hours.
4. Grill for 3 minutes per side.
5. Tips: Take the fish out of the refrigerator 30 minutes before cooking.

Cajun Catfish

Servings: 6
Cooking Time: 15 Minutes
Ingredients:
- 2½ pounds catfish fillets
- 2 tablespoons olive oil
- 1 batch Cajun Rub

Directions:

1. Supply your smoker with wood pellets and follow the manufacturer's specific start-up procedure. Preheat the grill, with the lid closed, to 300°F.
2. Coat the catfish fillets all over with olive oil and season with the rub. Using your hands, work the rub into the flesh.
3. Place the fillets directly on the grill grate and smoke until their internal temperature reaches 145°F. Remove the catfish from the grill and serve immediately

Oyster In Shells

Servings: 4
Cooking Time: 8 Minutes
Ingredients:
- 12 medium oysters
- 1 tsp oregano
- 1 lemon (juiced)
- 1 tsp freshly ground black pepper
- 6 tbsp unsalted butter (melted)
- 1 tsp salt or more to taste
- 2 garlic cloves (minced)
- 2 ½ tbsp grated parmesan cheese
- 2 tbsp freshly chopped parsley

Directions:
1. Remove dirt
2. Open the shell completely. Discard the top shell.
3. Gently run the knife under the oyster to loosen the oyster foot from the bottom shell.
4. Repeat step 2 and 3 for the remaining oysters.
5. Combine melted butter, lemon, pepper, salt, garlic and oregano in a mixing bowl.
6. Pour ½ to 1 tsp of the butter mixture on each oyster.
7. Start your wood pellet grill on smoke, leaving the lid opened for 5 minutes, or until fire starts.
8. Keep lid unopened to preheat in the set "HIGH" with lid closed for 15 minutes.
9. Gently arrange the oysters onto the grill grate.
10. Grill oyster for 6 to 8 minutes or until the oyster juice is bubbling and the oyster is plump.
11. Remove oysters from heat. Serve and top with grated parmesan and chopped parsley.
Nutrition Info: Calories: 200 Cal Fat: 19.2 g Carbohydrates: 3.9 g Protein: 4.6 g Fiber: 0.8 g

Wood Pellet Smoked Buffalo Shrimp

Servings: 6
Cooking Time: 5 Minutes
Ingredients:
- 1 lb raw shrimps peeled and deveined
- 1/2 tbsp salt
- 1/4 tbsp garlic salt
- 1/4 tbsp garlic powder
- 1/4 tbsp onion powder
- 1/2 cup buffalo sauce

Directions:
1. Preheat the wood pellet grill to 450°F.
2. Coat the shrimp with both salts, garlic and onion powders.
3. Place the shrimp in a grill and cook for 3 minutes on each side.
4. Remove from the grill and toss in buffalo sauce. Serve with cheese, celery and napkins. Enjoy.
Nutrition Info: Calories 57, Total fat 1g, Saturated fat 0g, Total Carbs 1g, Net Carbs 1g, Protein 10g, Sugar 0g, Fiber 0g, Sodium: 1106mg, Potassium 469mg.

Cajun Smoked Catfish

Servings: 4
Cooking Time: 2 Hours
Ingredients:
- 4 catfish fillets (5 ounces each)
- ½ cup Cajun seasoning
- 1 tsp ground black pepper
- 1 tbsp smoked paprika
- 1 /4 tsp cayenne pepper
- 1 tsp hot sauce
- 1 tsp granulated garlic
- 1 tsp onion powder
- 1 tsp thyme
- 1 tsp salt or more to taste
- 2 tbsp chopped fresh parsley

Directions:
1. Pour water into the bottom of a square or rectangular dish. Add 4 tbsp salt. Arrange the catfish fillets into the dish. Cover the dish and refrigerate for 3 to 4 hours.
2. Combine the paprika, cayenne, hot sauce, onion, salt, thyme, garlic, pepper and Cajun seasoning in a mixing bowl.
3. Remove the fish from the dish and let it sit for a few minutes, or until it is at room temperature. Pat the fish fillets dry with a paper towel.
4. Rub the seasoning mixture over each fillet generously.
5. Start your grill on smoke, leaving the lid opened for 5 minutes, or until fire starts.
6. Keep lid unopened and preheat to 200°F, using mesquite hardwood pellets.
7. Arrange the fish fillets onto the grill grate and close the grill. Cook for about 2 hours, or until the fish is flaky.
8. Remove the fillets from the grill and let the fillets rest for a few minutes to cool.
9. Serve and garnish with chopped fresh parsley.

Nutrition Info: Calories: 204 Cal Fat: 11.1 g Carbohydrates: 2.7 g Protein: 22.9 g Fiber: 0.6 g

Octopus With Lemon And Oregano

Servings: 4
Cooking Time: 1 Hour And 30 Minutes
Ingredients:
- 3 lemons
- 3 pounds cleaned octopus, thawed if frozen
- 6 cloves garlic, peeled
- 4 sprigs fresh oregano
- 2 bay leaves
- Salt and pepper
- 3 tablespoons good-quality olive oil
- Minced fresh oregano for garnish

Directions:
1. Halve one of the lemons. Put the octopus, garlic, oregano sprigs, bay leaves, a large pinch of salt, and lemon halves in a large pot with enough water to cover by a couple of inches. Bring to a boil, adjust the heat so the liquid bubbles gently but steadily, and cook, occasionally turning with tongs, until the octopus is tender 30 to 90 minutes. (Check with the tip of a sharp knife; it should go in smoothly.) Drain; discard the seasonings. (You can cover and refrigerate the octopus for up to 24 hours.)
2. Start the coals or heat a gas grill for direct hot cooking. Make sure the grates are clean.
3. Squeeze the juice 1 of the remaining lemons and whisk it with the oil and salt and pepper to taste. Cut the octopus into large serving pieces and toss with the oil mixture.
4. Put the octopus on the grill directly over the fire. Cover the grill and cook until heated through and charred, 4 to 5 minutes per side. Cut the remaining lemon in wedges. Transfer the octopus to a platter, sprinkle with minced oregano, and serve with the lemon wedges.

Nutrition Info: Calories: 139 Fats: 1.8 g Cholesterol: 0 mg Carbohydrates: 3.7 g Fiber: 0 g Sugars: 0 g Proteins: 25.4 g

Cured Cold-smoked Lox

Servings: 6
Cooking Time: 6 Hours
Ingredients:
- ¼ cup salt
- ¼ cup sugar
- 1 tablespoon freshly ground black pepper
- 1 bunch dill, chopped
- 1 pound sashimi-grade salmon, skin removed
- 1 avocado, sliced

- 8 bagels
- 4 ounces cream cheese
- 1 bunch alfalfa sprouts
- 1 (5-ounce) jar capers

Directions:
1. In a small bowl, combine the salt, sugar, pepper, and fresh dill to make the curing mixture. Set aside.
2. On a smooth surface, lay out a large piece of plastic wrap and spread half of the curing salt mixture in the middle, spreading it out to about the size of the salmon.
3. Place the salmon on top of the curing salt.
4. Top the fish with the remaining curing salt, covering it completely. Wrap the salmon, leaving the ends open to drain.
5. Place the wrapped fish in a rimmed baking pan or dish lined with paper towels to soak up liquid.
6. Place a weight on the salmon evenly, such as a pan with a couple of heavy jars of pickles on top.
7. Put the salmon pan with weights in the refrigerator. Place something (a dishtowel, for example) under the back of the pan in order to slightly tip it down so the liquid drains away from the fish.
8. Leave the salmon to cure in the refrigerator for 24 hours.
9. Place the wood pellets in the smoker, but do not follow the start-up procedure and do not preheat.
10. Remove the salmon from the refrigerator, unwrap it, rinse it off, and pat dry.
11. Put the salmon in the smoker while still cold from the refrigerator to slow down the cooking process. You'll need to use a cold-smoker attachment or enlist the help of a smoker tube to hold the temperature at 80°F and maintain that for 6 hours to absorb smoke and complete the cold-smoking process.
12. Remove the salmon from the smoker, place it in a sealed plastic bag, and refrigerate for 24 hours. The salmon will be translucent all the way through.
13. Thinly slice the lox and serve with sliced avocado, bagels, cream cheese, alfalfa sprouts, and capers.

Grilled Tuna

Servings: 4
Cooking Time: 4 Minutes
Ingredients:
- 4 (6 ounce each) tuna steaks (1 inch thick)
- 1 lemon (juiced)
- 1 clove garlic (minced)
- 1 tsp chili
- 2 tbsp extra virgin olive oil
- 1 cup white wine
- 3 tbsp brown sugar

- 1 tsp rosemary

Directions:
1. Combine lemon, chili, white wine, sugar, rosemary, olive oil and garlic. Add the tuna steaks and toss to combine.
2. Transfer the tuna and marinade to a zip-lock bag. Refrigerate for 3 hours.
3. Remove the tuna steaks from the marinade and let them rest for about 1 hour
4. Start your grill on smoke, leaving the lid opened for 5 minutes, or until fire starts.
5. Do not open lid to preheat until 15 minutes to the setting "HIGH"
6. Grease the grill grate with oil and place the tuna on the grill grate. Grill tuna steaks for 4 minutes, 2 minutes per side.
7. Remove the tuna from the grill and let them rest for a few minutes.
Nutrition Info: Calories: 137 Cal Fat: 17.8 g Carbohydrates: 10.2 g Protein: 51.2 g Fiber: 0.6 g

Wood Pellet Teriyaki Smoked Shrimp

Servings: 6
Cooking Time: 10 Minutes
Ingredients:
- 1 lb tail-on shrimp, uncooked
- 1/2 tbsp onion powder
- 1/2 tbsp salt
- 1/2 tbsp Garlic powder
- 4 tbsp Teriyaki sauce
- 4 tbsp sriracha mayo
- 2 tbsp green onion, minced

Directions:
1. Peel the shrimps leaving the tails then wash them removing any vein left over. Drain and pat with a paper towel to drain.
2. Preheat the wood pellet to 450°F
3. Season the shrimp with onion, salt, and garlic then place it on the grill to cook for 5 minutes on each side.
4. Remove the shrimp from the grill and toss it with teriyaki sauce. Serve garnished with mayo and onions. Enjoy.
Nutrition Info: Calories 87, Total fat 0g, Saturated fat 0g, Total Carbs 2g, Net Carbs 2g, Protein 16g, Sugar 1g, Fiber 0g, Sodium: 1241mg

Halibut In Parchment

Servings: 4
Cooking Time: 15 Minutes
Ingredients:
- 16 asparagus spears, trimmed, sliced into 1/2-inch pieces

- 2 ears of corn kernels
- 4 ounces halibut fillets, pin bones removed
- 2 lemons, cut into 12 slices
- Salt as needed
- Ground black pepper as needed
- 2 tablespoons olive oil
- 2 tablespoons chopped parsley

Directions:
1. Switch on the grill, fill the grill hopper with flavored wood pellets, power the grill on by using the control panel, select 'smoke' on the temperature dial, or set the temperature to 450 degrees F and let it preheat for a minimum of 5 minutes.
2. Meanwhile, cut out 18-inch long parchment paper, place a fillet in the center of each parchment, season with salt and black pepper, and then drizzle with oil.
3. Cover each fillet with three lemon slices, overlapping slightly, sprinkle one-fourth of asparagus and corn on each fillet, season with some salt and black pepper, and seal the fillets and vegetables tightly to prevent steam from escaping the packet.
4. When the grill has preheated, open the lid, place fillet packets on the grill grate, shut the grill and smoke for 15 minutes until packets have turned slightly brown and puffed up.
5. When done, transfer packets to a dish, let them stand for 5 minutes, then cut 'X' in the center of each packet, carefully uncover the fillets an vegetables, sprinkle with parsley, and then serve.
Nutrition Info: Calories: 186.6 Cal ;Fat: 2.8 g ;Carbs: 14.2 g ;Protein: 25.7 g ;Fiber: 4.1 g

Lively Flavored Shrimp

Servings: 6
Cooking Time: 30 Minutes
Ingredients:
- 8 oz. salted butter, melted
- ¼ C. Worcestershire sauce
- ¼ C. fresh parsley, chopped
- 1 lemon, quartered
- 2 lb. jumbo shrimp, peeled and deveined
- 3 tbsp. BBQ rub

Directions:
1. In a metal baking pan, add all ingredients except for shrimp and BBQ rub and mix well.
2. Season the shrimp with BBQ rub evenly.
3. Add the shrimp in the pan with butter mixture and coat well.
4. Set aside for about 20-30 minutes.
5. Set the temperature of Grill to 250 degrees F and preheat with closed lid for 15 minutes.

6. Place the pan onto the grill and cook for about 25-30 minutes.
7. Remove the pan from grill and serve hot.
Nutrition Info: Calories per serving: 462; Carbohydrates: 4.7g; Protein: 34.9g; Fat: 33.3g; Sugar: 2.1g; Sodium: 485mg; Fiber: 0.2g

Summer Paella

Servings: 6
Cooking Time: 45 Minutes
Ingredients:
- 6 tablespoons extra-virgin olive oil, divided, plus more for drizzling
- 2 green or red bell peppers, cored, seeded, and diced
- 2 medium onions, diced
- 2 garlic cloves, slivered
- 1 (29-ounce) can tomato purée
- 1½ pounds chicken thighs
- Kosher salt
- 1½ pounds tail-on shrimp, peeled and deveined
- 1 cup dried thinly sliced chorizo sausage
- 1 tablespoon smoked paprika
- 1½ teaspoons saffron threads
- 2 quarts chicken broth
- 3½ cups white rice
- 2 (7½-ounce) cans chipotle chiles in adobo sauce
- 1½ pounds fresh clams, soaked in cold water for 15 to 20 minutes2 tablespoons chopped fresh parsley
- 2 lemons, cut into wedges, for serving

Directions:
1. Make the sofrito: On the stove top, in a saucepan over medium-low heat, combine ¼ cup of olive oil, the bell peppers, onions, and garlic, and cook for 5 minutes, or until the onions are translucent.
2. Stir in the tomato purée, reduce the heat to low, and simmer, stirring frequently, until most of the liquid has evaporated, about 30 minutes. Set aside. (Note: The sofrito can be made in advance and refrigerated.)
3. Supply your smoker with wood pellets and follow the manufacturer's specific start-up procedure. Preheat, with the lid closed, to 450°F.
4. Heat a large paella pan on the smoker and add the remaining 2 tablespoons of olive oil.
5. Add the chicken thighs, season lightly with salt, and brown for 6 to 10 minutes, then push to the outer edge of the pan.
6. Add the shrimp, season with salt, close the lid, and smoke for 3 minutes.
7. Add the sofrito, chorizo, paprika, and saffron, and stir together.

8. In a separate bowl, combine the chicken broth, uncooked rice, and 1 tablespoon of salt, stirring until well combined.
9. Add the broth-rice mixture to the paella pan, spreading it evenly over the other ingredients.
10. Close the lid and smoke for 5 minutes, then add the chipotle chiles and clams on top of the rice.
11. Close the lid and continue to smoke the paella for about 30 minutes, or until all of the liquid is absorbed.
12. Remove the pan from the grill, cover tightly with aluminum foil, and let rest off the heat for 5 minutes.
13. Drizzle with olive oil, sprinkle with the fresh parsley, and serve with the lemon wedges.

No-fuss Tuna Burgers

Servings: 6
Cooking Time: 15 Minutes
Ingredients:
- 2 lb. tuna steak
- 1 green bell pepper, seeded and chopped
- 1 white onion, chopped
- 2 eggs
- 1 tsp. soy sauce
- 1 tbsp. blackened Saskatchewan rub
- Salt and freshly ground black pepper, to taste

Directions:
1. Set the temperature of Grill to 500 degrees F and preheat with closed lid for 15 minutes.
2. In a bowl, add all the ingredients and mix until well combined.
3. With greased hands, make patties from mixture.
4. Place the patties onto the grill close to the edges and cook for about 10-15 minutes, flipping once halfway through.
5. Serve hot.
Nutrition Info: Calories per serving: 313; Carbohydrates: 3.4g; Protein: 47.5g; Fat: 11g; Sugar: 1.9g; Sodium: 174mg; Fiber: 0.7g

Grilled Tilapia

Servings: 6
Cooking Time: 2o Minutes
Ingredients:
- 2 tsp dried parsley
- ½ tsp garlic powder
- 1 tsp cayenne pepper
- ½ tsp ground black pepper
- ½ tsp thyme
- ½ tsp dried basil
- ½ tsp oregano
- 3 tbsp olive oil

- ½ tsp lemon pepper
- 1 tsp kosher salt
- 1 lemon (juiced)
- 6 tilapia fillets
- 1 ½ tsp creole seafood seasoning

Directions:
1. In a mixing bowl, combine spices
2. Brush the fillets with oil and lemon juice.
3. Liberally, season all sides of the tilapia fillets with the seasoning mix.
4. Preheat your grill to 325°F
5. Place a non-stick BBQ grilling try on the grill and arrange the tilapia fillets onto it.
6. Grill for 15 to 20 minutes
7. Remove fillets and cool down

Nutrition Info: Calories: 176 Cal Fat: 9.6 g Carbohydrates: 1.5 g Protein: 22.3 g Fiber: 0.5 g

Crab Stuffed Lingcod

Servings: 6
Cooking Time: 30 Minutes
Ingredients:
- Lemon cream sauce
- 4 garlic cloves
- 1 shallot
- 1 leek
- 2 tbsp olive oil
- 1 tbsp salt
- 1/4 tbsp black pepper
- 3 tbsp butter
- 1/4 cup white wine
- 1 cup whipping cream
- 2 tbsp lemon juice
- 1 tbsp lemon zest
- Crab mix
- 1 lb crab meat
- 1/3 cup mayo
- 1/3 cup sour cream
- 1/3 cup lemon cream sauce
- 1/4 green onion, chopped
- 1/4 tbsp black pepper
- 1/2 tbsp old bay seasoning
- Fish
- 2 lb lingcod
- 1 tbsp olive oil
- 1 tbsp salt
- 1 tbsp paprika
- 1 tbsp green onion, chopped
- 1 tbsp Italian parsley

Directions:
1. Lemon cream sauce
2. Chop garlic, shallot, and leeks then add to a saucepan with oil, salt, pepper, and butter.

3. Saute over medium heat until the shallot is translucent.
4. Deglaze with white wine then add whipping cream. Bring the sauce to boil, reduce heat and simmer for 3 minutes.
5. Remove from heat and add lemon juice and lemon zest. Transfer the sauce to a blender and blend until smooth.
6. Set aside 1/3 cup for the crab mix
7. Crab mix
8. Add all the ingredients in a mixing bowl and mix thoroughly until well combined.
9. Set aside
10. Fish
11. Fire up your to high heat then slice the fish into 6-ounce portions.
12. Lay the fish on its side on a cutting board and slice it 3/4 way through the middle leaving a 1/2 inch on each end so as to have a nice pouch.
13. Rub the oil into the fish then place them on a baking sheet. Sprinkle with salt.
14. Stuff crab mix into each fish then sprinkle paprika and place it on the grill.
15. Cook for 15 minutes or more if the fillets are more than 2 inches thick.
16. Remove the fish and transfer to serving platters. Pour the remaining lemon cream sauce on each fish and garnish with onions and parsley.

Nutrition Info: Calories 476, Total fat 33g, Saturated fat 14g, Total carbs 6g, Net carbs 5g Protein 38g, Sugars 3g, Fiber 1g, Sodium 1032mg

Seared Tuna Steaks

Servings: 2
Cooking Time: 10 Minutes
Ingredients:
- 2 (1½- to 2-inch-thick) tuna steaks
- 2 tablespoons olive oil
- Salt
- Freshly ground black pepper

Directions:
1. Supply your smoker with wood pellets and follow the manufacturer's specific start-up procedure. Preheat the grill, with the lid closed, to 500°F.
2. Rub the tuna steaks all over with olive oil and season both sides with salt and pepper.
3. Place the tuna steaks directly on the grill grate and grill for 3 to 5 minutes per side, leaving a pink center. Remove the tuna steaks from the grill and serve immediately.

Cider Salmon

Servings: 4

Cooking Time: 1 Hour
Ingredients:
- 1 ½ pound salmon fillet, skin-on, center-cut, pin bone removed
- For the Brine:
- 4 juniper berries, crushed
- 1 bay leaf, crumbled
- 1 piece star anise, broken
- 1 1/2 cups apple cider
- For the Cure:
- 1/2 cup salt
- 1 teaspoon ground black pepper
- 1/4 cup brown sugar
- 2 teaspoons barbecue rub

Directions:
1. Prepare the brine and for this, take a large container, add all of its ingredients in it, stir until mixed, then add salmon and let soak for a minimum of 8 hours in the refrigerator.
2. Meanwhile, prepare the cure and for this, take a small bowl, place all of its ingredients in it and stir until combined.
3. After 8 hours, remove salmon from the brine, then take a baking dish, place half of the cure in it, top with salmon skin-side down, sprinkle remaining cure on top, cover with plastic wrap and let it rest for 1 hour in the refrigerator.
4. When ready to cook, switch on the grill, fill the grill hopper with oak flavored wood pellets, power the grill on by using the control panel, select 'smoke' on the temperature dial, or set the temperature to 200 degrees F and let it preheat for a minimum of 5 minutes.
5. Meanwhile, remove salmon from the cure, pat dry with paper towels, and then sprinkle with black pepper.
6. When the grill has preheated, open the lid, place salmon on the grill grate, shut the grill, and smoke for 1 hour until the internal temperature reaches 150 degrees F.
7. When done, transfer salmon to a cutting board, let it rest for 5 minutes, then remove the skin and serve.

Nutrition Info: Calories: 233 Cal ;Fat: 14 g ;Carbs: 0 g ;Protein: 25 g ;Fiber: 0 g

Bacon-wrapped Scallops

Servings: 8
Cooking Time: 20 Minutes
Ingredients:
- 1 lb sea scallops
- 1/2 lb bacon
- Sea salt

Directions:

1. Preheat your to 375F.
2. Pat dry the scallops with a paper towel then wrap them with a piece of bacon and secure with a toothpick.
3. Lay the scallops on the grill with the bacon side down. Close the lid and cook for 5 minutes on each side.
4. Keep the scallops on the bacon side so that you will not get grill marks on the scallops.
5. Serve and enjoy.

Nutrition Info: Calories 261, Total fat 14g, Saturated fat 5g, Total carbs 5g, Net carbs 5g Protein 28g, Sugars 0g, Fiber 0g, Sodium 1238mg

Salmon With Avocado Salsa

Servings: 6
Cooking Time: 20 Minutes
Ingredients:
- 3 lb. salmon fillet
- Garlic salt and pepper to taste
- 4 cups avocado, sliced into cubes
- 1 onion, chopped
- 1 jalapeño pepper, minced
- 1 tablespoon lime juice
- 1 tablespoon olive oil
- ¼ cup cilantro, chopped
- Salt to taste

Directions:
1. Sprinkle both sides of salmon with garlic salt and pepper.
2. Set the wood pellet grill to smoke.
3. Grill the salmon for 7 to 8 minutes per side.
4. While waiting, prepare the salsa by combining the remaining ingredients in a bowl.
5. Serve salmon with the avocado salsa.
6. Tips: You can also use tomato salsa for this recipe if you don't have avocados.

Bbq Oysters

Servings: 4-6
Cooking Time: 16 Minutes
Ingredients:
- Shucked oysters - 12
- Unsalted butter - 1 lb.
- Chopped green onions - 1 bunch
- Honey Hog BBQ Rub or Meat Church "The Gospel" - 1 tbsp
- Minced green onions - ½ bunch
- Seasoned breadcrumbs - ½ cup
- Cloves of minced garlic - 2
- Shredded pepper jack cheese - 8 oz
- Heat and Sweet BBQ sauce

Directions:

1. Preheat the pellet grill for about 10-15 minutes with the lid closed.
2. To make the compound butter, wait for the butter to soften. Then combine the butter, onions, BBQ rub, and garlic thoroughly.
3. Lay the butter evenly on plastic wrap or parchment paper. Roll it up in a log shape and tie the ends with butcher's twine. Place these in the freezer to solidify for an hour. This butter can be used on any kind of grilled meat to enhance its flavor. Any other high-quality butter can also replace this compound butter.
4. Shuck the oysters, keeping the juice in the shell.
5. Sprinkle all the oysters with breadcrumbs and place them directly on the grill. Allow them to cook for 5 minutes. You will know they are cooked when the oysters begin to curl slightly at the edges.
6. Once they are cooked, put a spoonful of the compound butter on the oysters. Once the butter melts, you can add a little bit of pepper jack cheese to add more flavor to them.
7. The oysters must not be on the grill for longer than 6 minutes, or you risk overcooking them. Put a generous squirt of the BBQ sauce on all the oysters. Also, add a few chopped onions.
8. Allow them to cool for a few minutes and enjoy the taste of the sea!

Nutrition Info: Carbohydrates: 2.5 g Protein: 4.7 g Fat: 1.1 g Sodium: 53 mg Cholesterol: 25 mg

Teriyaki Smoked Shrimp

Servings: 6
Cooking Time: 20 Minutes
Ingredients:

- Uncooked shrimp - 1 lb.
- Onion powder - ½ tbsp
- Garlic powder - ½ tbsp
- Teriyaki sauce - 4 tbsp
- Mayo - 4 tbsp
- Minced green onion - 2 tbsp
- Salt - ½ tbsp

Directions:

1. Remove the shells from the shrimp and wash thoroughly.
2. Preheat the wood pellet grill to 450 degrees.
3. Season with garlic powder, onion powder, and salt.
4. Cook the shrimp for 5-6 minutes on each side.
5. Once cooked, remove the shrimp from the grill and garnish it with spring onion, teriyaki sauce, and mayo.

Nutrition Info: Carbohydrates: 2 g Protein: 16 g Sodium: 1241 mg Cholesterol: 190 mg

Wood Pellet Rockfish

Servings: 6
Cooking Time: 20 Minutes
Ingredients:

- 6 rockfish fillets
- 1 lemon, sliced
- 3/4 tbsp Himalayan salt
- 2 tbsp fresh dill, chopped
- 1/2 tbsp garlic powder
- 1/2 tbsp onion powder
- 6 tbsp butter

Directions:

1. Preheat your wood pellet grill to 375°F.
2. Place the rockfish in a baking dish and season with salt, dill, garlic, and onion.
3. Place butter on top of the fish then close the lid. Cook for 20 minutes or until the fish is no longer translucent.
4. Remove from grill and let sit for 5 minutes before serving. enjoy.

Nutrition Info: Calories 270, Total fat 17g, Saturated fat 9g, Total Carbs 2g, Net Carbs 0g, Protein 28g, Sugar 0g, Fiber 0g, Sodium: 381mg

Cajun-blackened Shrimp

Servings: 4
Cooking Time: 20 Minutes
Ingredients:

- 1 pound peeled and deveined shrimp, with tails on
- 1 batch Cajun Rub
- 8 tablespoons (1 stick) butter
- ¼ cup Worcestershire sauce

Directions:

1. Supply your smoker with wood pellets and follow the manufacturer's specific start-up procedure. Preheat the grill, with the lid closed, to 450°F and place a cast-iron skillet on the grill grate. Wait about 10 minutes after your grill has reached temperature, allowing the skillet to get hot.
2. Meanwhile, season the shrimp all over with the rub.
3. When the skillet is hot, place the butter in it to melt. Once the butter melts, stir in the Worcestershire sauce.
4. Add the shrimp and gently stir to coat. Smoke-braise the shrimp for about 10 minutes per side, until opaque and cooked through. Remove the shrimp from the grill and serve immediately.

Barbecued Shrimp

Servings: 4
Cooking Time: 10 Minutes

Ingredients:
- 1 pound peeled and deveined shrimp, with tails on
- 2 tablespoons olive oil
- 1 batch Dill Seafood Rub

Directions:
1. Soak wooden skewers in water for 30 minutes.
2. Supply your smoker with wood pellets and follow the manufacturer's specific start-up procedure. Preheat the grill, with the lid closed, to 375°F.
3. Thread 4 or 5 shrimp per skewer.
4. Coat the shrimp all over with olive oil and season each side of the skewers with the rub.
5. Place the skewers directly on the grill grate and grill the shrimp for 5 minutes per side. Remove the skewers from the grill and serve immediately.

OTHER FAVORITE RECIPES

Marinated Chicken Kabobs

Servings: 6
Cooking Time: 12 Minutes
Ingredients:
- Marinade
- 1/2 cup olive oi
- 2 tbsp white vinegar
- 1 tbsp lemon juice
- 1-1/2 tbsp salt
- 1/2 tbsp ground pepper
- 2 tbsp fresh chives, chopped
- 1-1/2 tbsp thyme, chopped
- 2 tbsp Italian parsley, chopped
- 1 tbsp minced garlic
- Kabobs
- 1-1/2 lb chicken breast
- 12 crimini mushrooms
- 1 each orange, red and yellow bell pepper
- Serve with
- Naan bread

Directions:
1. Mix all the marinade ingredients then toss the chicken and mushrooms until well coated.
2. Place in the fridge to marinate for 30 minutes.
3. Meanwhile, soak the skewers in water. And preheat your to 450F.
4. Assemble the kabobs and grill for 6 minutes on each side. Set aside.
5. Heat up the naan bread on the grill for 2 minutes .serve and enjoy.
Nutrition Info: Calories 165, Total fat 5g, Saturated fat 2g, Total carbs 1g, Net carbs 1g Protein 0g, Sugars 0g, Fiber 0g, Sodium 582mg

Smoked Hot Paprika Pork Tenderloin

Servings: 6
Cooking Time: 2 ½ To 3 Hours
Ingredients:
- 2-pound pork tenderloin
- 3/4 cup chicken stock
- 1/2 cup tomato-basil sauce
- 2 tbsp smoked hot paprika (or to taste)
- 1 tbsp oregano
- Salt and pepper to taste

Directions:
1. In a bowl, combine the chicken stock, tomato-basil sauce, paprika, oregano, salt, and pepper together.
2. Brush over tenderloin.
3. Smoke grill for 4-5 minutes. Pre head, lid closed for 10-14 minutes

4. Place pork for 2 ½ to 3 hours.
5. Rest for 10 minutes.
Nutrition Info: Calories: 360.71 Cal Fat: 14.32 g Carbohydrates: 3.21 g Protein: 52.09 g Fiber: 1.45 g

Rosemary-garlic Lamb Seasoning

Servings: 2
Cooking Time: 5 Minutes
Ingredients:
- 2 teaspoons dried rosemary leaves
- 2 teaspoons coarse kosher salt
- 1 teaspoon garlic powder
- 1 teaspoon freshly ground black pepper
- ½ teaspoon onion powder
- ½ teaspoon dried minced onion

Directions:
1. In a small airtight container or zip-top bag, combine the rosemary, salt, garlic powder, black pepper, onion powder, and minced onion.
2. Close the container and shake to mix. Unused seasoning will keep in an airtight container for months.

Barbecue Sandwich

Servings: 6
Cooking Time: 30 Minutes
Ingredients:
- 3 lb. steak
- ½ cup barbecue sauce
- 6 ciabatta rolls
- 6 slices cheddar cheese

Directions:
1. Preheat your wood pellet grill to 450 degrees F. for 15 minutes while the lid is closed.
2. Grill the steak for 30 minutes.
3. Let rest on a cutting board.
4. Slice thinly.
5. Coat with the barbecue sauce.
6. Stuff in ciabatta rolls with cheese.
7. Tips: You can also smoke the beef before grilling.

Tofu Smoothie

Servings: 2
Cooking Time: 5 Minutes
Ingredients:
- 1 Banana, sliced and frozen
- 3/4 cup Almond Milk
- 2 tbsp. Peanut Butter
- 1/2 cup Yoghurt, plain and low-fat

- 1/2 cup Tofu, soft and silken
- 1/3 cup Dates, chopped

Directions:
1. First, place tofu, banana, dates, yogurt, peanut butter, and almond milk in the blender pitcher.
2. After that, press the 'smoothie' button.
3. Finally, transfer to serving glass and enjoy it.

Nutrition Info: Fat: 0 g Calories: 330 Total Carbs: 0 g Fiber: 0 g Sugar: 0 g Protein: 0 g Cholesterol: 0

Venison Rib Roast

Servings: 6
Cooking Time: 25 Minutes
Ingredients:
- 2 pounds venison roast, about 8 ribs
- Rib rub as needed
- 1 tablespoon olive oil

Directions:
1. Switch on the grill, fill the grill hopper with hickory flavored wood pellets, power the grill on by using the control panel, select 'smoke' on the temperature dial, or set the temperature to 375 degrees F and let it preheat for a minimum of 5 minutes.
2. Meanwhile, brush roast with oil and then season with rib rub until well coated.
3. When the grill has preheated, open the lid, place food on the grill grate, shut the grill, and smoke for 25 minutes until the internal temperature reaches 125 degrees F.
4. When done, transfer roast to a cutting board, let it rest for 10 minutes, then cut into slices and serve.

Nutrition Info: Calories: 128 Cal ;Fat: 2.8 g ;Carbs: 0 g ;Protein: 24.8 g ;Fiber: 0 g

Grilled Lime Chicken

Servings: 6
Cooking Time: 45 Minutes
Ingredients:
- 2 teaspoon sugar
- 1 teaspoon chili powder
- 1 1/2 teaspoons granulated garlic
- 1 1/2 teaspoons ground cumin
- Salt and pepper to taste
- 12 chicken thighs, skin removed
- 1 1/2 tablespoons olive oil
- 1 1/2 tablespoons butter
- 4 tablespoons pineapple juice
- 4 tablespoons honey
- 1 1/2 tablespoons lime juice
- 1/4 teaspoon red pepper flakes
- 1 1/2 tablespoons hot sauce

Directions:
1. Set the grill to 375 degrees F.
2. Preheat it for 10 minutes.
3. In a bowl, mix the sugar, chili powder, garlic, cumin, salt and pepper.
4. Coat the chicken with the olive oil and sprinkle with the dry rub.
5. Grill the chicken for 7 minutes per side.
6. In a pan over medium heat, simmer the rest of the ingredients for 10 minutes.
7. Remove from heat and transfer to a bowl.
8. Brush the mixture on both sides of the chicken.
9. Cook for another 7 minutes per side.
10. Tips: Add more hot sauce to the glaze if you want your chicken spicier.

Belgian Ale-braised Brisket

Servings: 6
Cooking Time: 3 Hours
Ingredients:
- 1/4 cup Dijon mustard
- 2 bay leaves
- 1/4 cup all-purpose flour
- 1/4 cup dark brown sugar, packed
- 2 Tbsp bacon fat
- 2 medium onion, thinly sliced
- Kosher salt
- 4lb beef brisket, flat cut, untrimmed
- 1 Tbsp grated ginger
- 4 cups beef broth
- 750ml bottle Belgian style tripel ale

Directions:
1. Preheat wood pellet smoker-grill to 400°F.
2. Rub brisket in salt and leave in a reusable plastic bag for 8 hours at room temperature.
3. In a small bowl, mix ginger, brown sugar, and ginger.
4. Remove brisket from the bag, rub mustard over brisket, and place on the grill grate. Roast for 40 minutes, until the top, is brown.
5. Transfer brisket to a plate and set aside.
6. Reduce the temperature of the grill to 300°F.
7. Heat bacon fat in a cast-iron Dutch oven placed on the grill. Add onions and sprinkle in the salt. Stir continuously and cook until brown, about 10 minutes.
8. Reduce heat and stir in flour and cook for another 4 minutes. Add ale, bay leaves, and stock, and then allow to simmer. Put in brisket and cover the lid of the Dutch oven.
9. Braise brisket for 4 hours with the grill cover closed.
10. Remove bay leaves and place brisket on a platter. Allow resting of brisket for 20 minutes before carving.
11. Serve brisket with braising liquid.

Nutrition Info: Per Serving:Calories: 387kcal,Carbs: 35g,Fat: 21g, Protein: 14g

Red Wine Beef Stew

Servings: 8
Cooking Time: 3 Hours 30 Minutes
Ingredients:
- 1-1/2 tsp kosher salt
- 4lb chuck roast, cut into 2-inch pieces
- 1 Tsp ground black pepper
- 1/4 cup tomato paste
- 1 Tsp olive oil
- 2 cups dry red wine
- 2 bay leaves
- 4 spring's fresh thyme
- 2 lb carrots, peeled and chopped
- 1lb red potatoes, cut into half
- 4 cups chicken broth
- 3 Tsp all-purpose flour

Directions:
1. Preheat wood pellet smoker-grill to 325^{0}F, with the lid closed for about 15 minutes
2. Place meat in a bowl and sprinkle in salt, pepper, and flour. Toss together until meat is adequately seasoned.
3. Heat oil in a cast-iron Dutch oven and cook the meat at Medium for about 8 minutes, until brown.
4. Remove meat and place on a plate. Add wine, broth, tomato paste, thyme, bay leaves, and 1/4 of carrots into the Dutch oven and bring to a boil. Transfer meat to Dutch oven and place on the grill grate for direct cooking. Cook meat for about 2 hours.
5. Remove cooked vegetables from Dutch oven and add remaining carrots and potatoes. Cook until meat is fork-tender, about 1 hour.
6. Serve.

Nutrition Info: Per Serving: Calories: 402kcal,Carbs: 17.3g,Fat: 15.4g, Protein: 35.5g

Mouthwatering Cauliflower

Servings: 8
Cooking Time: 30 Minutes
Ingredients:
- 2 large heads cauliflower head, stem removed and cut into 2-inch florets
- 3 tbsp. olive oil
- Salt and freshly ground black pepper, to taste
- ¼ C. fresh parsley, chopped finely

Directions:
1. Set the temperature of Grill to 500 degrees F and preheat with closed lid for 15 minutes.

2. In a large bowl, add cauliflower florets, oil, salt and black pepper and toss to coat well.
3. Divide the cauliflower florets onto 2 baking sheets and spread in an even layer.
4. Place the baking sheets onto the grill and cook for about 20-30 minutes, stirring once after 15 minutes.
5. Remove the vegetables from grill and transfer into a large bowl.
6. Immediately, add the parsley and toss to coat well.
7. Serve immediately.

Nutrition Info: Calories per serving: 62; Carbohydrates: 3.6g; Protein: 1.4g; Fat: 5.3g; Sugar: 1.6g; Sodium: 40mg; Fiber: 1.7g

Satisfying Veggie Casserole

Servings: 10
Cooking Time: 3 Hours
Ingredients:
- 5 tbsp. olive oil, divided
- 6 C. onions, sliced thinly
- 1 tbsp. fresh thyme, chopped and divided
- Salt and freshly ground black pepper, to taste
- 1 tbsp. unsalted butter
- 1¼ lb. Yukon gold potatoes, peeled and 1/8-inch thick slices
- ½ C. heavy cream
- 2¼ lb. tomatoes, cut into ¼-inch thick slices
- ¼ cup black olives, pitted and sliced

Directions:
1. In a large cast iron pan, heat 3 tbsp.of oil and over high heat and cook onions, 1 tsp. of thyme, salt and black pepper for about 5 minutes, stirring occasionally.
2. Add the butter and cook over medium heat for about 15 minutes.
3. Reduce the heat to low and cook for about 10 minutes.
4. Set the temperature of Grill to 350 degrees F and preheat with closed lid for 15 minutes.
5. Meanwhile, in a bowl, add potatoes slices, cream, 1 tsp. of thyme, salt and black pepper and toss to coat.
6. In another bowl, add tomato slices, salt and black pepper and toss to coat.
7. Transfer half of the caramelized onions into a small bowl.
8. In the bottom of the cast iron pan, spread the remaining onion slices evenly and top with 1 layer of potatoes and tomatoes.
9. Drizzle with 2 tbsp. of cream from potato mixture and 1 tbsp. of olive oil.
10. Sprinkle with a little salt, black pepper and ½ tsp. of thyme.

11. Spread remaining caramelized onions on top, followed by potatoes, tomatoes and olives.
12. Drizzle with remaining cream from the potatoes and remaining tbsp. of olive oil.
13. Sprinkle with a little salt, black pepper and remaining ½ tsp. of thyme.
14. With a piece of foil, cover the cast iron pan tightly.
15. Place the pan onto the grill and cook for about 2 hours.
16. Remove from grill and uncover the cast iron pan.
17. Now, set the temperature of Grill to 450 degrees F.
18. Place the cast iron pan,uncovered onto the grill and cook for about 25-30 minutes.
19. Remove from grill and serve hot.
Nutrition Info: Calories per serving: 158; Carbohydrates: 14.8g; Protein: 2.3g; Fat: 11.1g; Sugar: 5.8g; Sodium: 65mg; Fiber: 3.2g

Ginger And Chili Grilled Shrimp

Servings: 6
Cooking Time: 1 Hour 15 Minutes
Ingredients:
- 1 tsp of salt, kosher
- 2 mangos, riped, peeled, and chopped
- 1 Tbsp of fresh ginger, grated
- 2 cloves of garlic, crushed
- 1-1/4 pound of jumbo shrimp, deveined and peeled.
- 2 jalapenos, chopped
- 1/2 cup of buttermilk, low-fat
- 1/2 tsp of black pepper, ground
- 1 lime, small and also cut into wedges (6)

Directions:
1. Set the grill for direct cooking at 150°F. Use hickory wood pellets for a robust taste.
2. Pour the ginger into a bowl, add buttermilk, jalapenos, garlic, pepper, and salt. Mix thoroughly.
3. Put shrimps inside the same bowl, and mix well with a wooden spoon. Allow it to marinate in the refrigerator for an hour
4. Arrange 2 mango chops, 3 shrimps on a water-soaked wooden skewer. Do this for the other 5 skewers.
5. Place shrimp skewers on the grates and grill for 10 minutes, or until the shrimps turn opaque. Serve immediately with the lime wedge
Nutrition Info: Per Serving: Calories: 80kcal, Protein: 20g, Fat:1.3g, Carb: 1.2g

Smoked Pork Tenderloin With Mexican Pineapple Sauce

Servings: 6
Cooking Time: 3 Hours And 55 Minutes
Ingredients:
- Pineapple Sauce
- 1 can (11 oz) unsweetened crushed pineapple
- 1 can (11 oz) roasted tomato or tomatillo
- 1/2 cup port wine
- 1/4 cup orange juice
- 1/4 cup packed brown sugar
- 1/4 cup lime juice
- 2 tbsp Worcestershire sauce
- 1 tsp garlic powder
- 1/4 tsp cayenne pepper
- PORK
- 2 pork tenderloin (1 pound each)
- 1 tsp ground cumin
- 1/2 tsp pepper
- 1/4 tsp cayenne pepper
- 2 tbsp lime juice (freshly squeezed)

Directions:
1. Combine cumin, pepper, cayenne pepper and lime juice and rub over tenderloins.
2. Smoke grill for 4-5 minutes. Preheat, lid closed for 10-15 minutes
3. Smoke tenderloin for 2 ½ to 3 hours.
4. Rest for 5 minutes
5. For Sauce:
6. Combine ingredients and boil for 25 minutes
7. Remove from heat and cool.
8. Serve pork slices with pineapple sauce and lime wedges.
Nutrition Info: Calories: 277.85 Cal Fat: 3.49 g Carbohydrates: 24.31 g Protein: 32.42 g Fiber: 0.67 g

Classic Apple Pie

Servings: 8
Cooking Time: 2 Hours
Ingredients:
- 2 Tbsp all-purpose flour
- 2 pie dough rounds
- 6 cups of apple, peeled and sliced
- 1 Tbsp lemon juice
- 3/4 cup of sugar
- 1/4 tsp powdered nutmeg
- 1/2 tsp powdered cinnamon
- 1/2 tsp salt

Directions:
1. Set the wood pellet smoker-grill to indirect cooking at 425 F
2. In a large bowl, combine all your ingredients (except for the pie dough) and mix well. Gently press

one of the pie dough unto a 10-inch pie dough plate. Make sure it is firm and covers the sides.

3. Pour in your apple mixture. Cover the filling with the second pie dough, gently clip the two doughs together. Make a crosshatch slit on the top with a knife—transfer dough plate to the cooking grid.

4. Bake for 45-60 minutes or until the crust browns. Allow to cool for 1 hour before serving.

Nutrition Info: Per Serving: Calories: 542kcal, Carbs: 41g, Fat: 20g, Protein: 10g

Coconut Dipping Sauce

Servings: 4
Cooking Time: 10 Minutes
Ingredients:
- 4 tablespoons coconut milk
- 1 tablespoon curry paste
- 2 tablespoons lime juice
- 2 tsp soy sauce
- 1 oz. parsley
- 2 tablespoons olive oil

Directions:
1. In a blender place all ingredients and blend until smooth
2. Pour sauce in a bowl and serve

Buttered Green Peas

Servings: 1-2
Cooking Time: 30 Minutes
Ingredients:
- 1/2 cup butter, melted
- Kosher salt
- 24 oz green beans, trimmed
- 1/4 cup veggie rub

Directions:
1. Preheat the wood pellet smoker-grill to 345°F using pellets of your choice
2. Pour the beans into a baking pan lined with parchment sheets and rub melted butter over the beans. Season with salt. Place the baking pan on the cooking grid.
3. Arrange the beans on the pan with a tong and pour the veggie rub over it.
4. Braise the beans until tender and lightly browned. Flip after 20 minutes.
5. Serve.

Nutrition Info: Per Serving: Calories: 93kcal,Carbs: 9.5g, Fat: 3.8g, Protein: 3.8g

Rosemary Cheese Bread

Servings: 30
Cooking Time: 12 Minutes
Ingredients:
- 1½ cup sunflower seeds
- ½ tsp sea salt
- 1egg
- 1tsp fresh rosemary (finely chopped)
- 2tsp xanthan gum
- 2tbsp cream cheese
- 2cups grated mozzarella

Directions:
1. Preheat the grill to 400°F with the lid closed for 15 minutes.
2. Toss the sunflower seeds into a powerful blender and blend until it smooth and flour-like.
3. Transfer the sunflower seed flour into a mixing bowl and add the rosemary and xanthan gum. Mix and set aside.
4. Melt the cheese in a microwave. To do this, combine the cream cheese and mozzarella cheese in a microwave-safe dish.
5. Place the microwave-safe dish in the grill and heat the cheese on high for 1 minute.
6. Bring out the dish and stir. Place the dish in the grill and heat for 30 seconds. Bring out the dish and stir until smooth.
7. Pour the melted cheese into a large mixing bowl.
8. Add the sunflower flour mixture to the melted cheese and stir the ingredients are well combined.
9. Add the salt and egg and mix thoroughly to form a smooth dough.
10. Measure out equal pieces of the dough and roll into sticks.
11. Grease a baking sheet with oil and arrange the breadsticks into the baking sheet in a single layer.
12. Use the back of a knife or metal spoon to make lines on the breadsticks.
13. Place the baking sheet on the grill and make for about 12 minutes or until the breadsticks turn golden brown.
14. Remove the baking sheet from the grill and let the breadsticks cool for a few minutes.
15. Serve.

Nutrition Info: Calories: 23 Total Fat: 1.9 g Saturated Fat: 0.5 g Cholesterol: 7 mg Sodium: 47 mg Total Carbohydrate: 0.6 g Dietary Fiber: 0.2 g Total Sugars: 0.1 g Protein: 1.2 g

Sandwich With Roasted Beef

Servings: 4
Cooking Time: 25 Minutes
Ingredients:
- Butter

- Barbecue sauce
- 1 pound of beef roast
- 4 hamburger buns

Directions:
1. Set the grill for direct cooking at 300°F. Use hickory pellets.
2. Roast the beef on the grill for 20 minutes or until internal temperature reads 135°F.
3. Lightly rub butter on the hamburger buns, then arrange the roasted beef between the buttered buns. You can also put the barbecue sauce well on the meat.
4. Serve immediately.

Nutrition Info: Per Serving: Calories: 340kcal, Protein: 22g, Fat:12.9g, Carb: 32.9g.

Pork And Portobello Burgers

Servings: 4
Cooking Time: 30 Minutes
Ingredients:
- 1 pound ground pork
- 1 tablespoon minced garlic
- 1 teaspoon minced fresh rosemary, fennel seed or parsley
- Salt and ground black pepper
- 4 large portobello mushroom caps, stems removed
- Olive oil
- 4 burger buns
- Any burger fixings you like

Directions:
1. Combine the ground pork, garlic, rosemary and a sprinkle of salt and pepper. Use a spoon to lightly scrape away the gills of the mushrooms and hollow them slightly. Drizzle the mushrooms (inside and out) with olive oil and sprinkle with salt and pepper. Press 1/4 of the mixture into each of the hollow sides of the mushrooms; you want the meat to spread all the way across the width of the mushrooms. They should look like burgers.
2. Grill the burgers, meat side down, until the pork is well browned, 4 to 6 minutes. Flip and cook until the top side of the mushrooms are browned and the mushrooms are tender, another 6 to 8 minutes. If you like, use an instant-read thermometer to check the interior temperature of the pork, which should be a minimum of 145 degrees.
3. Serve the burgers on buns (toasted, if you like) with any fixings you like.

Hot Sauce With Cilantro

Servings: 4
Cooking Time: 10 Minutes
Ingredients:
- ½ tsp coriander
- ½ tsp cumin seeds
- ¼ tsp black pepper
- 2 green cardamom pods
- 2 garlic cloves
- 1 tsp salt
- 1 oz. parsley
- 2 tablespoons olive oil

Directions:
1. In a blender place all ingredients and blend until smooth
2. Pour sauce in a bowl and serve

Texas-style Brisket Rub

Servings: 1
Cooking Time: 15 Minutes
Ingredients:
- 2 tsp Sugar
- 2 Tbsp Kosher salt
- 2 tsp Chilli powder
- 2 Tbsp Black pepper
- Tbsp Cayenne pepper
- Tbsp Powdered garlic
- tsp Grounded cumin
- 2 Tbsp Powdered onion
- 1/4 cup paprika, smoked

Directions:
1. Mix all the ingredients in a small bowl until it is well blended.
2. Transfer to an airtight jar or container. Store in a cool place.

Nutrition Info: Per Serving: Calories: 18kcal, Carbs: 2g, Fat: 1g, Protein: 0.6g

All-purpose Dry Rub

Servings: 2 And ½ Cups
Cooking Time: 5 Minutes
Ingredients:
- ½ cup paprika, or 1/3 cup smoked paprika
- ¼ cup kosher salt
- ¼ cup freshly ground black pepper
- ¼ cup brown sugar
- ¼ cup chile powder
- 3 tablespoons ground cumin
- 2 tablespoons ground coriander
- 1 tablespoon cayenne pepper, or to taste

Directions:
1. Combine all ingredients in a bowl and mix well with a fork to break up the sugar and combine the spices. Mixture will keep in an airtight container, out of the light, for a few months.

Beef Pot Roast

Servings: 6
Cooking Time: 3 Hours 10 Minutes
Ingredients:
- 3 cup beef stock
- 1 cup carrots, chopped
- 1 Tbsp garlic, minced
- 1/4 cup softened butter
- 1 Tsp ground black pepper
- 2 red onions, chopped
- 4lb chuck roast
- 1 Tbsp kosher salt
- 1Tbsp sage, chopped
- 1/2 cup red wine

Directions:
1. Preheat Grill & Smoker to 300°F with the cover of the grill closed for 10 minutes.
2. In a stockpot, put in red wine, beef stock, butter, garlic, carrot, red onion, sage, and chuck roast—season with pepper and salt. Stir the contents and cover the pot.
3. Transfer stockpot to the preheated grill; close the grill lid and leave to cook for 3 hours, until the roast reaches an internal temperature of 203°F.
4. Serve.

Nutrition Info: Per Serving: Calories: 487kcal, Carbs: 19g, Fat: 17g, Protein: 6.0g

Seared Venison Chops With Marsala

Servings: 6
Cooking Time: 1 Hour 10 Minutes
Ingredients:
- 1 cup marsala wine
- Venison chops
- 3 Tbsp unsalted butter
- 2 Tbsp olive oil
- 1 cup of beef stock
- 1 tsp fresh sage, finely chopped
- 1 cup of beef stock
- Salt and pepper to taste
- peeled shallot

Directions:
1. Set the wood pellet smoker-grill to direct cooking at 300 F
2. Rinse the venison and pat dry with a paper towel. Season with salt and pepper.
3. Grill both sides of venison for 30 minutes, then set aside and increase the temperature of the grill to High.
4. Place a skillet over cooking grates, add oil and sear venison for 4 minutes per side. Set aside.
5. Place a small pot over cooking grates, melt 1 tbsp of butter and sauté the shallot for 5 minutes, or until they are brown.

6. Add the stock, marsala, and sage and allow it to simmer for 15-20 minutes. Add the remaining butter, season with salt and pepper.
7. Serve with the venison.

Nutrition Info: Per Serving: Calories: 345kcal, Carbs: 24g, Fat: 23.5g, Protein: 45g

Smoking Burgers

Servings: 8
Cooking Time: 4o Minutes
Ingredients:
- For the topping:
- 3 apples, peeled and cut into slices
- 75g blueberries
- 25g salted butter
- 2 tablespoons maple syrup
- For the cake:
- 75g butter, cut into cubes
- 75g organic virgin coconut oil, cut into cubes
- 100g cane sugar
- 2 large free-range eggs, beaten
- 75g buckwheat flour
- 75g ground almonds
- ½ teaspoon bicarbonate of soda
- 1 teaspoon baking powder
- 1 teaspoon cinnamon

Directions:
1. Preheat oven to 180°C. Caramelize the apples.
2. Add the blueberries last. Set aside. Place the sugar, butter and coconut oil into a mixing bowl and cream until pale and fluffy.
3. Gradually add the beaten eggs, adding a bit of flour if the mixture begins to curdle. Continue to beat the mixture until fluffy. Fold in the remaining flour, ground almonds, baking powder and cinnamon.
4. Transfer the apple and blueberry mixture into the bottom of a greased Bundt cake mold, leveling well with the back of a spoon. Then pour the cake mixture over the top. Bake for about 40 minutes or until a skewer comes out clean. Leave to cool. Delicious served with Greek yogurt.

Nutrition Info: Calories: 275 Cal Fat: 10 g Carbohydrates: 31 g Protein: 14 g Fiber: 4 g

Grilled Pineapple With Chocolate Sauce

Servings: 6 To 8
Cooking Time: 25 Minutes
Ingredients:
- 1pineapple
- 8 oz bittersweet chocolate chips
- 1/2 cup spiced rum
- 1/2 cup whipping cream

128

- 2tbsp light brown sugar

Directions:
1. Preheat pellet grill to 400°F.
2. De-skin the pineapple and slice pineapple into 1 in cubes.
3. In a saucepan, combine chocolate chips. When chips begin to melt, add rum to the saucepan. Continue to stir until combined, then add a splash of the pineapple's juice.
4. Add in whipping cream and continue to stir the mixture. Once the sauce is smooth and thickening, lower heat to simmer to keep warm.
5. Thread pineapple cubes onto skewers. Sprinkle skewers with brown sugar.
6. Place skewers on the grill grate. Grill for about 5 minutes per side, or until grill marks begin to develop.
7. Remove skewers from grill and allow to rest on a plate for about 5 minutes. Serve alongside warm chocolate sauce for dipping.

Nutrition Info: Calories: 112.6 Fat: 0.5 g Cholesterol: 0 Carbohydrate: 28.8 g Fiber: 1.6 g Sugar: 0.1 g Protein: 0.4 g

Savory Applesauce On The Grill

Servings: 2
Cooking Time: 45 Minutes
Ingredients:
- 1½ pounds whole apples
- Salt

Directions:
1. Start the coals or heat a gas grill for medium direct cooking. Make sure the grates are clean.
2. Put the apples on the grill directly over the fire. Close the lid and cook until the fruit feels soft when gently squeezed with tongs, 10 to 20 minutes total, depending on their size. Transfer to a cutting board and let sit until cool enough to touch.
3. Cut the flesh from around the core of each apple; discard the cores. Put the chunks in a blender or food processor and process until smooth, or put them in a bowl and purée with an immersion blender until as chunky or smooth as you like. Add a generous pinch of salt, then taste and adjust the seasoning. Serve or refrigerate in an airtight container for up to 3 days.

Nutrition Info: Calories: 15 Fats: 0 g Cholesterol: 0 mg Carbohydrates: 3 g Fiber: 0 g Sugars: 3 g Proteins: 0 g

Reverse-seared Halibut

Servings: 4
Cooking Time: 50 Minutes
Ingredients:

- halibut fillet (skin removed)
- 1 tsp of salt
- 1 tsp grounded black pepper
- 1 tsp of dried basil
- 1 tbsp lemon juice
- Pinch of chopped parsley
- tbsps olive oil.

Directions:
1. Preheat the wood pellet smoker-grill for direct cooking at 300 F.
2. In a large bowl, add the fillets, salt, basil, olive oil, salt, pepper, and lemon juice. Cover and refrigerate for 30 minutes.
3. Grill the halibut for 30 minutes, then set aside.
4. Increase the temperature to 450 F and allow the temperature of the grill to rise.
5. Sear halibut for 3 minutes per side. Remove and garnish with parsley.

Nutrition Info: Per Serving: Calories: 517kcal, Carbs: 2g, Fat: 23g, Protein: 37g

Cajun Rub

Servings: 3
Cooking Time: 5 Minutes
Ingredients:
- 1 teaspoon freshly ground black pepper
- 1 teaspoon onion powder
- 1 teaspoon coarse kosher salt
- 1 teaspoon garlic powder
- 1 teaspoon sweet paprika
- ½ teaspoon cayenne pepper
- ½ teaspoon red pepper flakes
- ½ teaspoon dried oregano leaves
- ½ teaspoon dried thyme
- ½ teaspoon smoked paprika

Directions:
1. In a small airtight container or zip-top bag, combine the black pepper, onion powder, salt, garlic powder, sweet paprika, cayenne, red pepper flakes, oregano, thyme, and smoked paprika.
2. Close the container and shake to mix. Unused rub will keep in an airtight container for months.

Grilled Bacon Dog

Servings: 4 To 6
Cooking Time: 25 Minutes
Ingredients:
- 16 Hot Dogs
- 16 Slices Bacon, sliced
- 2 Onion, sliced
- 16 hot dog buns
- As Needed The Ultimate BBQ Sauce

- As Needed Cheese

Directions:

1. When ready to cook, set the to 375°F and preheat, lid closed for 15 minutes.
2. Wrap bacon strips around the hot dogs, and grill directly on the grill grate for 10 minutes each side. Grill onions at the same time as the hot dogs, and cook for 10 -15 minutes.
3. Open hot dog buns and spread BBQ sauce, the grilled hot dogs, cheese sauce and grilled onions. Top with vegetables. Serve, enjoy!

Twice- Baked Potatoes With Smoked Gouda And Grilled Scallions

Servings: 6
Cooking Time: 1hours 15 Minutes
Ingredients:

- 3 large potatoes
- 8 TbspUnsalted butter
- Tbsp Of barbeque rub
- 1-1/2 cup of smoked gouda cheese (grated)
- 1/4 cup of extra-virgin olive oil
- 3/4 cup heavy cream
- Salt and pepper to taste
- 1/4 cup chopped scallions

Directions:

1. Set the wood pellet smoker-grill to indirect cooking at 400 F
2. Brush the potatoes with olive oil, make incisions with fork and season with salt. Wrap with aluminum foil paper and bake on grill grates for 30 minutes per side. Transfer to a rimmed sheet and allow to cool.
3. Cut the potatoes lengthwise, scoop out the flesh into a bowl. Add butter and 1 cup of cheese. Set aside. Place a small pot over low-medium heat, add cream, then heat for 1 minute. Add the scallions and the barbeque rub and mix well
4. Add the scallion mixture to the potatoes and cheese in the bowl, combine until it is evenly mixed. Scoop the mixture back into the potato shell and top with cheese.
5. Bake for 5 minutes or until the cheese melts.

Nutrition Info: Per Serving: Calories: 276kcal, Carbs: 28g, Fat: 14.5g, Protein: 3g

Smoked Chuck Roast

Servings: 6
Cooking Time: 5 Hours
Ingredients:

- 3 lb. chuck roast
- 3 tablespoons sweet and spicy rub
- 3 cups beef stock, divided

- 1 yellow onion, sliced

Directions:

1. Add the chuck roast to a baking pan.
2. Coat with the sweet, spicy rub.
3. Cover with foil. Refrigerate and marinate overnight.
4. Set the wood pellet grill to smoke.
5. Preheat it to 225 degrees F.
6. Add the chuck roast to the grill.
7. Close the lid.
8. Smoke the chuck roast for 3 hours.
9. Brush with 1 cup beef stock every 1 hour.
10. Add the onion slices to a baking pan.
11. Pour the remaining beef stock.
12. Transfer the chuck roast on top of the onions.
13. Increase the heat to 250 degrees F.
14. Smoke for 3 hours.
15. Cover the chuck roast with the foil.
16. Smoke for another 2 hours and 30 minutes.
17. Let the chuck roast rest for 10 minutes.
18. Serving Suggestion: Serve with mashed potatoes.

Nutrition Info: Calories: 201 Fat: 13 g Cholesterol: 71 mg Carbohydrates: 0 g Fiber: 0 g Sugars: 0 g Protein: 21 g

North American Pot Pie

Servings: 10
Cooking Time: 1 Hour 25 Minutes
Ingredients:

- 2 tbsp. cornstarch
- 2 tbsp. water
- 3 C. chicken broth
- 1 C. milk
- 3 tbsp. butter
- 1 tbsp. fresh rosemary, chopped
- 1 tbsp. fresh thyme, chopped
- Salt and freshly ground black pepper, to taste
- 2¾ C. frozen chopped broccoli, thawed
- 3 C. frozen peas, thawed
- 3 C. chopped frozen carrots, thawed
- 1 frozen puff pastry sheet

Directions:

1. Set the temperature of Grill to 375 degrees F and preheat with closed lid for 15 minutes.
2. In a small bowl, dissolve cornstarch in water. Set aside.
3. In a pan, add broth, milk, butter and herbs over medium heat and bring to a boil.
4. Add the cornstarch mixture and stir to combine well.
5. Stir in salt and black pepper and remove from the heat.
6. In a large bowl, add the vegetables and milk sauce and mix well.

7. Transfer mixture into a cast iron skillet.
8. With the puff pastry, cover the mixture and cut excess from edges.
9. Place the skillet onto the grill and cook for about 80 minutes.
10. Remove the pan from grill and set aside for about 15 minutes before serving.
11. Cut the pie into desired-sized portions and serve.
Nutrition Info: Calories per serving: 257; Carbohydrates: 26.1g; Protein: 7.6g; Fat: 14g; Sugar: 5.8g; Sodium: 408mg; Fiber: 4.7g

Tea Injectable

Servings: 2 Cups
Cooking Time: 30 Minutes
Ingredients:
- ¼ cup favorite spice rub or shake
- 2 cups water

Directions:
1. Place the rub in a standard paper coffee filter and tie it up with kitchen string to seal.
2. In a small pot over high heat, bring the water to a boil.
3. Drop the filter into the boiling water and remove the pot from the heat. Let it steep for 30 minutes.
4. Remove and discard the filter. Discard any unused tea after injecting the meat.

Smoked Pork Chops Marinated With Tarragon

Servings: 4
Cooking Time: 4-6 Hours
Ingredients:
- 1/2 cup olive oil
- 4 Tbsp of fresh tarragon chopped
- 2 tsp fresh thyme, chopped
- salt and grated black pepper
- 2 tsp apple-cider vinegar
- 4 pork chops or fillets

Directions:
1. Whisk the olive oil, tarragon, thyme, salt, pepper, apple cider and stir well. Place the pork chops in a container and pour with tarragon mixture.
2. Refrigerate for 2 hours. Start pellet grill on, lid open, until the fire is established (4-5 minutes).
3. The temperature must rise to 250 degrees Fahrenheit with the lid closed until 15 minutes
4. The temperature must rise up to 250 degrees Fahrenheit and must be preheated for at most 15 minutes. Remove chops from marinade and pat dry on kitchen towel. Arrange pork chops on the grill rack and smoke for about 3 to 4 hours. Transfer

chops on a serving platter and let rest 15 minutes before serving.
Nutrition Info: Calories: 528.8 Cal Fat: 35 g Carbohydrates: 0.6 g Protein: 51 g Fiber: 0.14 g

Alder Wood Smoked Bony Trout

Servings: 4
Cooking Time: 2 Hours
Ingredients:
- 4 fresh boned whole trout with their skin on
- For trout Brine
- 4 cups of filtered water
- 1 cup of soy sauce
- ½ a cup of pickling kosher salt
- ½ a cup of brown sugar
- 2 tablespoon of garlic powder
- 2 tablespoon of onion powder
- 1 teaspoon of cayenne pepper

Directions:
1. Combine all of the ingredients listed under trout brine in two different 1-gallon bags.
2. Store it in your fridge.
3. Place your trout in the sealable bag with trout brine and place the bag in a shallow dish.
4. Let it refrigerate for about 2 hours, making sure to rotate it after 30 minutes.
5. Remove them from your brine and pat them dry using kitchen towels.
6. Air Dry your brine trout in your fridge uncovered for about 2 hours.
7. Preheat your smoker to a temperature of 180 degrees Fahrenheit using alder pellets.
8. The pit temperature of should be 180 degrees Fahrenheit and the cold smoke should be 70 degrees Fahrenheit.
9. Cold smoke your prepared trout for 90 minutes.
10. After 90 minutes transfer the cold smoked boned trout pellets to your smoker grill are and increase the smoker temperature to 225 degrees Fahrenheit.
11. Keep cooking until the internal temperature reaches 145 degrees Fahrenheit in the thickest parts.
12. Remove the trout from the grill and let them rest for 5 minutes.
13. Serve!
Nutrition Info: Calories: 508 Cal Fat: 23 g Carbohydrates: 47 g Protein: 15 g Fiber: 0 g

Grilled Flank Steak

Servings: 6
Cooking Time: 2 Hours 15 Minutes
Ingredients:
- 1/2 cup of soy sauce

- 1-1/2 pound of flank steak.
- 1/2 cup of bourbon
- 1/2 cup of water

Directions:

1. Set the grill for direct cooking at 300°F. Use hickory wood pellets for a strong taste and aroma.
2. Pour the soy sauce, 1/2 cup of water, and bourbon in a bowl. Whisk together to make a marinade. Pour the marinade inside a food storage bag and add the steak to the bag. Keep in the refrigerator for 2 hours to allow flavors to combine and penetrate steak.
3. Remove from the refrigerator and dry with a paper towel.
4. Grill the steak for about 30 minutes, flipping every five minutes to ensure both sides are equally cooked.
5. Cover the steak with foil paper and allow it to rest for about 5 minutes.
6. Serve.

Nutrition Info: Per Serving: Calories: 370kcal, Carbs: 45g, Protein: 25.5g, Fat: 32 g.

Baked Apple Crisp

Servings: 7
Cooking Time: 30 Minutes
Ingredients:
- Butter for greasing
- 1/2 cup flour
- 1/2 cup rolled oats
- 1 stick butter, sliced into cubes
- 1 cup brown sugar
- 1 1/2 teaspoon ground cinnamon
- 1/4 cup walnuts, chopped
- 3 lb. apples, sliced thinly
- ½ cup dried cranberries
- 2 1/2 tablespoons bourbon
- 1/2 cup brown sugar
- 1 tablespoon lemon juice
- 1/4 cup honey
- 1 teaspoon vanilla
- 1 1/2 teaspoons ground cinnamon
- Pinch salt

Directions:

1. Grease cast iron pan with butter.
2. Add flour, oats, butter cubes, 1 cup sugar, cinnamon and walnuts to a food processor. Pulse until crumbly.
3. In a bowl, mix the apples with the rest of the ingredients.
4. Pour apple mixture into the greased pan.
5. Spread flour mixture on top.
6. Bake in the wood pellet grill at 350 degrees F for 1 hour.

7. Tips: Use freshly squeezed lemon juice.

Thai Dipping Sauce

Servings: 4
Cooking Time: 10 Minutes
Ingredients:
- 6 tsp garlic sauce
- 2 tablespoons fish sauce
- 2 tablespoons lime juice
- 1 tablespoon brown sugar
- 1 tsp chili flakes

Directions:

1. In a blender place all ingredients and blend until smooth
2. Pour sauce in a bowl and serve

Veggie Lover's Burgers

Servings: 6
Cooking Time: 51 Minutes
Ingredients:
- ¾ C. lentils
- 1 tbsp. ground flaxseed
- 2 tbsp. extra-virgin olive oil
- 1 onion, chopped
- 2 garlic cloves, minced
- Salt and freshly ground black pepper, to taste
- 1 C. walnuts, toasted
- ¾ C. breadcrumbs
- 1 tsp. ground cumin
- 1 tsp. paprika

Directions:

1. In a pan of boiling water, add the lentils and cook for about 15 minutes or until soft.
2. Drain the lentils completely and set aside.
3. In a small bowl, mix together the flaxseed with 4 tbsp. of water. Set aside for about 5 minutes.
4. In a medium skillet, heat the oil over medium heat and sauté the onion for about 4-6 minutes.
5. Add the garlic and a pinch of salt and pepper and sauté for about 30 seconds.
6. Remove from the heat and place the onion mixture into a food processor.
7. Add the ¾ of the lentils, flaxseed mixture, walnuts, breadcrumbs and spices and pulse until smooth.
8. Transfer the mixture into a bowl and gently, fold in the remaining lentils.
9. Make 6 patties from the mixture.
10. Place the patties onto a parchment paper-lined plate and refrigerate for at least 30 minutes.

11. Set the temperature of Grill to 425 degrees F and preheat with closed lid for 15 minutes, using charcoal.

12. Place the burgers onto the grill and cook for about 8-10 minutes flipping once halfway through.

13. Serve hot.

Nutrition Info: Calories per serving: 324; Carbohydrates: 28.9g; Protein: 13.6g; Fat: 18.5g; Sugar: 13.6g; Sodium: 130mg; Fiber: 10.3g

Sweet Sensation Pork Meat

Servings: 3
Cooking Time: 3 Hours
Ingredients:
- 2 tsp of nutmeg, ground
- 1/4 cup of allspice
- 2 tsp of thyme, dried
- 1/4 cup of brown sugar
- 2 pounds of pork
- 2 tsp of cinnamon, ground
- 2 Tbsp of salt, kosher or sea

Directions:
1. Preheat the grill for 15 minutes at 225°F. Use hickory wood pellets
2. Combine all the ingredients (except pork) in a bowl. Mix thoroughly.
3. Slice the sides of the pork meat in 4-5 places. Put some of the ingredients into the slices and rub the rest over the pork.
4. Place the pork on the preheated grill and smoke for 3 hours or until internal temperature reads 145°F.
5. Allow it to rest before serving.

Nutrition Info: Per Serving: Calories: 300kcal, Protein: 36g, Carbs: 45g, Fat: 31g

Cinnamon Sugar Donut Holes

Servings: 4
Cooking Time: 35 Minutes
Ingredients:
- 1/2 cup flour
- 1tbsp cornstarch
- 1/2 tsp baking powder
- 1/8 tsp baking soda
- 1/8 tsp ground cinnamon
- 1/2 tsp kosher salt
- 1/4 cup buttermilk
- 1/4 cup sugar
- 11/2 tbsp butter, melted
- 1egg
- 1/2 tsp vanilla
- Topping
- 2tbsp sugar

- 1tbsp sugar
- 1tsp ground cinnamon

Directions:
1. Preheat pellet grill to 350°F.
2. In a medium bowl, combine flour, cornstarch, baking powder, baking soda, ground cinnamon, and kosher salt. Whisk to combine.
3. In a separate bowl, combine buttermilk, sugar, melted butter, egg, and vanilla. Whisk until the egg is thoroughly combined.
4. Pour wet mixture into the flour mixture and stir. Stir just until combined, careful not to overwork the mixture.
5. Spray mini muffin tin with cooking spray.
6. Spoon 1 tbsp of donut mixture into each mini muffin hole.
7. Place the tin on the pellet grill grate and bake for about 18 minutes, or until a toothpick can come out clean.
8. Remove muffin tin from the grill and let rest for about 5 minutes.
9. In a small bowl, combine 1 tbsp sugar and 1 tsp ground cinnamon.
10. Melt 2 tbsp of butter in a glass dish. Dip each donut hole in the melted butter, then mix and toss with cinnamon sugar. Place completed donut holes on a plate to serve.

Nutrition Info: Calories: 190 Fat: 17 g Cholesterol: 0 Carbohydrate: 21 g Fiber: 1 g Sugar: 8 g Protein: 3 g

Espresso Brisket Rub

Servings: 1/2 Cup
Cooking Time: 5 Minutes
Ingredients:
- 3 tablespoons coarse kosher salt
- 2 tablespoons ground espresso coffee
- 2 tablespoons freshly ground black pepper
- 1 tablespoon garlic powder
- 1 tablespoon light brown sugar
- 1½ teaspoons dried minced onion
- 1 teaspoon ground cumin

Directions:
1. In a small airtight container or zip-top bag, combine the salt, espresso, black pepper, garlic powder, brown sugar, minced onion, and cumin.
2. Close the container and shake to mix. Unused rub will keep in an airtight container for months.

Smoked Beef Stew

Servings: 6-8
Cooking Time: 4 Hours
Ingredients:
- 2 ½ lbs. Beef Roast, sliced into 1 -inch cubes

- 2 Potatoes for boiling, cut into pieces (peeled)
- 4 Carrots cut into pieces (peeled)
- 1 ½ tsp. Thyme, dried
- 1 - 2 Bay leaves
- 2 tsp. of Worcestershire sauce
- 1 tbsp. of Tomato paste
- 2 Garlic cloves, minced
- 1 onion sliced lengthwise
- 3 cups Beef broth, low sodium
- Optional: ½ cup of Red wine
- 2 tbsp. Oil
- Black pepper and salt
- 2 tbsp. of Flour
- 2 - 3 tbsp. Potato flakes
- For serving: Buttered noodles or Biscuits
- For Garnish: Parsley, chopped

Directions:
1. In a bag add the flour, salt, and black pepper to taste. Add the meat pieces. Toss and coat.
2. Heat the oil in a large pot until hot. Add the meat pieces. Cook until browned. Add the wine, broth and scrape the brown bits using a wooden spoon. Add thyme, bay leaves, Worcestershire, tomato paste, garlic, and onion. Cover the pot.
3. Preheat the grill to 300F with the lid closed.
4. Put pot on grate and cook 2 hours. After 2 hours add the potatoes and carrots. Cook until the veggies and meat are tender, 2 hours more.
5. If you need to thicken the gravy add 2 - 3 tbsp. Potato flakes.
6. Serve garnished with parsley.

Nutrition Info: Calories: 240 Cal Fat: 11 g Carbohydrates: 17 g Protein: 19 g Fiber: 3 g

Eastern North-carolina Bbq Sauce

Servings: 1 Cup
Cooking Time: 5 Minutes
Ingredients:
- ½ cup white vinegar
- ½ cup cider vinegar
- ½ tablespoon sugar
- ½ tablespoon crushed red pepper flakes
- ½ tablespoon Tabasco sauce
- Salt and freshly cracked black pepper to taste

Directions:
1. Whisk ingredients together in a bowl. Drizzle on barbecued meat. Covered, sauce will keep about 2 months.

Avocado With Lemon

Servings: 4
Cooking Time: 20 Minutes

Ingredients:
- 2 ripe avocados
- Good-quality olive oil for brushing
- 1 lemon, halved
- Salt and pepper

Directions:
1. Start the coals or heat a gas grill for medium direct cooking. Make sure the grates are clean.
2. Cut the avocados in half lengthwise. Carefully strike a chef's knife into the pit, then wiggle it a bit to lift and remove it. Insert a spoon underneath the flesh against the skin and run it all the way around to separate the entire half of the avocado. Repeat with the other avocado. Brush with oil, then squeeze one of the lemon halves over them thoroughly on both sides, so they don't discolor. Cut the other lemon half into 4 wedges.
3. Put the avocados on the grill directly over the fire, cut side down. Close the lid and cook, turning once, until browned in places, 5 to 10 minutes total. Serve the halved avocados as is, or slice and fan them for a prettier presentation. Sprinkle with salt and pepper and garnish with the lemon wedges.

Nutrition Info: Calories: 50.3 Fats: 4.6 g Cholesterol: 0 mg Carbohydrates: 2.8 g Fiber: 1.7 g Sugars: 0.2 g Proteins: 0.6 g

Roasted Korean Short Ribs

Servings: 4
Cooking Time: 8 Hours
Ingredients:
- 1 cup beef stock
- 1/2 cup soy sauce
- 3 cloves garlic, peeled
- 1 tablespoon ginger, minced
- 1 tablespoon beef and brisket dry rub
- 2 tablespoons brown sugar
- 1 tablespoon hot sauce
- 4 beef short ribs

Directions:
1. In a bowl, mix all the ingredients except the short ribs.
2. Add the ribs to a baking pan.
3. Pour the mixture on top of the ribs.
4. Cover and marinate in the refrigerator for 4 hours.
5. Set your wood pellet grill to 250 degrees F.
6. Roast the ribs for 4 hours.

Nutrition Info: Calories: 270 Fat: 22 g Cholesterol: 45 mg Carbohydrates: 8 g Fiber: 0 g Sugars: 0 g Protein: 11 g

Pizza Dough Roll

Servings: 6
Cooking Time: 1hour 15 Minutes
Ingredients:
- 1 tsp Yeast
- 1 cup of warm water
- 2-1/2 cups of all-purpose flour
- 1 tsp Kosher salt
- Tbsp Virgin olive oil
- 1 tsp Sugar

Directions:
1. Set the wood pellet smoker-grill to indirect cooking at 400 F
2. Combine all your ingredients and mix until the mixture is sticky and has a shaggy texture. Knead the dough for 3-5 minutes, then set aside and cover. Keep for 1 hour at room temperature or until it doubles in size.
3. Divide the dough into six equal parts and roll into a ball using a floured hand. Cover the baking pan with a parchment paper, place the roll on it, then cover and allow to rise for 30 minutes. Transfer the baking pan to the cooking grid, then cover.
4. Bake for 15-20min or until the rolls are golden brown. Allow to cool before serving.
Nutrition Info: Per Serving: Calories: 506kcal, Carbs: 46g, Fat:251g, Protein: 10.1g

Pork Dry Rub

Servings: 1
Cooking Time: 15 Minutes
Ingredients:
- Tbsp Kosher salt
- 2 Tbsp Powered onions
- Tbsp Cayenne pepper
- 1tsp Dried mustard
- 1/4 cup brown sugar
- Tbsp Powdered garlic
- Tbsp Powdered chili pepper
- 1/4 cup smoked paprika
- 2 Tbsp Black pepper

Directions:
1. Combine all the ingredients in a small bowl.
2. Transfer to an airtight jar or container.
3. Keep stored in a cool, dry place.
Nutrition Info: Per Serving: Calories: 16kcal, Carbs: 3g, Fat:0.9g, Protein: 0.8g

Roasted Buffalo Wings

Servings: 6
Cooking Time: 1 Hour
Ingredients:
- 4 lb. chicken wings
- 1 tablespoon cornstarch
- Salt to taste
- Chicken rub
- 6 tablespoon butter
- 1/2 cup hot sauce
- 1/4 cup spicy mustard

Directions:
1. Preheat the wood pellet grill to 375 degrees F for 15 minutes while the lid is closed.
2. In a bowl, mix the cornstarch, salt and chicken rub.
3. Sprinkle the chicken with this mixture.
4. Roast the chicken for 16 minutes per side.
5. In a pot over medium heat, simmer the rest of the ingredients for 15 minutes.
6. Dip the wings in the butter mixture.
7. Cook for 10 more minutes.
8. Serving Suggestion: Serve with blue cheese dressing.
9. Tips: Pat the chicken wings dry with paper towels before seasoning.

Curried Chicken Roast With Tarragon And Custard

Servings: 4
Cooking Time: 1 Hour 45 Minutes
Ingredients:
- 3 Tbsp of olive oil
- 1 Tbsp of salt, kosher
- 1 4pounds chicken
- 1/2 cup of grain mustard, whole
- 3 Tbsp of tarragon, freshly chopped
- 1 tsp of black pepper, freshly ground
- 1 Tbsp of curry powder

Directions:
1. Preheat the grill for direct cooking at 420°F (High). Use hickory wood pellets for a robust taste.
2. Mix the salt, olive oil, mustard, tarragon, pepper, and curry powder in a bowl. Coat the prepared rub all over the chicken with a grill brush. Put the chicken inside a Ziploc bag and refrigerate for an hour.
3. Roast the chicken on the preheated grill for 35 minutes. With a tong, flip the chicken and roast for another 15 minutes, or until the internal temperature of the thigh reads between 168-1690F.
4. Allow cooling for about 10 minutes before slicing and serving.
Nutrition Info: Per Serving: Calories: 330kcal, Protein: 34.1g, Carbs: 48g, Fat: 39g

Lemon And Thyme Roasted With Bistro Chicken

Servings: 4
Cooking Time: 25 Hours
Ingredients:
- 1 4pounds chicken
- 3 Tbsp of unsalted butter, melted
- 1 lemon
- 1 Tbsp of thyme, fresh and chopped.
- Salt and ground black pepper, to taste

Directions:
1. Season chicken with salt and pepper as desired. Make sure to rub seasoning all over, including the inner cavities. Refrigerate seasoned chicken, uncovered, for 24 hours.
2. Preheat the grill for direct cooking at 420°F (High). Use mesquite wood pellets for a distinctive, strong woody taste.
3. Put the lemon zest, chopped thyme, and butter in a bowl, then mix. Rub the mixture all over the chicken, and put half lemon in the chicken.
4. Place the chicken in a roasting pan and roast for about 35 minutes. Turn it to the other side and roast for 15 minutes or until internal temperature reads 160°F.
5. Cool for 10 minutes before slicing and serving.

Nutrition Info: Per Serving: Calories: 388.9kcal, Protein: 41.8g, Carbs: 73.4g, Fat: 52g.

Crispy Fish Sticks

Servings: 6
Cooking Time: 5 Minutes
Ingredients:
- Olive oil
- 1 ½ lb. halibut, sliced into strips
- 1/2 cup all-purpose flour
- Salt and pepper to taste
- 2 eggs, beaten
- 1 1/2 cup panko breadcrumbs
- 2 tablespoon dried parsley
- 1 teaspoon dried dill weed

Directions:
1. Preheat the wood pellet grill to high for 15 minutes while the lid is closed.
2. Pour olive oil to a pan.
3. Add pan on top of the grill.
4. Add flour, salt and pepper to a bowl. Mix well.
5. Add the eggs to another bowl.
6. In another bowl, mix the breadcrumbs and herbs.
7. Dip the fish strips in the flour mixture, eggs and breadcrumb mixture.
8. Place in oil and fry for 5 minutes or until golden.
9. Tips: Beat the egg white first until frothy before stirring in egg yolk. This makes it easier for breadcrumbs to stick to the fish.

Traegerbeef Pot Pie

Servings: 8
Cooking Time: 60 Minutes
Ingredients:
- 1 pie crust
- Pot Pie
- 2 cups potatoes, diced
- 3 cups leftover pot roast
- 1 cup corn
- 1 cup carrots
- 1/2 cup peas
- 1/2 cup green beans
- Gravy
- 1/4 cup butter +2 tbsp
- 1/4 cup flour
- 3 cups beef broth
- 1/4 tbsp sherry
- 1/2 tbsp onion powder
- 1/8 tbsp garlic powder
- 1/4 thyme
- Egg Wash
- 1 egg yolk
- 1 tbsp water

Directions:
1. Preheat your to 350F.
2. Take the potatoes and drizzle with some oil then sprinkle with salt. Microwave them for 4 minutes.
3. Place the pot pie ingredients in a cast iron pan.
4. Melt butter in a nonstick skillet, then whisk in flour until there are no lumps.
5. Stir cook the mixture for 7 minutes over medium heat. Whisk in broth, sherry, onion powder, garlic powder, and thyme.
6. Pour the mixture over the meat and vegetables. Top everything with a pie crust and slits for vents.
7. Whisk together the egg wash ingredients and brush the mixture at the top of the bowl.
8. Place the pie in the Traeger, close the lid, and cook for 1 hour or until the internal temperature reaches 165F. Cover the pie with a foil if it gets too much dark.
9. Let rest for 10 minutes before serving.

Nutrition Info: Calories 371, Total fat 20g, Saturated fat 8g, Total carbs 33g, Net carbs 29g Protein 16g, Sugars 5g, Fiber 4g, Sodium 671mg

Roasted Almonds

Servings: 6

Cooking Time: 1 Hour And 30 Minutes
Ingredients:
- 1 egg white
- Salt to taste
- 1 tablespoon ground cinnamon
- 1 cup granulated sugar
- 1 lb. almonds

Directions:
1. Beat the egg white in a bowl until frothy.
2. Stir in salt, cinnamon and sugar.
3. Coat the almonds with this mixture.
4. Spread almonds on a baking pan.
5. Set your wood pellet grill to 225 degrees F.
6. Preheat for 15 minutes while the lid is closed.
7. Roast the almonds for 90 minutes, stirring every 10 minutes.
8. Tips: Store in an airtight container with lid for up to 1 week.

Keto Quiche

Servings: 6
Cooking Time: 45 Minutes
Ingredients:
- 12 tbsp unsalted butter (soften)
- 12 large eggs
- 8 ounces grated cheddar cheese (divided)
- 4 ounces cream cheese
- ½ tsp salt or to taste
- ½ tsp ground black pepper or to taste
- 1 yellow onion (diced)
- 1 green bell pepper (chopped)
- 3 cups broccoli florets (chopped)
- 1 tbsp olive oil

Directions:
1. Preheat the grill to 325°F with the lid closed for 15 minutes.
2. Heat up the olive oil in a skillet over high heat.
3. Add the chopped onion, broccoli, and green pepper. Cook for about 8 minutes, stirring constantly.
4. Remove the skillet from heat.
5. Process the egg and cheese in a food processor, adding the melted butter in a bit while processing.
6. Combine 4ounce grated cheddar cheese, salt, and pepper in a quiche pan.
7. Toss the cooked vegetable into the pan and mix.
8. Pour the egg mixture over the ingredients in the quiche pan.
9. Sprinkle the remaining grated cheese over it.
10. Place the pan in the preheated grill and bake for 45 minutes.
11. Remove and transfer the quiche to a rack to cool.
12. Slice and serve.
Nutrition Info: Calories: 615 Total Fat: 54.7 g Saturated Fat: 30.1 g Cholesterol: 494 mg Sodium:

804 mg Total Carbohydrate 8.1 g Dietary Fiber 1.9 g Total Sugars: 3.6 g Protein: 25.4 g

Smoked Mac And Cheese

Servings: 8
Cooking Time: 1 Hour
Ingredients:
- 1/2 cup salted butter
- 1/3 cup flour
- 6 cups whole milk
- 1/2 tbsp salt
- 1/2 tbsp dry mustard
- A dash of Worcestershire
- White sauce
- noodles
- 1 lb small shells, cooked in saltwater
- 2 cups cheddar jack cheese
- 2 cups white cheddar, smoked
- 1 cup ritz, crushed

Directions:
1. Startup the and set it to smoke with the lid open. Let it run for 10 minutes then turn the grill up to 325F with the lid closed.
2. Meanwhile, melt butter in a saucepan over medium heat. Whisk in flour, reduce heat and continue whisking for 6 minutes or until it turns into light tan color.
3. Stir in milk, salt, dry mustard, and Worcestershire. increase the heat to medium and cook while stirring until the sauce has thickened.
4. Stir in white sauce, noodles, small shells, and all cheeses in 1 cup in a baking dish sprayed with cooking spray.
5. Top with ritz and the remaining cheese. Place the baking dish in the and bake for 30 minutes.
Nutrition Info: Calories 628, Total fat 42g, Saturated fat 24g, Total carbs 38g, Net carbs 37g Protein 25g, Sugars 11g, Fiber 1g, Sodium 807mg

Baked Asparagus & Bacon

Servings: 8
Cooking Time: 20 Minutes
Ingredients:
- 3 eggs
- 1 cup heavy cream
- 1 tablespoon chopped fresh chives
- 1/4 cup goat cheese
- 4 tablespoons Parmesan cheese
- 8 oz. fresh asparagus, trimmed
- 8 oz. bacon, cooked crispy and chopped
- ¼ teaspoon lemon zest

Directions:

1. Preheat the wood pellet grill to 375 degrees F for 15 minutes while the lid is closed.
2. In a bowl, beat the eggs and stir in cream, chives, goat cheese and Parmesan cheese.
3. Arrange the asparagus in a baking pan.
4. Spread cream mixture on top.
5. Sprinkle bacon bits and lemon zest on top.
6. Bake for 20 minutes.
7. Tips: You can also use this recipe for other vegetables like broccoli.

Smoked Pork Cutlets In Citrus-herb Marinade

Servings: 4
Cooking Time: 1 Hour And 45 Minutes
Ingredients:
- 4 pork cutlets
- 1 fresh orange juice
- 2 large lemons freshly squeezed
- 10 twigs of coriander chopped
- 2 Tbs of fresh parsley finely chopped
- 3 cloves of garlic minced
- 2 Tbs of olive oil
- Salt and ground black pepper

Directions:
1. Place the pork cutlets in a large container along with all remaining ingredients; toss to cover well.
2. Refrigerate at least 4 hours, or overnight. When ready, remove the pork cutlets from marinade and pat dry on kitchen towel. Start pellet grill on, lid open, until the fire is established (4-5 minutes).
3. The temperature must rise up to 250 degrees Fahrenheit and preheat until 15 minutes at most. Place pork cutlets on grill grate and smoke for 1 1/2 hours.
Nutrition Info: Calories: 260 Cal Fat: 12 g
Carbohydrates: 5 g Protein: 32.2 g Fiber: 0.25 g

Potluck Favorite Baked Beans

Servings: 10
Cooking Time: 3 Hours 5 Minutes
Ingredients:
- 1 tbsp. butter
- ½ of red bell pepper, seeded and chopped
- ½ of medium onion, chopped
- 2 jalapeño peppers, chopped
- 2 (28-oz.) cans baked beans, rinsed and drained
- 8 oz. pineapple chunks, drained
- 1 C. BBQ sauce
- 1 C. brown sugar
- 1 tbsp. ground mustard

Directions:

1. Set the temperature of Grill to 220-250 degrees F and preheat with closed lid for 15 minutes.
2. In a non-stick skillet, melt butter over medium heat and sauté the bell peppers, onion and jalapeño peppers for about 4-5 minutes.
3. Remove from heat and transfer the pepper mixture into a bowl.
4. Add remaining ingredients and stir to combine.
5. Transfer the mixture into a Dutch oven.
6. Place the Dutch oven onto the grill and cook for about 2½-3 hours.
7. Remove from grill and serve hot.
Nutrition Info: Calories per serving: 364; Carbohydrates: 61.4g; Protein: 9.4g; Fat: 9.8g; Sugar: 23.5g; Sodium: 1036mg; Fiber: 9.7g

Sweet Tooth Carving Rhubarb Crunch

Servings: 8
Cooking Time: 1 Hour
Ingredients:
- 1 C. oatmeal
- 1 C. flour
- 1 C. brown sugar
- ½ C. butter, melted
- ¼ tsp. salt
- 4 C. raw rhubarb, chopped finely
- 1 C. white sugar
- 2 tbsp. cornstarch
- 1 C. cold water
- 1 tsp. vanilla extract

Directions:
1. Set the temperature of Grill to 350 degrees F and preheat with closed lid for 15 minutes.
2. In a bowl, add oatmeal, flour, brown sugar, butter and salt and mix until well combined.
3. In a pan, add white sugar, cornstarch, cold water and vanilla extract and cook until sugar is dissolves, stirring continuously.
4. Place half of the four mixture into a 9x12-inch pan and top with chopped rhubarb evenly.
5. Place sugar mixture over rhubarb evenly and top with remaining flour mixture.
6. Place the pan onto the grill and cook for about 1 hour.
7. Remove from grill and place the crunch onto a wire rack to cool in the pan for about 10 minutes.
8. Cut into desired-sized slices and serve warm.
Nutrition Info: Calories per serving: 382; Carbohydrates: 66.3g; Protein: 3.7g; Fat: 12.5g; Sugar: 43.5g; Sodium: 164mg; Fiber: 2.6g

Smoked Tuna

Servings: 6

Cooking Time: 3 Hours
Ingredients:
- 2 cups water
- 1 cup brown sugar
- 1 cup salt
- 1 tablespoon lemon zest
- 6 tuna fillets

Directions:
1. Mix water, brown sugar, salt and lemon zest in a bowl.
2. Coat the tuna fillets with the mixture.
3. Refrigerate for 6 hours.
4. Rinse the tuna and pat dry with paper towels.
5. Preheat the wood pellet grill to 180 degrees F for 15 minutes while the lid is closed.
6. Smoke the tuna for 3 hours.
7. Tips: You can also soak tuna in the brine for 24 hours.

Special Mac And Cheese

Servings: 8
Cooking Time: 1 Hour
Ingredients:
- 4 strips bacon, cooked crispy and chopped
- 2 cups breadcrumbs
- 2 tablespoons fresh parsley, minced
- Salt and pepper to taste
- 2 tablespoons olive oil
- 1 white onion, chopped
- 3 cloves garlic, crushed and minced
- 1/2 cup melted butter
- 5 tablespoons all-purpose flour
- 12 oz. cheddar cheese, shredded
- 4 oz. brie cheese
- 4 oz. mozzarella cheese, shredded
- 12 oz. raclette
- 8 oz. gruyere cheese, grated
- 1 cup heavy cream
- 4 oz. milk
- 8 cups cooked macaroni pasta
- 1 teaspoon freshly grated nutmeg

Directions:
1. In a bowl, mix the bacon bits, breadcrumbs, parsley, salt, and pepper. Set aside.
2. Preheat your wood pellet grill to 350 degrees F with the lid closed.
3. Pour the olive oil into a pan over medium heat.
4. Cook the onion and garlic for 2 minutes.
5. Add the jalapeño and cook for 1 more minute.
6. Stir in the butter and flour.
7. Cook while stirring for 5 minutes.
8. Add all the cheeses along with the cream and milk.

9. Reduce heat to low and cook while stirring for 7 minutes.
10. Add the pasta and stir to coat evenly with the sauce.
11. Season with the salt and pepper.
12. Pour the mixture to a cast-iron pan.
13. Cover with foil.
14. Place on top of the wood pellet grill.
15. Bake for 20 minutes.
16. Sprinkle the breadcrumb mixture on top.
17. Bake for another 20 minutes.
Nutrition Info: Calories: 470 Fat: 31 g Cholesterol: 0 mg Carbohydrates: 33 g Fiber: 1 g Sugars: 0 g Protein: 17 g

Grilled Plantains

Servings: 2
Cooking Time: 6 Minutes
Ingredients:
- 2Plantains, cut and sliced horizontally
- 1tablespoon coconut oil, melted

Directions:
1. Put the grill grate inside the grill and set the timer to 8 minutes at high for preheating.
2. Once, the grill is preheated, open the unit.
3. Brush the plantains with coconut oil and add to the hot grill.
4. Close the unit and cook for 3 minutes at medium.
5. Flip to cook from the other side and cook for an additional 3 minutes.
6. Once done, serve.
Nutrition Info: Calories: 277 Total Fat: 7.5g Saturated Fat: 6.1g Cholesterol: 0mg Sodium: 7mg Total Carbohydrate: 57.1g Dietary Fiber 4.1g Total Sugars: 26.9g Protein: 2.3g

Bradley Maple Cure Smoked Salmon

Servings: 6
Cooking Time: 1 Hour And 30 Minutes
Ingredients:
- 1 large sized salmon fillet
- 1 quart of water
- ½ a cup of pickling and canning salt
- ½ a cup of maple syrup
- ¼ cup of dark rum
- ¼ cup of lemon juice
- 10 whole cloves
- 10 whole allspice berries
- 1 bay leaf

Directions:
1. Take a medium sized bowl and add the brine ingredients. Mix them well. Place the salmon fillet in a cover with brine. Cover it up and let it refrigerate

for about 2 hours. Remove the Salmon and pat dry then air dry for 1 hour. Preheat your smoker to a temperature of 180 degrees Fahrenheit and add Bradley Maple-Flavored briquettes. Smoke the salmon for about 1 and a ½ hour.
Nutrition Info: Calories: 223 Cal Fat: 7 g Carbohydrates: 15 g Protein: 21 g Fiber: 0 g

Pan-seared Ribeye Steak With Parsley Potatoes

Servings: 6
Cooking Time: 60 Minutes
Ingredients:
- 2 pork tenderloin
- medium potatoes (peeled and sliced)
- 3 tbsps extra-virgin olive oil
- 2 Tbsp Fresh parsley (chopped)
- Salt and pepper to taste.

Directions:
1. Preheat the wood pellet smoker-grill for direct cooking at 300 F using any pellets
2. Rinse the meat and pat dry, then season with salt and pepper.
3. Grill pork for 20 minutes, then set aside and increase the temperature of the grill to High.
4. Place an iron skillet on grill grates, add the oil and heat for 1 minute. Sear the meat for 3 minutes per side or until brown. Allow it to rest before serving.
5. Rearrange the grill for indirect cooking at 300 F
6. Place a pot on grates and fill with water, add the potatoes and allow to boil, reduce the heat and simmer for 15 minutes or until the potatoes become soft. Drain the water. Transfer to a bowl, add parsley, and olive oil.
7. Serve with pork.
Nutrition Info: Per Serving: Calories: 354kcal, Carbs: 27.8g, Fat: 21.5g, Protein: 36g

Garlic Aioli And Smoked Salmon Sliders

Servings: 12
Cooking Time: 1 Hour And 30 Minutes
Ingredients:
- For Brine:
- Water as needed
- ½ a cup of salt
- 1 tablespoon of dried tarragon
- 1 and a ½ pound of salmon fillets
- For Aioli:
- 1 cup of mayonnaise
- 3 tablespoon of fresh lemon juice
- 3 minced garlic cloves

- 1 and a ½ teaspoon of ground black pepper
- ½ a teaspoon of lemon zest
- Salt as needed
- ½ a cup of apple wood chips
- 12 slide burger buns

Directions:
1. Take a large sized baking dish and add ½ a cup of salt alongside about half water
2. Add tarragon, salmon in the brine mix and keep adding more water
3. Cover up the dish and freeze for 2-12 hours. Take a small bowl and add lemon juice, mayonnaise, pepper, garlic, 1 pinch of salt and lemon zest.
4. Mix and chill for 30 minutes
5. Remove your Salmon from the brine and place it on a wire rack and let it sit for about 30 minutes.
6. Smoke them over low heat for 1 and a ½ to 2 hours. Assemble sliders by dividing the salmon among 12 individual buns.
7. Top each of the pieces with a spoonful of aioli and place another bun on top
Nutrition Info: Calories: 320 Cal Fat: 22 g Carbohydrates: 13 g Protein: 22 g Fiber: 0 g

Lobster Butter

Servings: 1/2 Cup
Cooking Time: 40 Minutes
Ingredients:
- Shells of cooked lobsters, crushed into small pieces
- 8 tablespoons (1 stick) unsalted butter per lobster

Directions:
1. Heat grill to 300 degrees. Put lobster shells on the largest sheet pan you can fit in the oven, and allow them to dry and roast, about 15 to 20 minutes. Remove and set aside.
2. Meanwhile, melt 1 stick butter per lobster in a large bowl or double boiler set over simmering water, making sure bowl does not touch the surface of water. Add lobster shells to the melted butter and simmer gently, without boiling, for about 20 minutes.
3. Strain the melted butter through a cheesecloth-lined sieve into another bowl, then set that bowl into ice to chill. Cover bowl and refrigerate to set, then skim off the top and discard any liquids. Use within a few days, or freeze for up to a few weeks.

Bison Burgers

Servings: 6
Cooking Time: 17 To 19 Minutes
Ingredients:
- 2 pounds ground bison

- 2 tablespoons steak seasoning
- 4 tablespoons (½ stick) unsalted butter, cut into pieces
- 1 large onion, finely minced
- 6 slices Swiss cheese
- 6 ciabatta buns, split
- Sweet and Spicy Jalapeño Relish, for serving
- Lettuce and sliced tomatoes, for serving

Directions:
1. Supply your smoker with wood pellets and follow the manufacturer's specific start-up procedure. Preheat, with the lid closed, to 425°F.
2. In a large bowl, combine the ground bison and steak seasoning until well blended.
3. Shape the meat mixture into 6 patties and make a thumb indentation in the center of each. Set aside.
4. Place a rimmed baking sheet on the grill and add the butter and onion. Sauté for 5 minutes, or until the onion is translucent. Top with the bison burger patties, indention-side down.
5. Close the lid and smoke for 6 to 7 minutes, then flip the burgers and smother them in the sautéed onion. Close the lid again and continue smoking for 6 to 7 minutes. During the last few minutes of cooking, top each burger with a slice of Swiss cheese. For safe consumption, the internal temperature should reach between 140°F (medium) and 160°F (well-done).
6. Lightly toast the ciabatta buns, split-side down, on one side of the smoker.
7. Serve the onion-smothered cheeseburgers on the toasted buns with jalapeño relish, lettuce, and tomato—or whatever toppings you like.

Grilled Brussels Sprouts

Servings: 8
Cooking Time: 20 Minutes
Ingredients:
- 1/2 lb bacon, grease reserved
- 1 b Brussels Sprouts
- 1/2 tbsp pepper
- 1/2 tbsp salt

Directions:
1. Cook bacon until crispy on a stovetop, reserve its grease then chop into small pieces.
2. Meanwhile, wash the Brussels sprouts, trim off the dry end and remove dried leaves, if any. Half them and set aside.
3. Place 1/4 cup reserved grease in a pan, cast-iron, over medium-high heat.
4. Season the Brussels sprouts with pepper and salt.
5. Brown the sprouts on the pan with the cut side down for about 3-4 minutes.
6. In the meantime, preheat your pellet grill to 350-375F.

7. Place bacon pieces and browned sprouts into your grill-safe pan.
8. Cook for about 20 minutes.
9. Serve immediately.
Nutrition Info: Calories: 153 Total Fat: 10 g Saturated Fat: 3 g Total Carbs: 5 g Net Carbs: 3 g Protein: 11 g Sugars: 1 g Fiber: 2 g Sodium: 622mg

Wood-fired Burger Seasoning

Servings: 2
Cooking Time: 5 Minutes
Ingredients:
- 1 teaspoon coarse kosher salt
- 1 teaspoon garlic powder
- 1 teaspoon dried minced onion
- 1 teaspoon onion powder
- 1 teaspoon freshly ground black pepper
- ½ teaspoon sweet paprika
- ¼ teaspoon mustard powder
- ¼ teaspoon celery seed

Directions:
1. In a small airtight container or zip-top bag, combine the salt, garlic powder, minced onion, onion powder, black pepper, sweet paprika, mustard powder, and celery seed.
2. Close the container and shake to mix. Unused burger shake will keep in an airtight container for months.

Spicy Tofu Marinade

Servings: 1/2 Cup
Cooking Time: 5 Minutes
Ingredients:
- ¼ cup soy sauce
- 1 tablespoon rice vinegar
- 1 teaspoon brown sugar
- 2 tablespoons mirin (sweet Japanese rice wine)
- 1 to 2 garlic cloves, to taste, minced or puréed
- 1 tablespoon minced or grated fresh ginger
- 1 teaspoon Asian chili paste or cayenne to taste
- 2 tablespoons dark sesame oil

Directions:
1. Whisk together all of the ingredients in a bowl. Use as a marinade and/or dipping sauce for pan-seared, grilled or plain tofu.

Steak Kabobs

Servings: 6
Cooking Time: 10 Minutes
Ingredients:

- 3 lb steak
- 2 small zucchini
- 1 onion
- 2 small yellow squash
- Salt and pepper
- 1 cup teriyaki sauce
- 3 tbsp sesame seeds, toasted

Directions:
1. Preheat your to 400F.
2. Cut the steak and veggies into skewable pieces.
3. Place the meat and veggies on the skewers then sprinkle with salt and pepper.
4. Place the skewers on the grill and cook for 5 minutes per side.
5. Remove the skewers, drizzle teriyaki sauce and top with sesame seeds.
6. Serve when hot. Enjoy.

Nutrition Info: Calories 727, Total fat 44g, Saturated fat 17g, Total carbs 15g, Net carbs 13g Protein 64g, Sugars 10g, Fiber 2g, Sodium 2011mg

Roasted Lamb

Servings: 8
Cooking Time: 1 Hour And 30 Minutes
Ingredients:
- 1 leg of lamb
- 8 cloves garlic, minced
- 1 sprig oregano, chopped
- 2 sprigs rosemary, chopped
- 6 tablespoons olive oil
- 2 tablespoons lemon juice
- Salt and pepper to taste

Directions:
1. Make slits on the lamb leg.
2. Combine the garlic and herbs.
3. Mash to form a paste.
4. Stuff mixture inside the slits.
5. Add the lamb leg to a roasting pan.
6. Drizzle it with olive oil and lemon juice.
7. Cover with foil and refrigerate for 10 hours.
8. When ready to cook, sprinkle lamb with salt and pepper.
9. Set the wood pellet grill to 400 degrees F.
10. Preheat for 15 minutes while the lid is closed.
11. Open the lid and let it establish fire for 5 minutes.
12. Roast the leg of lamb for 30 minutes.
13. Reduce temperature to 350 degrees F and cook for 1 hour.
14. Let rest before slicing and serving.
15. Tips: You can also use a food processor to create a paste from the garlic and herbs.

Veal Paprikash

Servings: 6
Cooking Time: 1 Hour 25 Minutes
Ingredients:
- 3lb Veal, cut into 1-inch piece
- 1 yellow onion, chopped
- 1 tsp cayenne pepper
- 1 small red pepper, finely chopped
- Kosher salt
- 1 cup regular sour cream
- 1 Tsp all-purpose flour
- 1 medium ripe tomato
- 1 Tsp paprika
- 2 Tbsp vegetable oil
- 2 Tbsp butter

Directions:
1. Preheat wood pellet smoker-grill to 350^0F, with the lid closed for about 15 minutes
2. Heat oil and melt butter in a Dutch oven, add the onion and cook until tender, about 3 minutes.
3. Add veal, and then season onion with paprika and cayenne pepper. Cover the lid of the Dutch oven and allow the meat to cook for about 10 minutes.
4. Add tomato, bell pepper, and season with salt. Stir and leave to cook for 45 minutes, until tender.
5. Combine the flour and sour cream in a small bowl. Stir in the flour mixture into the Dutch oven and cook for another 10 minutes.
6. Remove pot from the cooking grid and enjoy the dish.

Nutrition Info: Per Serving: Calories: 400kcal,Carbs: 39g, Fat: 10g, Protein: 38g

Breakfast Sausage

Servings: 6
Cooking Time: 9 Hours
Ingredients:
- 20/22 millimeter natural sheep casings, rinsed
- Warm water
- 2 lb. ground pork
- Apple butter rub
- Pinch dried marjoram
- 1/2 teaspoon ground cloves
- 1 tablespoon brown sugar
- 1/3 cup ice water
- Pepper to taste

Directions:
1. Soak the sheep casings in warm water for 1 hour.
2. In a bowl, mix all the ingredients.
3. Use a mixer set on low speed to combine the ingredients.
4. Cover and refrigerate the mixture for 15 minutes.
5. Insert the casings into the sausage stuffer.

6. Stuff the casings with the ground pork mixture.
7. Twist into five links.
8. Remove bubbles using a pricker.
9. Put the sausages on a baking pan.
10. Refrigerate for 24 hours.
11. Set your wood pellet grill to smoke.
12. Hang the sausages on hooks and put them in the smoking cabinet.
13. Set the temperature to 350 degrees F.
14. Smoke the sausages for 1 hour.
15. Increase the temperature to 425 degrees F.
16. Cook for another 30 minutes.
Nutrition Info: Calories: 220 Fat: 19 g Cholesterol: 45 mg Carbohydrates: 1 g Fiber: 0 g Sugars: 1 g Protein: 11 g

Greek Leg Of Lamb

Servings: 12 To 16
Cooking Time: 20 To 25 Minutes
Ingredients:
- 2 tablespoons finely chopped fresh rosemary
- 1 tablespoon ground thyme
- 5 garlic cloves, minced
- 2 tablespoons sea salt
- 1 tablespoon freshly ground black pepper
- Butcher's string
- 1 whole boneless (6- to 8-pound) leg of lamb
- ¼ cup extra-virgin olive oil
- 1 cup red wine vinegar
- ½ cup canola oil

Directions:
1. In a small bowl, combine the rosemary, thyme, garlic, salt, and pepper; set aside.
2. Using butcher's string, tie the leg of lamb into the shape of a roast. Your butcher should also be happy to truss the leg for you.
3. Rub the lamb generously with the olive oil and season with the spice mixture. Transfer to a plate, cover with plastic wrap, and refrigerate for 4 hours.
4. Remove the lamb from the refrigerator but do not rinse.
5. Supply your smoker with wood pellets and follow the manufacturer's specific start-up procedure. Preheat, with the lid closed, to 325°F.
6. In a small bowl, combine the red wine vinegar and canola oil for basting.
7. Place the lamb directly on the grill, close the lid, and smoke for 20 to 25 minutes per pound (depending on desired doneness), basting with the oil and vinegar mixture every 30 minutes. Lamb is generally served medium-rare to medium, so it will be done when a meat thermometer inserted in the thickest part reads 140°F to 145°F.
8. Let the lamb rest for about 15 minutes before slicing to serve.

Smoked Bacon

Servings: 6
Cooking Time: 30 Minutes
Ingredients:
- 1-pound thick cut bacon

Directions:
1. Preheat your wood pellet grill to 375 degrees.
2. Line a huge baking sheet. Place a single layer of thick-cut bacon on it.
3. Bake for 20 minutes and then flip it to the other side.
4. Cook for another 10 minutes or until the bacon is crispy.
5. Take it out and enjoy your tasty grilled bacon.
Nutrition Info: Calories: 80 Cal Fat: 10 g Carbohydrates: 18 g Protein: 9 g Fiber: 0 g

Bearnaise Sauce With Marinated London Broil

Servings: 4
Cooking Time: 50 Minutes
Ingredients:
- 2 cups of Rory's marinade
- 1-1/2 cups of béarnaise sauce
- 2-1/2 pound of London broil

Directions:
1. Place London broil in a big baking dish, pour marinade over the steak, then refrigerate it over the night.
2. Set the grill for direct cooking at 300°F. Use maple pellets for a robust woody taste.
3. Remove London broil from the marinade the following morning. Place it on the preheated grill and cook for 15 minutes before flipping and grilling the other side for 10 minutes. Serve immediately with béarnaise sauce.
Nutrition Info: Per Serving: Calories: 367g, Fat: 39g, Carbs: 53g, Protein: 32g

Chipotle Honey Smoked Beef Roast

Servings: 10
Cooking Time: 4 Hours And 20 Minutes
Ingredients:
- Beef roast (5-lbs., 2.3-kg.)
- The Rub Vegetable oil – 2 tablespoons
- Black pepper – 1 ½ tablespoons
- Salt – 1 ½ tablespoons
- Brown sugar – ¾ tablespoon
- Onion powder – ¾ tablespoon
- Mustard – 1 teaspoon

- Garlic powder – 1 ½ teaspoons
- Chipotle powder – 1 ½ teaspoons
- The Glaze Honey – ½ cup
- Water – 2 tablespoons
- Minced garlic – 1 ½ tablespoons

Directions:

1. Place the rub ingredients—vegetable oil, black pepper, salt, brown sugar, onion powder, mustard, garlic powder, and chipotle powder in a bowl then mix until combined.
2. Rub the beef roast with the spice mixture then set aside. Plug the wood pellet smoker and place wood pellet inside the hopper.
3. Turn the switch on. Set the "Smoke" setting and prepare the wood pellet smoker for indirect heat.
4. Wait until the smoke is ready and adjust the temperature to 275°F (135°C). Once the wood pellet smoker has reached the desired temperature, place the seasoned beef roast directly on the grate inside the wood pellet smoker and smoke for 2 hours.
5. In the meantime, combine honey, water, and minced garlic in a bowl then stir until incorporated. After 2 hours, take the beef roast out of the wood pellet smoker and place on as sheet of aluminum foil.
6. Leave the wood pellet smoker on and adjust the temperature to 300°F (149°C). Baste the beef roast with the glaze mixture then wrap it with the aluminum foil. Return the wrapped beef roast to the wood pellet smoker then smoke for another 2 hours.
7. Once the internal temperature of the smoked beef roast has reached 165°F (74°C), remove it from the wood pellet smoker.
8. Let the smoked beef roast rest for about 10 minutes then unwrap it. Transfer the smoked beef roast to a serving dish then serve. Enjoy!

Nutrition Info: Calories: 90 Cal Fat: 3 g Carbohydrates: 1 g Protein: 14 g Fiber: 0 g

Grilled Cocoa Steak

Servings: 8
Cooking Time: 10 Minutes
Ingredients:

- 1 tablespoon cocoa powder
- 1 1/2 tablespoons brown sugar
- 1 teaspoon chipotle chili powder
- 2 teaspoons chili powder
- 1/2 teaspoon onion powder
- 1/2 teaspoon garlic powder
- 1 tablespoon smoked paprika
- 1 tablespoon ground cumin
- Salt and pepper to taste
- 2 lb. flank steak
- Olive oil

Directions:

1. Make the dry rub by mixing the cocoa powder, sugar, spices, salt and pepper.
2. Coat the flank steak with olive oil.
3. Sprinkle dry rub on both sides.
4. Preheat your wood pellet grill to high for 15 minutes while the lid is closed.
5. Grill the steak for 5 minutes per side.
6. Let rest for 10 minutes before slicing and serving.
7. Tips: Slice against the grain after a few minutes of resting.

Delicious Donuts On A Grill

Servings: 6
Cooking Time: 10 Minutes
Ingredients:

- 1-1/2 cups sugar, powdered
- 1/3 cup whole milk
- 1/2 teaspoon vanilla extract
- 16 ounces of biscuit dough, prepared
- Oil spray, for greasing
- 1cup chocolate sprinkles, for sprinkling

Directions:

1. Take a medium bowl and mix sugar, milk, and vanilla extract.
2. Combine well to create a glaze.
3. Set the glaze aside for further use.
4. Place the dough onto the flat, clean surface.
5. Flat the dough with a rolling pin.
6. Use a ring mold, about an inch, and cut the hole in the center of each round dough.
7. Place the dough on a plate and refrigerate for 10 minutes.
8. Open the grill and install the grill grate inside it.
9. Close the hood.
10. Now, select the grill from the menu, and set the temperature to medium.
11. Set the time to 6 minutes.
12. Select start and begin preheating.
13. Remove the dough from the refrigerator and coat it with cooking spray from both sides.
14. When the unit beeps, the grill is preheated; place the adjustable amount of dough on the grill grate.
15. Close the hood, and cook for 3 minutes.
16. After 3 minutes, remove donuts and place the remaining dough inside.
17. Cook for 3 minutes.
18. Once all the donuts are ready, sprinkle chocolate sprinkles on top.
19. Enjoy.

Nutrition Info: Calories: 400 Total Fat: 11g Saturated Fat: 4.2g Cholesterol: 1mg Sodium: 787mg Total Carbohydrate: 71.3g Dietary Fiber 0.9g Total Sugars: 45.3g Protein: 5.7g

Smoked Irish Bacon

Servings: 7
Cooking Time: 3 Hours
Ingredients:
- 1 bay leaf
- 2/4 cup of water
- 2/3 cup of sugar
- 6 star anise, whole
- 1 cup of fresh fennel, preferably bulb and fronds
- 2 spring thyme, fresh
- 1 clove of garlic
- 2 tsp of curing salt
- 2-1/2 pound of pork loin
- 1-1/2 tsp of peppercorns, black
- 1-1/2 tsp of fennel seed

Directions:
1. In a big stockpot, mix the fennel seeds, peppercorn, star anise, and pork roast for about 3 minutes. Also, mix the sugar, water, thyme, garlic, curing salt, coarse salt, and bay leaves in a pot and, boil for 3 minutes until the salt and sugar dissolves.
2. Place the pork loin in a Ziploc bag, seal it, and put it in a roasting pan. Keep refrigerated for 4 days.
3. Preheat the grill for 15 minutes at 250°F. Use pecan wood pellets.
4. Remove the pork from the brine and place on the grates of the grill. Smoke it for 2 hours 30 minutes or until internal temperature reads 145°F.
5. Serves immediately or when it is cool.
Nutrition Info: Per Serving: Calories: 309kcal, Fat: 7g, Protein: 30.6g, Carbs: 40g

Salt-seared Kobe Beef With Tarragon Shallot Butter

Servings: 4
Cooking Time: 40 Minutes
Ingredients:
- 1 (8-inch) square salt block
- 3 Tbsp Unsalted butter
- 2 finely chopped shallot
- 12 oz. Kobe beef, boneless, trimmed, then boiled
- Grounded black pepper to taste
- 1/4 cup of dry vermouth
- Finely chopped tarragon leaves (1 sprig)

Directions:
1. Preheat the wood pellet smoker-grill for direct cooking at 400 F using any pellet
2. Heat the salt block on the smoker-grill for 10 minutes, increase the temperature to 450 F (High), and heat for another 10 minutes. While the salt is heating, transfer your beef to a freezer for 10-15 minutes. Do not allow to freeze.
3. Place a medium skillet on the cooking grate, then add the vermouth and shallot. Stir occasionally to prevent the shallot from boiling dry. Boil until 1 tbsp of shallot remains in the skillet, stir in the pepper and tarragon. Allow to cool and mix with butter.
4. Remove the beef and slice to about 1/4 -inch-thickness. Sear for 5 minutes per side on the salt block. Serve with shallot-tarragon butter.
Nutrition Info: Per Serving: Calories: 342kcal, Carbs: 16g, Fat: 12g, Protein: 32g

Venison Meatloaf

Servings: 6
Cooking Time: 1 Hour And 15 Minutes
Ingredients:
- For the Meatloaf:
- 1 medium white onion, peeled, diced
- 2 pounds ground venison
- 1 cup bread crumbs
- 1 teaspoon salt
- 1 tablespoon Worcestershire sauce
- ½ teaspoon ground black pepper
- 2 tablespoons onion soup mix
- 1 egg, beaten
- 1 cup milk, unsweetened
- For the Glaze:
- 1/4 cup brown sugar
- 1/4 cup ketchup
- 1/4 cup apple cider vinegar

Directions:
1. Switch on the grill, fill the grill hopper with big game blend wood pellets, power the grill on by using the control panel, select 'smoke' on the temperature dial, or set the temperature to 350 degrees F and let it preheat for a minimum of 15 minutes.
2. Meanwhile, take a large bowl, place all the ingredients for the meatloaf in it, and stir until just combined; don't overmix.
3. Take a loaf pan, grease it with oil, place meatloaf mixture in it, and spread evenly.
4. Prepare the glaze and for this, take a small bowl, place all of its ingredients in it, stir until combined, and then spread evenly on top of meatloaf.
5. When the grill has preheated, open the lid, place loaf pan on the grill grate, shut the grill and smoke for 1 hour and 15 minutes until the internal temperature reaches 165 degrees F.
6. Serve straight away.
Nutrition Info: Calories: 186.5 Cal ;Fat: 7.2 g ;Carbs: 7.7 g ;Protein: 21.6 g ;Fiber: 0.4 g

Texas Styled Smoked Flounder

Servings: 6
Cooking Time: 20 Minutes
Ingredients:
- 1 whole flounder
- 1 halved lemon
- Ground black pepper as needed
- 2 tablespoons of chopped up fresh dill
- 1 tablespoon of olive oil
- 1 cup of soaked wood chips

Directions:
1. Preheat your smoker to a temperature of 350 degrees Fahrenheit.
2. Slice half of your lemon and place them into the slices. Rub the fish with a coating of olive oil. Squeeze another half of the lemon all over the fish. Season with some black pepper.
3. Rub 1 tablespoon of dill into the slits and insert the lemon slices firmly. Place the flounder on top of a large piece of aluminum foil and fold the sides all around the fish.
4. Place the fish in your smoker and throw a couple handful of soaked wood chips into the coals. And smoke for 10 minutes Once done, seal up the foil and smoke it until it is fully done. Remove fish and garnish with some extra dill
Nutrition Info: Calories: 226 Cal Fat: 4 g
Carbohydrates: 28 g Protein: 28 g Fiber: 0 g

Berry Smoothie

Servings: 1
Cooking Time: 1 Minutes
Ingredients:
- 2 scoops Protein Powder
- 2 cups Almond Milk
- 4 cups Mixed Berry
- 2 cups Yoghurt

Directions:
1. First, place mixed berry, protein powder, yogurt, and almond milk in the blender pitcher.
2. Then, select the 'smoothie' button.
3. Finally, pour the smoothie to the serving glass.
Nutrition Info: Calories: 112 Fat: 2 g Total Carbs: 26 g Fiber: 0 g Sugar: 0 g Protein: 1 g Cholesterol: 0

Mushroom With Fennel Dressed With Roasted Chicken

Servings: 4
Cooking Time: 22 Hours 50 Minutes
Ingredients:
- 8 sun-dried tomatoes, oil-packed
- 4pound chicken
- Salt with black pepper
- 1-1/2 Tbsp of thyme
- 10 ounces of mushroom, preferably white button
- 1/2 pound of crusty bread
- 4 cloves of garlic, preferably smashed
- 1 Tbsp of balsamic vinegar
- 2 Tbsp of butter without salt.
- 1 fennel bulb

Directions:
1. Rub black pepper and salt all over the chicken, including cavities. Keep in the refrigerator for 22 hours.
2. Remove chicken from the refrigerator and rub with butter. In a big bowl, mix sun-dried tomato, mushroom, fennel, garlic, thyme, salt, and pepper. Then put the mixture into the roasting pan along with the chicken.
3. Roast the chicken on the preheated grill for 35 minutes. Flip the chicken with a tong and roast for another 15 minutes, or until the internal temperature of the thigh reads between 165-170F.
Nutrition Info: Per Serving: Calories: 290kcal, Carbs: 35g, Fat: 42g, Protein: 38g

Prosciutto-wrapped Melon

Servings: 8
Cooking Time: 25 Minutes
Ingredients:
- 1ripe cantaloupe
- Salt and pepper
- 16thin slices prosciutto

Directions:
1. Start the coals or heat a gas grill for medium direct cooking. Make sure the grates are clean.
2. Cut the cantaloupe in half lengthwise and scoop out all the seeds. Cut each half into 8 wedges, then cut away the rind from each wedge. Sprinkle with salt and pepper and wrap each wedge with a slice of prosciutto, covering as much of the cantaloupe as possible.
3. Put the wedges on the grill directly over the fire. Close the lid and cook, turning once, until the prosciutto shrivels, browns, and crisps in places, 2 to 3 minutes per side. Serve hot or at room temperature.
Nutrition Info: Calories: 118.3 Fats: 5.4 g
Cholesterol: 0 mg Carbohydrates: 12.5 g Fiber: 1.1 g Sugars: 0 g Proteins: 6.7 g

Wood Pellet Grill Chicken Flatbread

Servings: 6
Cooking Time: 30 Minutes
Ingredients:

146

- 6 mini breads
- 1-1/2 cups divided buffalo sauce
- 4 cups cooked and cubed chicken breasts
- For drizzling: mozzarella cheese

Directions:

1. Preheat your pellet grill to 375 - 400F.
2. Place the breads on a surface, flat, then evenly spread 1/2 cup buffalo sauce on all breads.
3. Toss together chicken breasts and 1 cup buffalo sauce then top over all the breads evenly.
4. Top each with mozzarella cheese.
5. Place the breads directly on the grill but over indirect heat. Close the lid.
6. Cook for about 5-7 minutes until slightly toasty edges, cheese is melted and fully hated chicken.
7. Remove and drizzle with ranch or blue cheese.
8. Enjoy!

Nutrition Info: Calories 346, Total fat 7.6g, Saturated fat 2g, Total Carbs 33.9g, Net Carbs 32.3g, Protein 32.5g, Sugars 0.8g, Fiber 1.6g, Sodium 642mg, Potassium 299mg

Crusty Artisan Dough Bread

Servings: 6
Cooking Time: 2 Hours
Ingredients:

- 3 cups all-purpose flour
- 1/2 tsp Yeast
- 1-1/2 cups of warm water
- 1-1/2 tsp salt

Directions:

1. In a large bowl, combine all your ingredients and mix until it is sticky and has a shaggy texture. Cover with plastic wrap and allow to rest for 12 hours
2. After 12 hours, set the wood pellet smoker-grill to indirect cooking at 425 F, using any pellet. Preheat the Dutch oven.
3. Transfer prepared mixture to a dry, floured surface and mold into a ball. Open the Dutch oven and place the dough in the middle—cover and bake for 30 minutes.
4. Remove the lid and bake for an additional 20 minutes.
5. Remove and allow to cool.

Nutrition Info: Per Serving: Calories: 462kcal, Carbs: 41g, Fat: 18g, Protein: 5g

Smoked Cheddar Cheese

Servings: 2
Cooking Time: 5 Hour
Ingredients:

- 2, 8-oz, cheddar cheese blocks

Directions:

1. Preheat and set your pellet grill to 90F.
2. Place the cheese blocks directly on the grill grate and smoke for about 4 hours.
3. Remove and transfer into a plastic bag, resealable. Refrigerate for about 2 weeks to allow flavor from smoke to permeate your cheese.
4. Now enjoy!

Nutrition Info: Calories 115, Total fat 9.5g, Saturated fat 5.4g, Total carbs 0.9g, Net carbs 0.9g, Protein 6.5g, Sugars 0.1g, Fiber 0g, Sodium 185mg, Potassium 79mg

Smoked Chicken With Perfect Poultry Rub

Servings: 2
Cooking Time: 3 Hours 15 Minutes
Ingredients:

- 2 Tbsp of onion, powder
- 1/4 cup of black pepper, freshly ground
- 2 Tbsp of dry mustard
- 3/4 cup of paprika
- 4pound chicken
- 3 lemon
- 2 tsp of cayenne
- 1/4 cup of sugar
- 1/4 cup of celery salt

Directions:

1. In a bowl, mix the onion powder, paprika, black pepper, dry mustard, cayenne, sugar, celery, salt, and 2 lemons.
2. Add your chicken to the rub and slice some parts so that the ingredients will find their way in.
3. Preheat the grill for 15 minutes at 225°F. Use apple wood pellets for a distinctive, strong woody taste.
4. Place the coated chicken on the preheated grill and smoke for 3 hours or until internal temperature reads 160°F.
5. Allow chicken to cool, then serve.

Nutrition Info: Per Serving: Calories: 255kcal, Protein: 35g, Carbs: 42g, Fat: 35g.

Black Bean Dipping Sauce

Servings: 4
Cooking Time: 10 Minutes
Ingredients:

- 2 tablespoons black bean paste
- 2 tablespoons peanut butter
- 1 tablespoon maple syrup
- 2 tablespoons olive oil

Directions:

1. In a blender place all ingredients and blend until smooth
2. Pour sauce in a bowl and serve

Hickory Smoked Green Beans

Servings: 10
Cooking Time: 3 Hours
Ingredients:
- 6 cups fresh green beans, halved and ends cut off
- 2 cups chicken broth
- 1 tbsp pepper, ground
- 1/4 tbsp salt
- 2 tbsp apple cider vinegar
- 1/4 cup diced onion
- 6-8 bite-size bacon slices
- Optional: sliced almonds

Directions:
1. Add green beans to a colander then rinse thoroughly. Set aside.
2. Place chicken broth, pepper, salt, and apple cider in a pan, large. Add green beans.
3. Blanch over medium heat for about 3-4 minutes then remove from heat.
4. Transfer the mixture into an aluminum pan, disposable. Make sure all mixture goes into the pan, so do not drain them.
5. Place bacon slices over the beans and place the pan into the wood pellet smoker,
6. Smoke for about 3 hours uncovered.
7. Remove from the smoker and top with almonds slices.
8. Serve immediately.

Nutrition Info: Calories: 57 Total Fat: 3 g Saturated Fat: 1 g Total Carbs: 6 g Net Carbs: 4 g Protein: 4 g Sugars: 2 g Fiber: 2 g Sodium: 484 mg

Amazing Irish Soda Bread

Servings: 10
Cooking Time: 1½ Hours
Ingredients:
- 4 C. flour
- 1 C. raisins
- ½ C. sugar
- 1 tbsp. caraway seeds
- 2 tsp. baking powder
- 1 tsp. baking soda
- ¾ tsp. salt
- 1¼ C. buttermilk
- 1 C. sour cream
- 2 eggs

Directions:
1. Set the temperature of Grill to 350 degrees F and preheat with closed lid for 15 minutes.
2. Grease a 9-inch round cake pan.
3. Reserve 1 tbsp. of flour in a bowl.
4. In a large bowl, mix together remaining flour, raisins, sugar, caraway seeds, baking powder, baking soda and salt.
5. In another small bowl, add buttermilk, sour cream and eggs and beat until well combined.
6. Add egg mixture into flour mixture and mix until just moistened.
7. With your hands, knead the dough until sticky.
8. Place the dough into the prepared pan evenly and cut a 4x¾-inch deep slit in the top.
9. Dust the top with reserved flour.
10. Place the pan onto the grill and cook for about 1½ hours or until a toothpick inserted in the center comes out clean.
11. Remove from grill and place the pan onto a wire rack to cool for about 10 minutes.
12. Carefully, invert the bread onto the wire rack to cool completely before slicing.
13. Cut the bread into desired-sized slices and sere.

Nutrition Info: Calories per serving: 340; Carbohydrates: 63g; Protein: 8.6g; Fat: 6.6g; Sugar: 20.3g; Sodium: 361mg; Fiber: 2.2g

Breakfast Sausage Casserole

Servings: 6
Cooking Time: 30 Minutes
Ingredients:
- 1 pound ground sausage
- 1 tsp ground sage
- ¼ cup green beans (chopped)
- 2 tsp yellow mustard
- 1 tsp cayenne
- 8 tbsp mayonnaise
- 1 large onion (diced)
- 2 cups diced zucchini
- 2 cups shredded cabbage
- 1 ½ cup shredded cheddar cheese
- Chopped fresh parsley to taste

Directions:
1. Preheat the grill to 360°F and grease a cast iron casserole dish.
2. Heat up a large skillet over medium to high heat.
3. Toss the sausage into the skillet, break it apart and cook until browned, stirring constantly.
4. Add the cabbage, zucchini, green beans, and onion and cook until the vegetables are tender, stirring frequently.
5. Pour the cooked sausage and vegetable into the casserole dish and spread it.
6. Break the eggs into a mixing bowl and add the mustard, cayenne, mayonnaise, and sage. Whish until well combined.
7. Stir in half of the cheddar cheese.
8. Pour the egg mixture over the ingredients in the casserole dish.

9. Sprinkle with the remaining shredded cheese.
10. Place the baking dish on the grill and bake for 30 minutes or until the top of the casserole turns golden brown.
11. Garnish with chopped fresh parsley.
Nutrition Info: Calories: 472 Total Fat: 37.6 g Saturated Fat: 13.9 g Cholesterol: 98 mg Sodium: 909 mg Total Carbohydrate 10.7 g Dietary Fiber 1.9 g Total Sugars: 4 g Protein: 23.1 g

Spatchcocked Quail With Smoked Fruit

Servings: 4
Cooking Time: 1 Hour
Ingredients:
- 4 quail, spatchcocked
- 2 teaspoons salt
- 2 teaspoons freshly ground black pepper
- 2 teaspoons garlic powder
- 4 ripe peaches or pears
- 4 tablespoons (½ stick) salted butter, softened
- 1 tablespoon sugar
- 1 teaspoon ground cinnamon

Directions:
1. Supply your smoker with wood pellets and follow the manufacturer's specific start-up procedure. Preheat, with the lid closed, to 225°F.
2. Season the quail all over with the salt, pepper, and garlic powder.
3. Cut the peaches (or pears) in half and remove the pits (or the cores).
4. In a small bowl, combine the butter, sugar, and cinnamon; set aside.
5. Arrange the quail on the grill grate, close the lid, and smoke for about 1 hour, or until a meat thermometer inserted in the thickest part reads 145°F.
6. After the quail has been cooking for about 15 minutes, add the peaches (or pears) to the grill, flesh-side down, and smoke for 30 to 40 minutes.
7. Top the cooked peaches (or pears) with the cinnamon butter and serve alongside the quail.

APPENDIX : RECIPES INDEX

Smoked Stuffed Mushrooms 30
Smoked Texas Bbq Brisket 90
Smoked Tofu 20
Smoked Tuna 138
Smoked Turkey Breast 36
Smoked Turkey Wings 41
Smoked Watermelon 10
Smoked Whole Chicken 44
Smoked Whole Duck 42
Smoked, Candied, And Spicy Bacon 94
Smoke-roasted Chicken Thighs 60
Smokey Roasted Cauliflower 12
Smoking Burgers 128
Smoking Duck With Mandarin Glaze 39
Southern Slaw 25
Spatchcocked Quail With Smoked Fruit 149
Spatchcocked Turkey 38
Special Mac And Cheese 139
Special Occasion's Dinner Cornish Hen 49
Spicy Pork Chops 76
Spicy Shrimp 111
Spicy Shrimps Skewers 109
Spicy Tofu Marinade 141
Spinach Soup 28
Split Pea Soup With Mushrooms 18
Sriracha Salmon 98
St. Patrick Day's Corned Beef 73
Strip Steak With Onion Sauce 77
Stuffed Grilled Zucchini 28
Stuffed Shrimp Tilapia 112
Stunning Prime Rib Roast 95
Succulent Duck Breast 55
Summer Paella 117
Summertime Pork Chops 91
Super-tasty Trout 106
Supper Beef Roast 94
Sweet And Spicy Smoked Wings 58
Sweet Potato Chips 8
Sweet Potato Fries 31
Sweet Sensation Pork Meat 133
Sweet Smoked Country Ribs 75
Sweet Sriracha Bbq Chicken 59
Sweet Tooth Carving Rhubarb Crunch 138
Sweetheart Steak 76

T

Tea Injectable 131
Teriyaki Beef Jerky 65

Teriyaki Smoked Shrimp 120
Texas Smoked Brisket 66
Texas Styled Smoked Flounder 146
Texas-style Brisket Rub 127
Thai Beef Salad 78
Thai Dipping Sauce 132
Thanksgiving Dinner Turkey 56
Tofu Smoothie 122
Togarashi Smoked Salmon 103
Traditional Bbq Chicken 61
Traditional Tomahawk Steak 72
Asian Miso Chicken Wings 53
Bacon-wrapped Scallops 119
Beef Jerky 68
Beef Short Rib Lollipop 71
Blackened Pork Chops 89
Chicken Breast 60
Chile Lime Chicken 43
Crown Rack Of Lamb 89
Fries With Chipotle Ketchup 24
Grill Bbq Chicken Breasts 62
Grilled Buffalo Chicken 43
Grilled Buffalo Chicken Legs 64
Grilled Chicken 35
Grilled Lamb With Sugar Glaze 80
Grilled Lingcod 111
Grilled Vegetables 26
Kalbi Beef Short Ribs 69
Lobster Tail 104
Marinated Chicken Kabobs 122
Rockfish 98
Salmon With Togarashi 101
Sheet Pan Chicken Fajitas 36
Shredded Pork Tacos 89
Smoked Beef Roast 96
Smoked Chicken And Potatoes 53
Smoked Cornish Hens 61
Smoked Mac And Cheese 137
Smoked Mushrooms 7
Smoked Shrimp 106
Spot Prawn Skewers 103
Steak Kabobs 141
Stuffed Peppers 79
Teriyaki Pineapple Pork Tenderloin Sliders 70
Traegerbeef Pot Pie 136
Trager New York Strip 72
Trager Smoked Spatchcock Turkey 40

CPSIA information can be obtained
at www.ICGtesting.com
Printed in the USA
LVHW060954270321
682676LV00005B/553